THE DEATH [illegible] AND THE MEANING OF LIFE

THE DEATH OF GOD AND THE MEANING OF LIFE

Julian Young

LONDON AND NEW YORK

First published 2003
by Routledge
2 Park Square, Milton Park, Abingdon, Oxon, OX14 4RN

Simultaneously published in the USA and Canada
by Routledge
270 Madison Ave, New York NY 10016

Routledge is an imprint of the Taylor & Francis Group

Transferred to Digital Printing 2010

Typeset in Sabon by RefineCatch Limited, Bungay, Suffolk

British Library Cataloguing in Publication Data
A catalogue record for this book is available from the British Library

Library of Congress Cataloging in Publication Data
Young, Julian.
The death of God and the meaning of life / by Julian Young.
p. cm.
Includes bibliographical references and index.
1. Life–History. 2. Meaning (Philosophy)–History.
3. Spiritual life–History of doctrines. 4. Nihilism
(Philosophy)–History. 5. Death of God–History of doctrines.
6. Philosophy–History. I. Title.

BD431.Y59 2003
128–dc21 2002037166

ISBN 0–415–30789–9 (hbk)
ISBN 0–415–30790–2 (pbk)

I should like to dedicate this book to the Haematology Department and the staff of Ward 6A at Auckland Hospital, without whose extraordinary skill, enterprise, dedication and good humour it would not exist.

Contents

Introduction

Nietzsche once remarked that when people talk a lot about 'values' one knows that values are in trouble. The same is true of the meaning of life. That we talk, make nervous, Woody Allenish jokes, write and read books such as this one about it suggests that we are troubled by the topic. Such talk, however, is a relatively recent phenomenon. For most of our Western history we have not talked about the meaning of life. This is because we used to be quite certain that we knew what it was. We were certain about it because we thought we knew that over and above this world of doubtful virtue and happiness is another world: a world Nietzsche calls (somewhat ironically) the 'true world' or, alternatively expressed, 'God'.

A true world[1] is a destination; a destination such that to reach it is to enter (or perhaps re-enter) a state of 'eternal bliss', a heaven, paradise or utopia. Hence true-world philosophies (in a broad sense which includes religions) give meaning to life by representing it as a journey; a journey towards 'redemption', towards an arrival which will more than make up for the stress and discomfort of the travelling. Since journeys have a beginning, a middle and an end, a true-world account of the proper course of our lives is a kind of story, a narrative. And since true-world narratives (that, for example, of Christianity) are global rather than individual, since they narrate not just your life or mine, but rather all lives at all times and places, they are, as I shall call them, 'grand' narratives.

Part I of this study is concerned with true-world, grand-narrative philosophies. In Chapter 1, I trace the idea of the true world from its entry into philosophy in the dialogues of Plato to its heyday, its assumption of world-historical dominion, in the shape of medieval Christianity.

At the beginning of the modern period, however, the birth and success of experimental science presented the severest of challenges to traditional Christian belief. For it became clear that on the map of the cosmos as drawn by Copernicus, Galileo and Newton no plausible place remained at which to locate the Christian heaven and its inhabitants. Previously a kind of *terra incognita*, a kind of Australia though even further away, an unexplored continent beyond the stars, there now seemed to remain no unexplored part of the cosmos in which it could be said to be. In Chapter 2, I examine Kant's attempt, at the end of the eighteenth century, to deploy his metaphysical[2] distinction between appearance and reality to rescue traditional religious belief. There *is* no place, Kant admits, in the world that is mapped by science, for God, the angels or the souls of the saved. But this doesn't matter. For whereas the space–time world of nature that is (completely and correctly) described by science is a world of 'appearance', absolutely beyond the ken of science is another world, the world of ultimate reality, of the 'thing in itself'. So there is, after all, a place for God to inhabit, a 'supersensible' domain – supersensible not in the sense of being, like Australia, too far away for us to see, but in the sense, rather, of being, in principle, not the kind of thing that ever could be accessible to the physical senses.

Of course, says Kant, since the senses are the sole source of knowledge we cannot *know* anything about the supersensible. But we can at least have *faith* that the claims of Christianity are realised in it, can rest secure in the knowledge that the faith of our forefathers can never be challenged by natural science.

In Chapter 3, I look at Schopenhauer's critique of the Kantian attempt to save Christianity. Though he fully accepts Kant's distinction between the sensible world of appearance and supersensible world of the thing in itself, Schopenhauer argues compellingly that the omnipresence of cruelty and suffering in the former discloses the idea of the latter as inhabited by the Christian God of love as, at best, a bad-taste joke.

Surprisingly, though, Schopenhauer's demolition of the benevolent creator of Christian theology does not lead him to abandon the idea of a true world. Rather, it leads him to identify that world, entry into which is to redeem us from the miseries of this bad dream of a life, with *nirvana*, the a-theistic domain of Buddhistic 'nothingness'. In Chapter 4, I show how Schopenhauer's ardent disciple, the youthful Nietzsche, follows him, with some modifications, into this 'European Buddhism'.

In essence, 'European Buddhism' (later Nietzsche's derisive term for his youthful enthusiasm) is an exotic species of Kantianism. But the essence of Kantianism is the unknowability of reality 'in itself'. Why, then, even if we accept Kant's metaphysical duality between appearance and reality, should we believe entry into the supersensible world to constitute 'salvation' from suffering? The answer, implicit in Schopenhauer and explicit in Nietzsche, is that, since it is only in space and time that there can be a *plurality* of things, the thing in itself is 'beyond plurality'. But, since suffering requires a disjunction between desiring subject and recalcitrant object, suffering requires plurality. Beyond plurality, therefore, there can be no suffering.

This, however, I suggest, is not really a compelling argument. Since the essence of Kantianism is the unknowability of the thing in itself, one of the things that we cannot know about it is precisely the claim that it is non-spatio-temporal. There just might, for all we know, be a more or less complete correspondence between our image of reality and the way it actually is in itself. I conclude, at the end of Chapter 4, that we have no more reason to accept Schopenhauer and Nietzsche's *nirvana* than we have to accept Kant's heaven. This, however, is not the end of the true world – a resilient idea we have been extremely reluctant to abandon.

In Chapters 5 and 6, I turn to Hegel and, briefly, Marx. Both, I argue, propose a fully naturalistic philosophy: both accept the death of the supersensible world in its Kantian as well as its medieval form. Yet they do not abandon the true world. Rather, they relocate it, transport it from a supposed *other* world into the future of *this* world. The history of the (one and only) world is pictured as moving according to inexorably progressive, 'dialectical' laws towards a final utopia the arrival of which will bring history to an end. The old distinction between nature and super-nature is reinterpreted as a distinction between present and future.

The trouble with this final version of true-worldism, I argue at the end of Chapter 6, is that 'history', as conceived by Hegel and Marx, is a myth (albeit a potent one). I conclude that there is no version of the true-world answer to the question of the meaning of life that merits belief.

And, in fact, speaking of the character of our culture as a whole, there is none that receives it. When Nietzsche reported, in 1882, that 'God is dead', he articulated no more than the truth: the sociological fact (on account of which fundamentalist Islam despises us) that Western culture has ceased to be a religious culture.[3]

When a traditional structure in terms of which the meaning of life has been defined no longer commands belief, and when nothing takes its place, the result is 'nihilism', understood in Nietzsche's sense: 'What does nihilism mean? *That the highest values devalue themselves*. The aim is lacking . . .' (*The Will to Power* section 2).

Part II of this book looks at the responses to the threat of nihilism – to the appearance that life, in the absence of the true world, is meaningless – that are to be found in the works of philosophers from the end of the nineteenth century to the present day: specifically, in the works of the later Nietzsche (Chapters 7 and 8), of Sartre (Chapters 10 and 11), Camus (Chapter 12), Foucault (Chapter 13), Derrida (Chapter 14), and Heidegger (Chapters 9 and 15). Since the definition of 'Continental philosophy' as 'philosophy which, as its primary task, seeks to respond to the question of what can be said about the meaning of life in the light of the death of the God of Christianity' is more useful than most, this book may be regarded as a brief history of the highlights (and a few of the lowlights) of Continental philosophy. A brief and *critical* history, and one, moreover, that, in the final chapter, finds itself inclined towards an *answer* to the question.

Part I, being concerned with those philosophers who respond to the question of the meaning of life within the broad parameters of the traditional true-world structure, may be said to be concerned with the more 'conservative' side of Continental philosophy. Part II, being concerned with those philosophers who reject the true-world structure root and branch and start afresh, is concerned with its more 'radical' side. It may be observed that the rift between the conservative and the radical runs straight through Nietzsche's philosophy – which is what makes him so pivotal to the understanding of where we are now.

Why exactly is the question of the meaning of life interesting? Why is it important? We all sense its importance (even though we try to cover up our incompetence to answer it with Pythonesque jokes), but just what is it that we sense?

Camus famously begins *The Myth of Sisyphus* by saying that 'There is but one truly serious philosophical problem and that is suicide'. The question of whether or not one should commit suicide is, of course, the question of whether or not life is worth living. And what makes this a real issue for us, Camus claims, is the 'absurdity' of existence, the meaninglessness of life. Though the connection between the issue of meaning and that of worth is somewhat obscure in *The Myth*, the suggestion made in its opening pages is, I believe, fundamentally correct: my life[4] is worth living if, but only if, it is (to me, at least) meaningful. Let me try to justify the two parts of this claim.

First, why is it true that if my life is meaningful, then it is a life worth living? The meaning (point, purpose, goal) of my life, if it has one, is my fundamental project – whether that be to gain 'eternal bliss', to be virtuous, to become a famous rock star or simply to watch over my children's growth and development. But, intuitively, to say 'I possess a fundamental project and the capacity to pursue it, yet my life isn't worth living' fails to make sense. Why is this? Because, I think, 'my fundamental project' means 'project the realisation of which is more important to me than anything else'. Nietzsche says (taking a swipe at Bentham's 'Utilitarian' maxim that right action is action which promotes the greatest amount of pleasure for the greatest number): 'Man does not seek pleasure; only the Englishman does.' What 'man' seeks, he continues, is 'meaning'. But this, I think, by making the primacy of meaning seem a psychological or anthropological truth, misses the point. The real point is a conceptual one. There is, that is to say, an imperialism about the concept 'meaning of life': to acknowledge something as the meaning of my life is – conceptually – to acknowledge it as my highest value. It follows that, whatever sufferings I may endure, whatever 'evils' may befall me, so long as I have a life-meaning and retain the capacity to pursue it, my life is worth living.

Why, to turn to the second part of my claim, is it true that if life is worth living, then it must be meaningful? I shall return to this issue in discussing Camus (who actually purports to disagree with the claim). Here, let me simply assert that, however full of pleasure and free of pain a life may be, if it is a life that lacks the possibility of *growth*, a possibility that can only come from the possession of a life-project, then it represents a fundamentally tedious existence, one that cannot but be *boring*. But bearing in mind Schopenhauer's insight (later repeated by Heidegger) that boredom is not an inner sensation but rather the way *everything* in one's world shows up – grey, flat, unprofitable, dead – a life the overall character of which is boredom cannot be one that is worth living.

Part I

Before the death of God

1

Plato

Plato (about 428–347 BC), bachelor, aristocrat and sometime cavalry officer, belonged in his youth to the circle of Socrates, a group of young Athenian men who admired and loved the philosopher (in spite of his snub nose and bulging eyes) and learnt from him how philosophy was to be done. The most traumatic event in Plato's life, which occurred when he was 31, was the execution of Socrates, who was required to drink hemlock after his condemnation by the Athenian court on charges of 'irreligion' and of corrupting the minds of young men. Other significant events in Plato's life were his founding of the 'Academy', the first university (attended by, among others, Aristotle), and his three visits to Syracuse in Sicily. In his most famous work, the *Republic*, Plato argues that the ideal state can only come into being when the philosopher becomes king – or, presumably, when the king becomes a philosopher. The visits to Syracuse appear to have been an (unsuccessful) attempt to put theory into practice, to persuade the military dictator of Syracuse to govern his state according to the principles set out in the *Republic*. (A couple of millennia later, as we shall see, after Heidegger's resignation from his post as an important Nazi official, a friend remarked ruefully: 'Back from Syracuse?')

Plato wrote some two dozen compositions known as 'dialogues' on account of their conversational form. In almost all of them, the main character is 'Socrates'. Though modelled on the real person, it seems to be the case that, as Plato became older, 'Socrates' became ever-increasingly his own literary construction; a mouthpiece through which he expressed his own ideas rather than reporting those of the hero of his youth.

As observed in the Introduction, the true world first enters philosophy in Plato's mature dialogues. The most fundamental aspect of that philosophy, expressed most famously in the *Republic*, is the division of reality into two worlds. On the one hand, there is the world of everyday visibility – the world that we see, smell, hear, feel and touch – which, because it is always changing, he called the world of 'becoming'. On the other, there is the true world, the invisible, but none the less absolutely real, world of unchanging 'Being'.

The world of Being is the world of the 'Forms'. The Forms are what account for the division of the visible world into *kinds* of things: this and that are both trees because they are 'semblances' – copies or imitations – of the very same thing, the Form of the tree, 'the tree itself', as Plato calls it. This and that are both circles because they are copies of 'the circle itself', this and that person or action courageous or wise because they are copies of 'courage itself' or 'wisdom itself'.

The things of this world are always *imperfect* copies, *inferior* versions of their originals in the world of true Being. (However carefully you draw it, a physical circle will always have a kink in it somewhere, so it can only ever be an *approximate* circle.) In the *Republic*, Plato uses the image of the shadow to express the inferiority of everyday things to their originals. We physical creatures are like prisoners in a cave, chained so that we can only see the rock wall in front of us. Beyond the mouth of the cave behind us are real things which, because they are illuminated by the sun, cast shadows on the wall, shadows which most of us, because we cannot turn around, mistake for the real things themselves.

Though we cannot see the Forms physically, we can, with training, come to know them intellectually; we can see them in the 'mind's eye'. And in fact all human beings have a dim and confused knowledge of the Forms. This is the explanation of the defining human attribute, the ability to reason and communicate by means of language. The reason you can follow my instructions when I say 'Draw a circle' is that what you have in mind when you hear the word 'circle' is the very same thing – circularity, 'the circle itself' – as I have in mind when I say it. The Forms are the meanings of words.

Plato, then, distinguishes between the true world of Being and the 'apparent' world of becoming; 'apparent' because, whereas, for

Plato, things in the world of Forms are truly the things they are, things in the realm of nature are only approximately – i.e. *not* really – the things we take them to be. So far, this dichotomy looks to be a contribution to metaphysics and the philosophy of language. In fact, however, it is also the heart of a philosophy of life. To see why this is so, I want to examine one of Plato's later dialogues, the *Phaedrus*.

The dialogue is set in the countryside, a short walk outside Athens. The place is an enchanted one, for it is where, according to legend, the wind-god Boreas seized Orithyia from the river. The enchantment works its effect on Socrates. 'Truly', he says, noting, after a time, that his usually dry style of speech has become somewhat 'dithyrambic' (rapturous), 'there seems to be a divine presence in this spot' (238d).[1]

The conversation is between Socrates and Phaedrus, a bright but impressionable youth. The topic is love. What makes it relevant to our concerns is that, in the course of discovering the nature of love, Socrates (Plato) deploys his true-versus-apparent-world metaphysics in such a way as to provide, in effect, an answer to the question of the meaning of life – an answer which, in outline, was to dominate Western thought and feeling for the next two millennia.

Phaedrus pulls from under his cloak a scroll that records a speech given by one Lysias, a speech by which he is greatly impressed.

Lysias' speech is an attack on love. Though one senses that Lysias himself is not unlike the unattractive figure valorised in his speech, he attacks love principally in order to demonstrate his skill in rhetoric. As the 'speaker for the affirmative' in the school debating team might choose to defend the most absurd of positions in order to demonstrate his skill as a debater, so Lysias chooses the scandalous path of attacking love in order to display his rhetorical virtuosity. (Scandalous and indeed blasphemous, since love, for the Greeks, was a god – Eros. For the ordinary Greek, to fall in love was to fall under the power of Eros.)

When deciding with whom to spend his time, the boy, Lysias argues, should consort not with the lover but with the non-lover, with the man who frankly confesses to not being in love at all. Whereas the non-lover will offer a relationship of calmness and discretion, the lover will be jealous and possessive, cutting the boy off from friends and from other adult influences. When, however, the 'disease or madness' of love has passed, when the lover's sick passion has transferred itself to a new object – as it inevitably will – then he will cast the boy off, abandoning him to a miserable and lonely existence.

(The context of this speech is, of course, *homo*sexual. Though there was some uncertainty as to whether it should be allowed physical expression, love of boys was widespread among men of the Greek upper classes. Nothing of philosophical significance, however, hangs on this context. 'She's may be substituted for the 'he's at the appropriate places without, it seems to me, affecting the substance of the argument in any way at all.)

Lysias' speech (which I have radically abbreviated) is long, rambling, boring and ugly. How clever of Lysias 'to say the same thing twice, in different words, but with equal success', comments Socrates snidely. None the less, Phaedrus' enthusiasm for its style and substance remains undiminished, so Socrates decides that he must make a speech *in defence* of love.[2] With Lysias as counsel for the prosecution, Socrates appoints himself, as it were, counsel for the defence.

Socrates starts by admitting that, as Lysias had claimed, love is indeed a kind of 'madness'. But not all madness is bad. It is, indeed, precisely the opposite – mankind's 'greatest blessing' – when it is 'heaven sent' (244d). One example of heaven-sent madness is poetry. Great poetry happens only when a 'tender, virgin soul is seized . . . by the Muses who . . . stimulate it to rapt and passionate expression' (245a). (When it becomes, as it were, 'music' – the word means 'inspired by the Muses'.) Poetry that is merely the product of 'man-made skill' is entirely worthless. To produce great poetry, in other words, the poet must be 'taken over', 'inspired' by some supra-normal force. Poetry which is written out of an everyday state of mind is lifeless and second-rate.

Another example of heaven-sent madness, suggests Socrates, is love. But to prove the point, he says, he needs first to provide a metaphysical account of the soul; of its nature, origin and 'destiny' (where it will, or at least ought to, go). He provides this in the form of a narrative that abolishes the boundaries between poetry and prose, philosophy and religion.

The soul, the source of all movement and action, is, says Socrates, immortal. The proof is as follows. We know that the soul is the uncaused cause of action, for when we decide to do something we *freely* so decide – nothing *compels* us to make one decision rather than another. But that means that the soul can neither come into, nor go out of, existence. It cannot come into existence because then it would have to have, after all, a cause. And it cannot go out of existence because the only way something can cease to exist is through the removal of its originating and sustaining cause. As a 'first principle of motion', therefore, the soul is immortal (245c–246a). (This is actually a pretty dodgy argument, but I shall not labour the point.)

What, now, of the constitution of this immortal psyche? The soul, says Socrates, may be compared to:

> the union of powers in a team of winged steeds and their winged charioteer. Now all the gods' steeds and all their charioteers are good, and of good stock, but with other beings it is not wholly so. With us men, [whereas one steed] . . . is noble and good and of good stock . . . the other has the opposite character and his stock is opposite. Hence the task of our charioteer is difficult and troublesome.
>
> (246a–b)

Later on in the dialogue (drawing, perhaps, on his experience in the Athenian cavalry) Plato provides a fuller description of the two horses:

> The good horse is upright and clean-limbed, carrying his neck high, with something of a hooked nose; in colour he is white with black eyes; a lover of glory but with temperance and modesty, one that consorts with genuine renown, and needs no whip, being driven by the word of command.

The other horse, by contrast,

> is crooked of frame, a massive jumble of a creature, with thick short neck, snub nose, black skin, and grey eyes; hot-blooded and consorting with wantonness and vainglory: shaggy of ear, deaf, and hard to control with whip and goad.
>
> (253d–e)

As Plato conceives it, the soul is a quasi-political entity. (In the *Republic* he argues that the structures of the state and the soul exactly mirror each other.) The charioteer represents 'reason . . . the soul's pilot' (247b). Reason, he holds, is the legislative power in the properly ordered soul. The business of 'command' belongs to it. The white horse, on the other hand, represents the executive, the power of action; or, rather, executive power in so far as its innate tendency is to be in harmony with the commands of reason. The 'massive jumble' of the black horse represents the many-headed monster of physical desire which Plato refers to as 'appetite'. It is, as it were, the rabble in the soul. As we shall see, disharmony in the soul, spiritual sickness, is always caused by rapacious 'appetite'.

Originally the soul belonged to the 'train' of one of the gods as it made its journey around the 'rim of the heavens'. (If, for example, one exhibits 'constancy', 'wisdom', and is a 'leader of men', then one probably belongs to the train of Zeus (252c–e); if one possesses a warlike disposition, then to that of Ares (ibid.); if musical, then that of Apollo; if gifted in speaking, to that of Hermes; if a natural home-maker, to that of Hestia; and so on.) From its vantage point on the rim of the heavens the soul was able, periodically, to receive its 'true nourishment' (247d), illumination by the Forms (Figure 1.1).

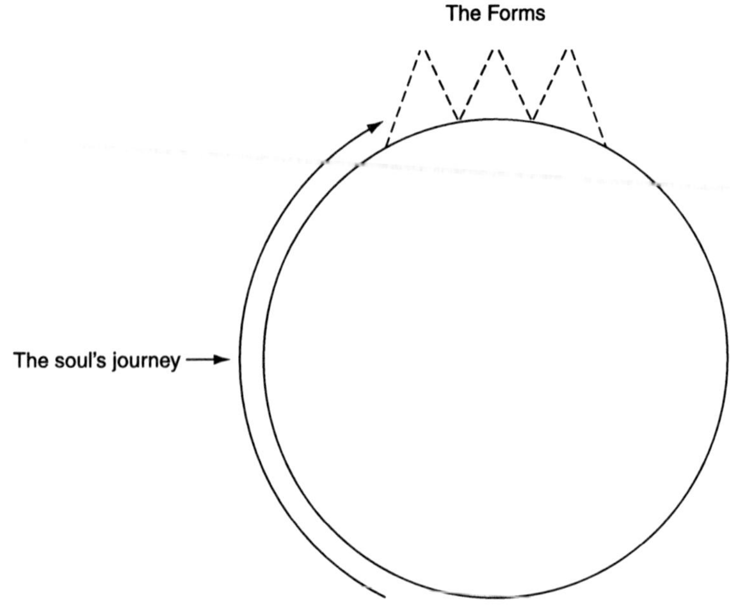

Figure 1.1

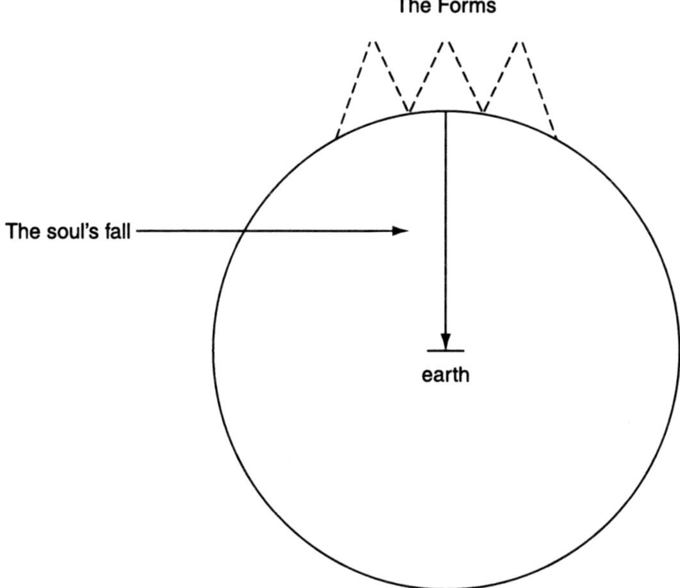

Figure 1.2

On account, however, of the struggle to control the black horse, some souls had their wings broken. No longer able to fly, they fell to earth where they became incarnate, entered into material bodies (Figure 1.2).

Normally, there is no return to the rim of the heavens (and to the soul's 'true nourishment') for ten thousand years. Rather, the soul is condemned to repeated reincarnations in bodily form, its current position in the order of things being determined by the merit or otherwise of its previous life. If, however, the soul has three times lived the best life – the 'philosophical life' – then the period that must be endured before a return to the heavens is abbreviated to three thousand years (248e–249a).

What is the 'philosophical life'? It is the life spent in the pursuit, not of power, fame, fortune or pleasure, but of *knowledge*, knowledge of the Forms. More exactly, it is the life that attempts to *remember* the Forms. Since all human souls once had direct experience of the Forms – as we have seen, they could not otherwise possess the distinctively human attribute of reason and understanding of language (249b) – knowing the Forms is really a matter of remembering them, just as, for instance, knowing the furnishings of one's childhood bedroom is a matter of remembering them.

The other central characteristic of the philosophical life is that it is virtuous. It is, indeed, the *only* truly virtuous life. The Forms, remember, are the standards, ideals or perfect examples of which things in the everyday world are at best imperfect copies. So the Form of the wise, the courageous, the just and the good are the standards of wisdom, courage, justice and goodness. Now, since, says Socrates, one obviously cannot consistently *do* what is good or wise unless one *knows* what is good or wise – knows the standard that makes an action good or wise – it follows that only the life devoted to *knowing* the good and the wise has any chance of *being* good and wise. (To gain an intuitive grasp of the idea of the Forms of justice, wisdom, goodness, etc., as standards or ideals, it may be helpful to think of 'role models', and to observe that people who become role models are always, *as* role models, better, more perfect, than they are in their everyday lives. No man, as the Duke of Wellington may have said, is a hero to his valet.)

What has all this to do with love? Where does love fit into the philosophical life?

Love, says Socrates, is essentially concerned with *beauty*. Now beauty, he argues, is unique among the Forms. In a difficult passage (250b–d), his argument appears to run as follows. As embodied beings, our typical and only easy access to things is through the physical senses. But beauty is the only Form that comes to presence in sense experience.[3] (To determine, for example, whether an action is just or wise or courageous one has to *think* about it, usually in quite complex ways. One cannot just *look and see* that an action is just. But one does determine that something is beautiful just by looking. Indeed, one might argue, this is the *only* way of determining whether or not something is beautiful.) Hence beauty represents a kind of fissure through which something from the realm of Forms leaks through, as it were, to the domain of sense. It is, therefore, especially likely to remind us of the Forms and our former proximity to them.

Seeing the beautiful is what love is. The man is suddenly 'captivated' by the sight of the beautiful boy. He loses all interest in anything else, allows his worldly affairs to go to rack and ruin. The result is that 'standing aside from the busy doings of mankind he is rebuked by the multitude as being out of his wits'. But what is really happening inside him is a kind of remembering. The earthly beauty of the boy has reminded him of true beauty, of the Form of beauty. In doing so it reminds him of his true home on the 'rim of the heavens', of that home we all inhabited when we were 'without taint of that prison house which we are now encompassed within, and call a body, fast bound therein as an oyster in its shell' (250c). The wings of the soul begin to grow again, the feeling of which is the 'bitter-sweet' feeling of love: bitter because the memory reminds us of our current homelessness, sweet because, as a hope, a promise, a goal, a meaning, homecoming has suddenly come closer to us.

Ravished by beauty, the lover has begun, therefore, a kind of self-transformation; he has begun to live the 'philosophical life' of knowing the Forms. The boy, in turn, suggests Plato, will become infected by the lover's love so that he, too, will turn towards the philosophical life. If this becomes established as the life that the two live together, then their souls are preparing themselves for a return to the heavens.

They prepare themselves, that is to say, if they live a life spent in spiritual contemplation, a life of meditation and reflection directed towards the Forms. Characteristic of such a life, a life directed away from the earthly and towards the heavenly, is asceticism, a disciplined aversion from things of the earth and of the flesh. Their life, therefore, is a life of abstention from physical enjoyment, from, in particular, enjoyment of each other's bodies. Such restraint demands particularly strenuous self-discipline, since the black horse in the soul strives, above all, for sexual satisfaction, lusts after 'a monstrous and forbidden act'. Time after time the charioteer must 'jerk back the bit in the mouth of the wanton horse . . . bespattering his railing tongue and jaws with blood' (254e). If the black horse is not subdued, an opportunity will have been missed, for then the two will have been diverted from their task of regrowing their wings. But if it is finally 'humbled', then they will have already begun their journey of spiritual homecoming, will 'stand victorious in the first of the three rounds of that truly Olympian struggle' (256b).

This, then, is the defence of love; of 'Platonic love', as we still say, referring to the fact that Plato's love is chaste, non-physical. Platonic love is a particular form of the philosophical life and, as such, the beginning of a return from exile.

By the standards of the everyday world such love is, indeed,

Socrates admits, a kind of madness. In reality, however, it is an understanding of the hollowness of those standards. True love is a meditation on 'ultimate things'. As such, it casts the cares and concerns of the everyday into a perspective from which they are seen to be matters of the utmost triviality. Who cares about fortune or reputation, who cares about the discretion offered by Lysias' seedy roué, when what is at stake is a return to 'the heavens'!

What is the intended status of Plato's myth? Though, like almost everything to do with Plato, this is a matter of scholarly debate, some points, I think, are clear. The first is that Plato certainly believed in the real existence of the Forms, the immortality of the soul, and in the latter's pre-natal exposure to the former. All of these doctrines are affirmed, and provided with 'proofs', in many other dialogues.[4] The second is that we are intended to take the myth of its fall and rise seriously. Early in the dialogue Phaedrus asks Socrates whether he believes the myth that Orithyia was raped and killed by Boreas at the place where they are. Socrates replies that, though one might expect him to go along with 'our clever men' and say that she was probably blown off a rock by the north wind, he finds this 'too clever and laboured', preferring to accept traditional beliefs at face value (229c). Plato was no 'de-mythologiser', was not disposed to rationalise myths out of existence. They communicate, for him, important truth.

On the other hand, this does not commit him to the literal truth of each and every detail of his own myth of the soul's journey. One of Socrates' most consistent assertions is that the only thing he is quite certain about is the extent of his own ignorance. And, of course, such ignorance would be at its maximum in relation to the afterlife. Given this, it would be absurd of him to claim to be certain about all the details of his story – the ten thousand years shortened to three thousand, and so on. All, I think, that is claimed to be true is the metaphysical framework of the myth, the dichotomy between the world of sense and the world of the Forms, and the general outline of the story – struggle, fall and recovery.

Were our primary concern with Plato criticism, we might, at this point, raise some challenging questions. Do we really need to believe in the supernatural world of the Forms to be able to explain the possibility of language? Does Plato really prove the soul to be immortal? Wouldn't the beauty of art do just as well as that of the boy to remind the lover of the Form of beauty? If so, is there not something inadequate in an account of love that cannot distinguish between love of a person and love of an artwork? Is true love really non-physical? Isn't there something disturbing about Plato's alienation from the physical in general, from our own bodies, and from sex in particular?[5]

But Plato-criticism is not my present concern, so I will pursue none of these questions. What I want rather to do is to draw attention to the way in which Plato uses his metaphysical dichotomy between the two worlds to give meaning to life.

One of the primary sources of meaning is narrative. And, typically, the way in which a narrative endows its hero's life with a goal or meaning is by reference to the past. A classic Western plot, for example, has the hero devoting his life to tracking down the Indians who burnt his house and murdered his family. A Jane Austen novel will explain the heroine's burning ambition to marry in terms of the married status of all her sisters and the modesty of her father's means. Providing meaning in terms of the past is the essential character of Plato's story of the soul's journey.

His story has, that is, a three-part structure. For it is a story of (*a*) an initial state of grace – a paradise – a place of integration, being at home, being in place, being in the *right* place, (*b*) a fall, a fall from grace to a place of alienation and exile, and (*c*) redemption. But redemption is simply homecoming, a return to the place from whence one came. The character, then, of a life's aim is determined by its past.

Notice that Plato's story does not simply explain life's goal or task. It does at least three other things. First, it explains the sense of alienation, exile ('thrownness', Heidegger calls it) to which we are sometimes vulnerable. (Of course, the true-world metaphysics – now revealed as a 'true-home' metaphysics – and the sense of alienation are mutually reinforcing.) Second, it explains the *justice* of our present condition – it is our own fault we are here since the fall is the result of our failure to control the black horse, the result of the disorderly state of our souls. And, third, it explains what we are to do, the kind of life we are to lead – the life of knowledge, virtue and ascetic self-discipline – if we are to achieve our goal.

Someone might say: Well, all this is certainly quaint – even, in its own way, quite engaging. The question is, however, what it has to do with *us*? The *Phaedrus* was, after all, written two-and-a-half millennia ago and we no longer believe in the things – the supernatural world, the immortal soul, reincarnation – in which Plato seems to have believed. Isn't, then, this excursion into Plato's dialogue, diverting though it might be, in the end just a piece of cultural archaeology?

The answer is that it is not. For Plato's *way* of giving meaning to life – if not the exact details of his story – has dominated virtually the entire history of Western thought and feeling.

I am referring, here, in the first instance, to Christianity – though, as we will see, Platonism (which I use as a synonym for 'true-worldism') continued, in disguised forms, to dominate Western thinking even in the materialist atmosphere of the post-Christian era. But let us attend, for now, to Christianity.

One does not, I think, need much convincing that Christianity (according to Nietzsche, the product of St Paul's grafting of Jesus' ethics on to Greek metaphysics) is basically a version of Platonism, of the true-world/true-home view of reality. There is, of course, not a complete identity between Platonism and Christianity. There is, for example, no omnipotent creator-God in Plato.[6] And neither is there anything corresponding to the crucifixion, to the idea of God's 'dying' in order to make it possible for us to achieve salvation. Yet in both the Platonic and the Christian story there is the same immortal, immaterial soul which figures in the same three-part story of sin, fall and redemption. In both stories there is the same metaphysical division between the natural and the supernatural worlds, between earth and heaven, with the latter portrayed as home and the former as a place of exile. In both stories, therefore, physical desire in general, and sex in particular, is presented as something deeply problematic, something to be avoided as much as possible. In both stories, moreover, the fall is our own fault (in the Christian story, it occurred because we disobeyed God's command and ate the forbidden fruit).

The historical importance of Christianity is, of course, that it achieved virtually complete hegemony over Western thinking from about the beginning of the fourth century until well into the eighteenth. The consequences of this will be discussed in the next chapter.

2

Kant and Christianity

From about the fourth to the eighteenth century Western thinking was Christian thinking. This meant that throughout this period the question of the meaning of life was a non-issue; a non-issue because the answer was *obvious*, self-evident, the topic completely sewn up by Christianity's version of Platonism. And if, perchance, one did threaten the prevailing meaning-giving story, then one got persecuted. (Hence Schopenhauer's sardonic remark that Christianity's single greatest argument has always been the stake.)

Though he was not burnt, a case in point is Galileo (1564–1642), who was persecuted by the Catholic Inquisition for saying (after Copernicus) that the earth rotates around the sun, precisely the opposite of what the Church had always taught.

One might wonder how Galileo could possibly bother the Vatican one way or another, how a theory of astronomy could possibly bother an institution that was in the meaning-of-life business, not that of science.

The answer is as follows. We saw that Plato's account of the cosmos is as is represented on the next page by Figure 2.1.

With a little more detail added, and with the substitution of God for the Forms, this becomes the metaphysics of medieval Christianity (Figure 2.2).

The thing to notice about this second map of the cosmos is that it represents *both* a theory of astronomy *and* an account of the meaning of life. To say that the picture is wrong, to say, as Galileo did, that the earth is not the centre of the universe, to say that the earth *moves*, is, therefore, not just to propose a new theory of astronomy. It is to threaten an entire meaning-giving world-view.

From its point of view, therefore, the Church was quite *right* to persecute Galileo, to demand, and eventually obtain, his retraction of the new astronomy. For what he threatened to bring into being

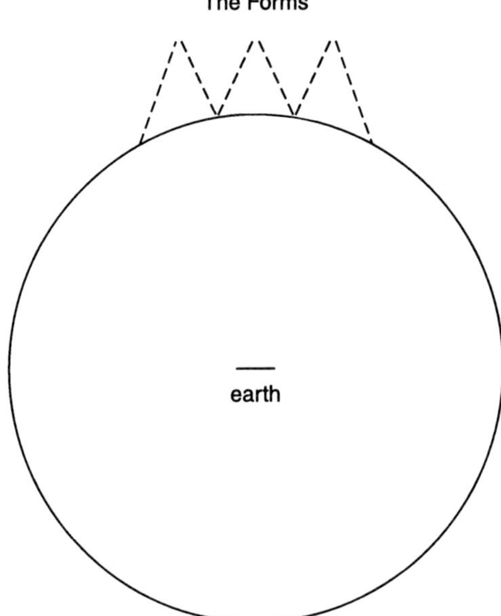

Figure 2.1

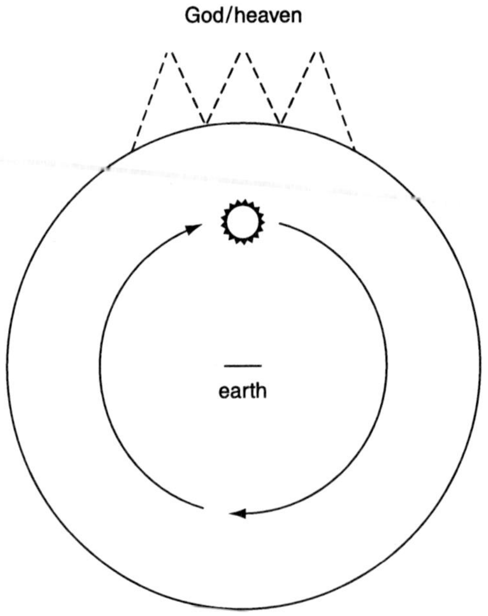

God/heaven

earth

Figure 2.2

(though any such consequence was certainly far from his conscious intentions) was a world in which no one knew the meaning of life any more, a new age of nihilism. It is noteworthy that Nietzsche, in seeking to describe the 'death of God' and the consequent meaninglessness he takes to characterise the modern age, takes his metaphor from Galileo's astronomy:

> The madman jumped into their midst and pierced them with his eyes. 'Whither is God?' he cried; 'I will tell you. *We have killed him* – you and I. All of us are his murderers. But how did we do this? How could we drink up the sea? Who gave us the sponge to wipe away the entire horizon? What were we doing when we unchained this earth from its sun? Whither is it moving now? Whither are we moving? Away from all suns? Are we not plunging continually? Backward, sideward, forward, in all directions? Is there still any up and down? Are we not straying through an infinite nothing? Do we not feel the breath of empty space? Has it not become colder? Is not night continually closing in on us? . . .'
>
> (*The Gay Science* section 125)

Yet, as the demise of communism at the end of the last century proved, persecution of dissenters cannot maintain an old worldview, an old ideology, indefinitely. Sooner or later new knowledge has to come out. In the long run Galileo was bound to win and the Vatican to lose. This meant that sooner or later the meaning of life had to re-emerge as an *issue*, as something needing to be newly thought out and answered in a new way.

The first of the great – of the really great – post-medieval philosophers to respond to this challenge was Immanuel Kant (1724–1804), whose greatest work, the *Critique of Pure Reason*,[1] appeared in 1781. (There is nothing at all to say about Kant's life save that he spent all of it in Königsberg (now Kaliningrad), where he was born, became professor at the University, wrote, never married, and died. So regular were his habits that the citizens of Königsberg are said to have corrected their clocks as he passed by on his afternoon walks.)

Kant saw that the old Platonic–Christian true-world story had become problematic, that its power to convince was waning. Now, in general, it seems to me, there are two possible strategies one may adopt in the face of the crumbling of a previously dominant ideology. On the one hand there is the *radical* response: to abolish the old ideology and put something entirely different in its place. If we think about the collapse of communism in the Soviet Union, we may (with considerable oversimplification) picture Boris Yeltsin as adopting this course: abolish communism and replace it with capitalism. On the other hand there is the *conservative* response: to retain the old ideology but reform it in such a way that it continues to be able to command belief and commitment in the current circumstances. Thinking again about the collapse of the Soviet Union, Mikhail Gorbachev stands out as a proponent of this strategy.

The important thing to know about Kant is that he adopted this second strategy, that he was a reformer rather than a revolutionary. With respect to the question of the meaning of life – with respect, that is, to the question of what to do about Christianity – Kant was a reforming conservative.

In what way, first of all, did Kant see the traditional meaning-giving story as having become problematic?

The fundamental fact about Kant's philosophy is that it was a response to the eighteenth-century 'Enlightenment' which Kant saw breaking out all around him. The basic character of the Enlightenment was a tremendous optimism about the power of human reason. No longer was knowledge, as it had been in the Middle Ages, God's dispensation, the product of divine revelation in the holy scriptures and the writings of the Church Fathers. Rather, it was humanity's own achievement, the product of human reasoning based on careful observation of the visible world. Eighteenth-century thinkers were led to this new optimism and self-confidence by, above all, the power of the new natural science worked out in the previous century, in part by the likes of Galileo but above all by Isaac Newton (1642–1727). To many of them it seemed that the new science, the new physics, had, in principle, the power to describe, explain and predict absolutely everything: that natural science had been completed by Newton.

What did the new science say? In brief, the cosmos, from the Newtonian perspective, turns out to be nothing but molecules in motion, a giant piece of molecular clockwork that operates, precisely, exceptionlessly and eternally, in accordance with Newton's laws of motion.

Given this outlook, nature ceases to be a place of surprise or mystery. There is no room left for miracles, for divine intervention in the world. (Perhaps someone is needed to wind the clock up in the first place; but, given that it is in perfect working order and never needs repairing, the divine clock-maker is not someone about whom we ever really need to think.) The same is true of the immortal soul. If my body is a bunch of molecules completely governed by the inexorable laws of physics, then my soul, even if it exists, is powerless to intervene in the workings of the world. Like God, it becomes, at best, an irrelevant *spectator* of those workings.

Under the impact of modern science, then, God and the soul fade into insignificance. Pretty soon, indeed, the thought presents itself that they *don't really exist at all*. Looked at in the harsh light of scientific reason, that is to say, the thought becomes ever more insistent that Plato's second world, the supernatural, immaterial, transcendent world, is nothing but a myth, a primitive, pre-scientific superstition.

Kant was a rationalist – he saw himself as belonging to the Enlightenment – but also, as I have said, a conservative. He was a man with one foot in the rationalist present – the 'Age of Reason' – and one foot in the medieval past – the 'Age of Faith'. As a member of the Enlightenment he was tremendously impressed by, and proud of, the achievements of the new science, but as a religious conservative (his upbringing was that of Pietism, a Quaker-like version of German Protestantism) he was concerned to retain the traditional Christian story, and to protect it from the threat posed by the new science.

The essence of Kant's strategy for retaining both traditional Christianity and modern science consists in establishing three propositions.

His first proposition says that nature, the world of things in space and time, is not 'real' but rather 'ideal'. (This technical term 'ideal' is potentially misleading. It is best thought of in connection not with 'perfect' but rather with 'idea'.) The world of shoes and ships, cabbages and kings – and the world, too, of quarks, electrons and black holes – is indeed, as the Enlightenment claims, completely fathomed by natural science. Yet, in the final analysis, this world is not reality itself but merely an 'appearance' of it, in the final analysis, a fiction unconsciously constructed by the human mind. Space, time and thingness (*our kind* of space, time and thingness, at least) are not really 'out there' in reality at all, but are, rather, mere 'forms of experience', filters through which the mind feeds all the input it receives from external reality. (Naturally the *Critique of Pure Reason* offers many detailed and complex *arguments* for this claim. In the 'Aesthetic' of the *Critique*, Kant argues that only the 'ideality' of nature can explain our knowledge of mathematics, in the 'Analytic' that it alone can explain our knowledge of physics, and in the 'Dialectic' that insoluble paradoxes about space and time arise if we adopt the opposite position. Here, however, we are concerned only with Kant's *conclusion*.)

Imagine you are wearing green-tinted sunglasses which you cannot remove since they are glued on to your head with supertough elephant glue. (This analogy is a cliché – Schopenhauer was already apologising for using it to elucidate Kant in the 1820s. But it is useful.) If you are wearing such glasses, then all the things you see are green, even though, in reality, only some, and perhaps none, of them are. Analogously, Kant argues that we all wear spatialising, temporalising and thing-ising filters 'hardwired' (to change the metaphor) into the computer that is our brain.

Kant's second proposition, argued for particularly in the 'Dialectic', is that reality – the 'thing in itself' – is *absolutely unknowable* by the human mind. To know what the world is *really* like – what it is like 'in itself' – one would have to be able to take the glasses off. But that we cannot do: they are irremovable, stuck on, as it were, with metaphysical glue. We can, in other words, never step outside the structure of our minds, never pierce the veil it interposes between us and the world. So reality itself is unknowable by us.

Kant's third proposition, argued for at the very end of the *Critique* (*A* 804–19), is that, though we can have no *knowledge* of reality itself, it can still be for us an object of *faith*, faith that it has the character attributed to it by traditional Christianity. (How, exactly, Kant thought the 'real', immaterial, non-natural world, the world beyond our kind of space and time, might be related to the 'apparent' world of matter in Newtonian motion is a complex matter I shall not, here, investigate.) Moreover, the faith in question is, in a certain sense, a *rational* faith – acceptable, therefore, to Enlightenment thinking. Kant's argument for this has to do with morality and runs roughly as follows.

We cannot but believe that there are some things we ought to do and others we ought not. Whether we act on it or not, we cannot help feeling the pressure of the moral 'ought'; of, as Kant calls it, the 'moral law'. But law is inextricably tied to sanctions, to punishment and reward, and cannot exist without it. We cannot, therefore, make sense of our commitment to morality unless we believe just God who, in the afterlife, punishes the wicked and rewards the virtuous. (It has to be an *after*life since, as we all know, in *this* life the wicked often prosper and the good die young.) But getting your just deserts in an afterlife means you have to be *around* in that life. Hence, we are constrained to believe, too, that we all have – are – immortal souls.

In a nutshell, Kant is claiming that Christian belief is 'rational' since, though we cannot prove it to be true, we need it to validate the inescapable sense that there is a moral task to which we are committed – and hence a meaning to our lives. Christian ethics does not make sense without Christian metaphysics. Since we cannot evade the former, we must not evade the latter, either.

In the introduction to the *Critique* Kant says: 'I have found it necessary to deny *knowledge* in order to make room for *faith*' (B xxx). This indicates the strategic bearing of his metaphysics on the threat to the traditional meaning-of-life story posed by modern science. Science, for Kant, *is* omniscient, all-knowing. Everything about nature is the way science says it is. In the final analysis, however, nature is mere appearance. Beyond – or, better, behind – it is another world: the supra-natural, ultimately real domain of the 'thing in itself'. Concerning this, science neither can nor, properly conducted, wishes to say anything at all. Hence science and religion, concerned as they are with distinct domains, cannot possibly come into conflict. In a word, Kant treats science in the way in which one treats a bright, but difficult, child who threatens to wreck everything: he puts it in a play-pen.

Kant's response to the existential predicament of his times was the product of spiritual seriousness and intellectual genius of the highest order. No subsequent philosopher has been able to ignore him. Arguments between philosophers about ultimate things have an uncanny knack of resolving themselves, sooner or later, into different interpretations of Kant. There are, however, two problematic features of Kant's version of Plato's 'true-world' metaphysics which, for our purposes, it is important to notice.

The first is that Kant's version of Platonism betrays a certain *lack of confidence*. For the medievals, the Christian heaven was not a problem. You could, after all, *see* it, at night, shining down through the holes in the 'rim of the heavens' – what we call the stars. (You could also *see* the circular path of the sun – its rising and setting – as it rotates about the earth. In persecuting Galileo, the Inquisition had not only religion but also 'common sense' on its side.) By the time we get to Kant, however, the Platonic world has become 'unknowable'. The confidence of knowledge has given way to the hesitancy of mere belief. In a section of *Twilight of the Idols* entitled 'How the "true world" finally became a fable', Nietzsche notes that Plato's 'sun' (the sun that shines outside the cave (p. 10 above)), though shining brightly in medieval Christianity, has, by the time we get to Kant, come to be 'seen through mist and scepticism', has become 'elusive, pale, Nordic, Königsbergian'. With Kant, the transcendent, supernatural world takes on a distinctly faded quality – like a much-loved pair of jeans that has been through the wash once too often.

The second thing to notice about Kant's attempted rescue of Christianity is that it is open to the following objection. If the world 'in itself', ultimate reality, is, in truth, unknowable, then we can, surely, make *various* guesses as to its true character. Why, then, should we prefer the Christian guess to that of rival candidates? (One rival candidate, as we shall see when we discuss Schopenhauer in the next chapter, is that ultimate reality is not divine but, rather, demonic.) Kant, of course, answers: because we cannot help believing in morality, and morality doesn't make sense without God and the soul. But could we not turn matters the other way round and say: We do not know there to be a God, so our moral commitments are nothing but old and irrational habits we should do our very best (e.g. through psychotherapy or 'deconstruction'[2]) to get rid of? If God is dead, are not all things permitted? And, if not, why not? I shall return to this last question in the final chapter.

3

Schopenhauer

Arthur Schopenhauer was born in Danzig (now Gdansk) in 1788, the son of a wealthy merchant and a mother, Johanna, who was a popular novelist. He was educated in Germany, France and England, and as a teenager already spoke and wrote French and English as well as his native German. His father died when Arthur was 17 – almost certainly by his own hand – and his mother – a woman whose combination of hardness and frivolity led acquaintances to describe her as without either heart or soul – disliked him on account of, as she put it, his morbid tendency to 'brood over the misery of things'. Independently wealthy, he never held a paid university post, making the point that independence of mind requires independence of means. He published his only major work of systematic philosophy, *The World as Will and Representation*, in 1819, to which he added a second volume in 1844.[1] He never married, and was given to making remarks of extreme political incorrectness about women. ('Women are qualified to be the nurses and governesses of our earliest childhood by the very fact that they are themselves childish, trifling, and short-sighted, in a word, are all their lives grown-up children; a kind of intermediate stage between the child and the man, who is the human being in the real sense.'[2]) Schopenhauer loved (of course) writing, conversation, poodles, playing the flute, and going to the opera in Frankfurt where he spent the final twenty-seven years of his life until his death in 1860.

Schopenhauer was the first, and almost the last, major European philosopher to be influenced by Eastern, in particular by Buddhist, thought. Though his influence on certain subsequent philosophers has been substantial – particularly on Nietzsche, Wittgenstein and Sartre – it has generally been unacknowledged on account of his scandalous reputation as a pessimist and nihilist. From artists, however, Schopenhauer has received more acknowledgement than probably any philosopher since Plato. Major figures who were his explicit admirers include Wagner, Tolstoy, Proust, Thomas Hardy and Thomas Mann. He had an important influence on the founder of psychoanalysis, Sigmund Freud.

Schopenhauer was a profound – though not uncritical – admirer of Kant. He explicitly called himself a 'Kantian', indeed often thought of himself as the only true Kantian left in an age devoted, under the cover of lip-service to the master, to abandoning his essential doctrine.

The first of Kant's major propositions, the ideal, merely apparent, status of the space–time world, Schopenhauer accepts without question. For Schopenhauer, to question the ideality of that world after Kant would be as absurd as questioning the heliocentric account of the cosmos after Galileo.

He did, however, make one modification to Kant's metaphysics of 'phenomenon' (appearance) and 'thing in itself'. Individuality and plurality, he suggests, are inconceivable apart from space and time. (If there are two distinct things, then either they must occupy different places or, if they occupy the same place, do so at different times.) Space and time are the principle of individuality – hence Schopenhauer's frequent reference to the phenomenal world as the world 'subject to the *principium individuationis*'. But what follows from this is that the thing in itself – Schopenhauer criticises Kant for speaking, on occasion, of thing*s* in themselves – is 'beyond plurality'. Since it lies outside of space and time it must be a unity, in some sense 'one' (WR I pp. 112–13, 128).

Like most of his fellow 'Post-Kantians', however, he found the second of Kant's propositions – the unknowability of the thing in itself – unacceptable. The reason was that it seems to entail the impossibility of metaphysics – the traditional heart of philosophy. Since metaphysics, as traditionally understood, is the attempt to gain knowledge of ultimate reality (or 'the absolute', as Schopenhauer's contemporaries tended to call the thing in itself), Kant's second proposition entailed, essentially, the end of philosophy.

Most of the Post-Kantians – or 'German Idealists' as they are also known – simply denied Kant's second proposition by claiming to have direct experience of the thing in itself – 'rational' or 'intellectual intuitions' of it. Not, however, Schopenhauer. Agreeing with Kant that there is no direct experience beyond the phenomenal, he argued that, none the less, metaphysics could still be pursued – that one could be a metaphysician and still retain a clear Kantian conscience.

Kant's fundamental argument for the unknowability of the thing in itself, it will be remembered, takes it to be a simple consequence of the ideality of the natural world. Since space and time (as well as substance and causality) are the sunglasses-like 'forms' of all our experience, we can have no experience of anything which falls outside those forms. But experience is the sole source of knowledge. It follows that we can have no knowledge of that which lies beyond space and time.

Schopenhauer's response to this argument is, in effect, to accept that sense experience is the sole source of knowledge, but to point out that knowledge can be grounded in experience in ways other, and more subtle, than being the product of direct *looking*. In particular, he argues, an account of things can be given which is (*a*) an account of the thing in itself and as such genuinely metaphysical, but (*b*) has its claim to constitute knowledge firmly grounded in experience.

How, then, is it that 'a science drawn from experience can lead beyond it, and thus merit the name *metaphysics*' (WR II p. 182)? The world, Schopenhauer answers,

> is like a cryptograph, and philosophy is like the deciphering of it, and the correctness of this is confirmed by the continuity and connexion that appear everywhere. If only this whole is grasped in sufficient depth, and inner experience is connected to outer, it must be capable of being *interpreted, explained* from itself.
>
> (ibid.)

To understand this, consider molecules. Why do we believe in them? Not because we can see them. Rather, because molecular theory provides a satisfying interpretation and explanation of things we can see – the release of steam by boiling water, the fracture of glass when dropped on the floor.

Metaphysics, suggests Schopenhauer, can be conceived in a similar way: its status as knowledge is based entirely on experience, yet because its topic lies beyond experience – in a way analogous to the way in which molecules lie beyond experience – it can count as genuinely metaphysical.

The similarity between physical theory and metaphysical 'theory' conceived à la Schopenhauer is particularly striking in his discussion of how one chooses between different and competing metaphysical theories. In science, what we demand of a theory is, above all, comprehensiveness: if one theory explains only some, while another explains all the observed phenomena, then we adopt the latter. Similarly, Schopenhauer says, with metaphysics,

> the deciphering of the world must be completely confirmed from itself. . . . This confirmation from itself is the characteristic stamp of its genuineness; for every false deciphering even though it suits some phenomena, will all the more glaringly contradict the remainder. Thus, for example, the optimism of Leibniz conflicts with the obvious misery of existence; Spinoza's doctrine that the world is the only possible and absolutely necessary substance is incompatible with our wonder and astonishment at its existence and essential nature; Wolff's doctrine that man has his *existentia* and *essentia* from a will foreign to him runs counter to our moral responsibility for actions. . . . The oft-repeated doctrine of a progressive development of mankind to ever higher perfection . . . is opposed to the *a priori* view that up to any point in time an infinite time has already elapsed, and consequently that all that is supposed to come with time is bound to have existed already.[3]
>
> (WR II p. 184)

Metaphysics, then, is possible: a rational, Kantian metaphysics that does not lapse into the charlatanry of purported 'intellectual intuitions' of the absolute. But what *is* the correct 'deciphering' of the world that will reveal to us the nature of the thing in itself?

Schopenhauer's answer consists in two steps. First of all he proposes an answer to the question of the essential nature of the thing in itself – it is, he claims, 'will' – and then he proceeds to 'decipher' the specific character of this will.

The most salient thing about the world, Schopenhauer suggests, is *striving*. Human beings are constantly in action, striving to achieve the goals they have set. Human beings are goal-directed beings. Similarly the animals, though in a simpler, more one-dimensional way: they are constantly in action striving simply to survive. Plants strive upwards for light and downwards for nutrition, and even (so-called) inorganic things strive to attract other things (gravity) or to repel penetration by them (hardness). Now, each of us, in our own case, has direct knowledge of the inner reality that underlies all our striving. It is 'will' – desire, lust, craving, yearning, repulsion, fear, hatred and so on. Hence we are constrained to conceive the same inner reality to underlie the striving of all beings. Of course, will, in the human case, is accompanied by intellect: we *calculate* how to achieve what we will. This is not the case in non-human nature. The will in non-human nature is mere instinct, 'blind'.

This might look more like landscape painting than philosophy, but Schopenhauer has another, strictly philosophical argument to the same conclusion. It arises out of reflection on the foundations of natural science; on, in particular, the inadequacy of the atomistic conception of matter. This he describes as a 'revolting absurdity' subscribed to mainly by the French on account of 'the backward state of [their] . . . metaphysics' (WR II p. 302) (a remark, one could be tempted to add, as true today as it was in 1844). Ultimate nature, he holds, cannot be conceived as a collection of tiny chunks of matter but must be understood, rather, as a flux of immaterial energy or 'force'.

Schopenhauer's argument, in a nutshell, is this. The ultimate entities of scientific theory must possess causal powers (gravity, resistance, and so on) in order to be able to explain anything at all. But since atomism holds that any power is grounded in atomic structure it is committed to an infinite regress of ever more fundamental structures of entities and can never, therefore, consistently claim to provide an account of ultimate nature. What follows is that we must abandon the attempt to ground every power in structure and accept powers ('forces') as *themselves* the ultimate constituents of reality.

The ultimate entities of science must, then, be conceived as 'forces'. But how can we make sense of the notion of force? The only possible way is by reference to our own inner experience of force in the form of our own will. Only by reference to our own cravings and yearnings can we make the notion of force intelligible to ourselves. We are, therefore, constrained to conceive ultimate natural reality as analogous to our own inner experience, as 'will'. By looking inward at the 'microcosm', as Schopenhauer often puts it, we discover the fundamental nature of the 'macrocosm'.

It is possible to suspect that sleight of hand is involved in moving from 'will' as the energy-like ultimate stuff of the physical universe to '*the* will' as the unitary, non-spatio-temporal thing in itself. None the less, what is really controversial about Schopenhauer is not the claim that the thing in itself is will but rather his characterisation of that will. When we have examined this characterisation we will see that, implicitly, Schopenhauer has another, quite different argument for identifying the thing in itself as will.

What is the overall character of the world as we know it? Until we have answered this question we will not be in a position to determine which metaphysical hypothesis best explains the existence and nature of that world.

Schopenhauer complains that, since the rise of Christianity, no Western philosopher has approached this question with a genuinely open mind. Saddled by the presumption that the world is the creation of a wholly powerful, all-knowing and completely benevolent God ('the omnigod' as some philosophers call it these days), they have been required to put a particular spin on things – to discover the world to be, as the philosopher Leibniz put it, 'the best of all possible worlds'. For obviously, if it is not the best, then either God is incompetent – lacks the *power* to create a first-rate world – or malevolent – lacks the *will* to do so. Or both. Whichever way one turns, heresy and persecution threaten someone who does not adopt Leibniz's, as Schopenhauer calls it, 'shallow optimism'.

If, however, one frees oneself from the theological pressure to come to this absurd conclusion – since Schopenhauer never held a paid university post, it was easier for him than for contemporaries such as Hegel to escape such pressure – then, claims Schopenhauer, we come to the unavoidable conclusion that there is one overwhelmingly salient characteristic which life thrusts under one's nose: suffering. Life, the impartial observer must conclude, is – overwhelmingly, although not exclusively – suffering. This is the 'pessimism' which gives Schopenhauer an almost unique position in the history of Western philosophy.

At one level, Schopenhauer's case for pessimism consists in the simple injunction: 'Don't think; just look.' All it needs to convince oneself that life is suffering is the honest, unflinching eye; the 'candid' eye, he calls it, alluding to the eponymous hero of Voltaire's satire on Leibniz's 'best of all possible worlds' hypothesis, *Candide* (WR II p. 583). Since, however, his claim is one about the *balance* between suffering and happiness – the former outweighs, vastly outweighs, the latter – he is aware of his vulnerability to the 'beer-glass' objection: the pessimist sees as half-empty what the optimist sees as half-full, there is no fact of the matter, it is all a matter of subjective interpretation, of projecting one's own particular temperament on to the world at large. In order, therefore, to escape the charge of selectively choosing examples so as to produce 'a mere declamation on human misery' which, as such, would be 'one-sided' (WR I p. 323), Schopenhauer produces a series of arguments which proceed, not by assembling examples of life's horrors, but rather from something 'universal' and '*a priori*' (WR I p. 324).

This universal, metaphysically necessary, feature is, of course, 'will'. Every being in the phenomenal world is, in its innermost nature, will. This fact inexorably condemns it to suffering. How so?

Consider, first, non-human life, the lives of the animals. Every animal has, as its most fundamental impulse, the will to survive. (Since survival is the fundamental goal of every will, Schopenhauer often refers to the will as 'the will to live'.) Yet in order to survive, he observes (anticipating by some fifty years central aspects of Darwin's *Origin of Species*), life must feed on life. The way, that is to say, that nature preserves her system of species is through over-population. She produces enough members of one species – antelopes – so that, in the first place, there are enough antelopes to ensure the survival of that species, but, in the second, a surplus left over adequate to ensure the survival of another species – lions. What follows from this, however, is that fear, terror, pain and death are not accidental or occasional malfunctions of a mainly benign order of things. They are, rather, written into, essential or structural features of, the order of things that is nature. Nature, that is to say, cares not a fig for the individual, but only for the species. The suffering and death of individuals are the horrendous means she has chosen in order to preserve her system of species (WR I sections 27–9, WR II chapter 28).

We are, perhaps, not generally accustomed to look on non-human nature with a moral eye. But if we do – as, of course, the Christian apologist's claim that this is the best of all possible worlds invites us to – then, says Schopenhauer, we are forced to the very opposite of the Christian judgement. Viewed with an honest eye, nature must be adjudged a *morally disgusting* phenomenon, something that 'ought not exist'. Schopenhauer finds the endless and pointless horror of animal life personified in the report of an early nineteenth-century visitor to Java, F. W. Junghuhn. Junghuhn records, says Schopenhauer (re-presenting the traveller's report in his own language),

> how he saw an immense field covered with skeletons, and

> took it to be a battlefield. However, they were nothing but skeletons of large turtles, five feet long, three feet broad, and of equal height. These turtles come this way from the sea, in order to lay their eggs, and are then seized by wild dogs (*canis rutilans*); with their united strength, these dogs lay them on their backs, tear open their lower armour, the small scales of the belly, and devour them alive. But then a tiger often pounces on the dogs. Now all this misery is repeated thousands and thousands of times, year in, year out. For this, then, are these turtles born. For what offence must they suffer this agony? What is the point of this whole scene of horror? The only answer is that the will-to-live thus objectifies [expresses] itself.[4]
>
> (WR II p. 354)

Animal life is, then, *bellum omnium contra omnes*, war, all against all. The will-to-live in one individual is locked in mortal combat with the will in another. It is the same with plants competing for light in the jungle, and the same even on the so-called inorganic level. Centrifugal force must overcome centripetal force in order to maintain itself, rigidity must overcome gravity in order to survive.

Turning now to human life, we find the same fundamental phenomenon of war, all against all, that pulsates through the rest of nature. Nations are either overtly or covertly at war with each other, individuals must strive to become overdogs to avoid becoming underdogs. As the ancients observed, *homo homini lupus*, man is a wolf for man (WR II p. 577).

Schopenhauer's principal and most interesting argument for pessimism with respect to the human condition – I shall call it the 'stress or boredom' argument – has to do, however, not with our interaction with others but rather with our own internal natures. According to this argument, even if we were to emigrate to an uninhabited South Sea Island (with a stock of good books, CDs and an unlimited supply of fine New Zealand wines) we would still suffer.

As with all living things, the essence of human existence is will. As human beings, what we are is 'objectified' (i.e. physiologically expressed) will: 'teeth, gullet and intestinal canal are objectified hunger, the genitals objectified sexual impulse; grasping hands and nimble feet correspond to the more indirect strivings of the will' (WR I p. 108). Since will is our essence, what we do – all of the time save when we are sleeping, and sometimes even then – is to will. Always, restlessly and tirelessly, we are needing, wanting, desiring, striving for and against things. Our willing, says Schopenhauer, 'can be fully compared to an unquenchable thirst'. 'The basis of all willing, however', he continues,

> is need, lack, and hence pain, and by its very nature and origin it [the human being] is therefore destined to pain. If on the other hand it lacks objects of willing, because it is . . . deprived of them by . . . satisfaction, a fearful emptiness and boredom comes over it; in other words, its being and its existence itself becomes an intolerable burden for it. Hence its life swings like a pendulum to and fro between pain and boredom, and these two are, in fact, its ultimate constituents.
>
> (WR I p. 312)

Schopenhauer is the first – and almost only – major Western philosopher to have paid serious attention to boredom. And he has some insightful things to say about it.

Boredom, he suggests – not the child's momentary tantrum but real, adult boredom ('depression' as we call it these days) – is marked by three essential characteristics. The first concerns the look of things, the look not of this or that, but rather of everything, of the world as a whole. In boredom, the world as a whole loses colour, becomes stale, flat and unprofitable, 'dreary' (WR I p. 314) and 'dead' (WR I p. 164). The second mark of boredom concerns the will. In unbored existence one experiences, always, the 'pressure of the will'. This pressure, however, *continues* when one is bored. But, since it can find no goal to latch on to, one experiences a terrible frustration, the suffering of 'a longing without any definite object' (WR I p. 164). (I think this observation must be understood as pointing out that, in boredom, we experience a second-order desire, a 'will to will' – a will to be engaged in, and therefore have targets of, first-order willing – which is unsatisfied.) The third mark of boredom is philosophical in character. Deprived of the ability to act, expelled, as it were, from the 'game' (ibid.) of life, one sees life as precisely that: like tiddlywinks, draughts, Go or golf, a set of moves which are entirely without point or purpose save that of filling in the tedious interval between now and death.[5] In boredom, life presents itself as an alien, meaningless phenomenon.

Boredom is, then, suffering – indeed, the most terrible of all forms of suffering, since, paradoxically, the suffering of unsatisfied desire, of the unsatisfied will to will, is incorporated into the suffering of satisfied desire. But life is either unsatisfied desire – 'stress' – or satisfied desire, boredom. Hence, life is suffering: it 'swings like a pendulum' between the suffering of stress and the suffering of boredom. (The former, observes Schopenhauer, is most commonly the fate of the poor, the latter of the rich. Hence it is among the latter, he says, that one usually finds addiction to time-killing devices such a card games, cigar smoking and drumming on the table with one's thumbs (WR I p. 313).)

For Schopenhauer, the paradigm of life's oscillation between stress and boredom is sexual love. Under the influence of the sexual instinct we magnify the virtues of the beloved out of all proportion to reality. He or she becomes *the* most perfect, desirable, beautiful object in existence; no other goal is worth pursuing. We suffer the agonies of unrequited love. Should, however, the beloved relent and at last smile on us so that finally we attain our goal, then, afterwards, she or he seems so ordinary that we wonder what all the fuss was about. 'Everyone is disappointed after sex,' runs the Roman proverb (WR I section 60, WR II chapter 44).

Life, then, is – overwhelmingly – suffering. But what has this to do with the character of the metaphysical will that is the thing in itself? (We have, remember, been discussing the character of the world as a preliminary to determining which account of the thing in itself best explains the world's existence and nature.) In contrast to the absurd Christian view that the world is the creation of a wholly benevolent divinity we are forced to conclude precisely the opposite: that the creative origin of the universe is 'not divine but demonic', 'devilish' (WR II p. 349). In opposition to 'the palpably sophistical proofs of Leibniz that this is the best of all possible worlds', suggests Schopenhauer, 'we may even oppose seriously and honestly the proof that it is the *worst* of all possible worlds'. For if it were but a little worse it could not exist at all (WR II p. 583). Traits, that is to say, which theists take to be proof that the world is created by a benevolent intelligence – the orderly progression of the planets, a climate conducive to life – are, in fact, conditions of its existence. A very modest increase in heat, for example, would result in the extermination of all life (ibid.). Schopenhauer thus ends up with an exact reversal of Christianity: the all-powerful creator of the universe represents, not absolute good, but absolute evil.

Though he never explicitly states it as such, we can now see Schopenhauer's most fundamental reason for designating the thing in itself 'will'. One of the most persuasive of the traditional arguments for the existence of God is the so-called 'argument from design', an argument which runs as follows. The world exhibits an intricate 'design' – for example, the adaptation of animals to their environment and vice versa – that could only have issued from an intelligent source. Moreover, this design is so benevolent – there is a wonderful harmony to the way in which all the parts of nature fit together with each other – that we must conclude this intelligence to possess an entirely benevolent will. Schopenhauer accepts the first part of this argument. There is indeed 'design' in the world, and this presupposes the wilful activity of an intelligent creator. But since this design is *malevolent* – the minimal order required to allow the existence of beings capable of suffering – we must conclude its creator to possess an entirely *malevolent* will. Schopenhauer's fundamental argument that the thing in itself is will is, it seems to me, this, as it were, mirror image of the theist's argument from design.

What are we to do about life's suffering? Though claiming to have arrived at his conclusions independently, Schopenhauer had an intense admiration for Buddhism.[6] And, in fact, his pessimism is identical with one of the major doctrines of Buddhism: the first of the Four Noble Truths in which the Buddha summed up his life's teaching is 'Life is suffering (*dhukka*)'. The second Truth is 'The origin of suffering is craving [i.e. willing]', which, as we have seen, is precisely Schopenhauer's analysis. The Buddha's third Truth maintains that 'The cessation of suffering is possible through the cessation of craving'. (The fourth, the 'eightfold path' to the cessation of craving, does not concern us here.) This, too, is precisely Schopenhauer's answer to the question of what we are to do about life's suffering, what we are to do in the face of the truth of pessimism. Since the source of suffering is willing, the solution to the 'riddle' of life (WR II chapter 17 *passim*), says Schopenhauer, lies in 'denial of the will'.

In the first instance, the transition from 'affirmation' to 'denial' of the will consists in a 'transition . . . to asceticism' (WR I p. 380). Someone who has seen the Schopenhauerian truth of things will turn from the life of ambitious striving to a life of as little willing as possible. The characteristics of such a life will be the traditional monastic virtues: poverty, chastity and obedience. (Notice, here, echoes of Plato's 'philosophical life' (see pp. 15–16 above).) But though, perhaps surprisingly, Schopenhauer rejects suicide,[7] the ultimate and complete solution to the problem of life consists in death, the most enlightened death being that of the ascetic who starves, not by a deliberate act, but simply because he has become too will-less to eat. (This should not be confused with anorexia, which, on most accounts, is a powerful *affirmation* of the will.)

But is this not the most abject nihilism? Is not death the entry into a mere 'nothingness'? And is not Schopenhauer, therefore, offering nothingness, becoming nothing, as the goal and meaning of life?

To be sure, Schopenhauer replies, to our finite minds 'what remains after the complete abolition of the will is . . . assuredly nothing' (WR I p. 412). But we only have to observe the 'deep tranquillity', the 'ocean-like calmness of the spirit' in the face of the mystic to 'banish the dark impression of that nothingness, which as the final goal hovers behind all virtue and holiness' (WR I p. 411). The mystics, in other words, know something that is inaccessible to ordinary minds. They know that what seems to us to be nothing is, in fact, a 'better place'. (Schopenhauer thinks that we can sometimes share in the mystics' insight through music. As did Franz Schubert who, in 'To Music', praises his 'blessed art' as that which 'transport[s] us to a better place'.)

As we have seen, Schopenhauer despises Christianity. What he in fact despises, however, is not Christianity as such but rather the idea of our world as the creation of an omnipotent God of love. Other aspects of Christianity, the idea that this world is a 'veil of tears' from which we need other-worldly 'salvation', he completely endorses. Surprisingly, therefore, Schopenhauer turns out to be, in the end, yet another 'true-world' theorist. Salvation consists in transcendence of the world of the *principium individuationis*, in breaking through the 'web of Mâyâ' (WR I p. 17), so as to achieve unification – or reunification – with the absolute. (Transcendence of individuality must be *unification*, because, remember, beyond the phenomena there is no plurality.) The only real difference between Schopenhauer and Christianity is that his true world is not populated by God and the angels, but is the a-theistic true world of Buddhism, in other language, *nirvana*. In the end, to use what the later Nietzsche deploys as a term of disparagement, Schopenhauer turns out to be a 'European Buddhist'.

How good is Schopenhauer's (and Buddhism's) case for pessimism? Let us look first at the case for pessimism in non-human nature. Nature, Schopenhauer claims, red in tooth and claw, is a scene of fear, pain and death. In fact, however, since most animals have no anticipation of the future beyond a few moments hence, they cannot experience anything but the brief terror and pain which comes at the point of death itself. To be set against this is the relatively pleasant condition in which most of their lives are quite often spent. That, at least, is what we generally suppose. The reason we take 'free-range' farming to be important is that we assume animals which range freely to enjoy a generally pleasant kind of existence.

Turning to the 'man is a wolf for man' argument, Schopenhauer seems to assume that social life must be more or less overt 'war, all against all' on account of the inevitability of competition for scarce resources. This, however, ignores the capacity of technology to create an adequacy, and even a surplus, of such resources.

The most interesting part of Schopenhauer's case for pessimism is, however, the 'stress or boredom' argument. What are we to make of it?

Let us, for ease of reference, set the argument out in a formal kind of way. It is, I suggest, the following:

(1) To live is to will.
(2) To will is to pursue a goal.
(3) Either one's goal is satisfied or it is not.
(4) If it is not, then one suffers a lack, i.e. suffers.
(5) If it is, then one is bored, i.e. suffers.

So

(6) Life is suffering.

Interesting though this argument is, it is possible to raise objections against it. Against (2) one might point out that, as human beings we will *many* goals. Hence, against (3), one might point out that satisfaction is not an all-or-nothing business. Some of one's goals might be unsatisfied, thereby warding off boredom, while others are satisfied, thereby producing an overall state which is unbored yet, on balance, pleasant. Against (4) one might point out that it is not really true that unsatisfied desire *always* amounts to suffering. Certainly the pangs of hunger may be an *ingredient* in one's pre-dinner condition, but the pleasant anticipation of the excellent pheasant in orange sauce at one's favourite German restaurant surely outweighs those pangs. Certainly the heart may pine for the absent beloved, but the pleasure of looking forward to the evening together, on the bench, in the park, under the moon, surely outweighs any suffering involved. Many unsatisfied desires have, that is, a bitter-sweet quality to them. And the sweetness often outweighs the bitterness. Against (5) one might point out that even if one ultimately becomes bored with an attained goal there may be a period of genuine enjoyment before boredom sets in, during which time a new goal may have emerged to ward off boredom.

The most telling objection to (5), however, is the following. Schopenhauer's argument assumes that the satisfaction of a desire constitutes its immediate elimination, together with the goal it provides. He has to make this assumption for otherwise boredom – goal-lessness – cannot be the automatic consequence of the satisfaction of desire. Of many desires this is perfectly true. Once one has satisfied one's hunger, then (as a matter of physiology) the desire to eat disappears. Once one has become the first man on the moon or the conqueror of Everest, then (as a matter of logic) the desire to achieve that goal disappears. But there is a very important range of desires which are capable of satisfaction *without* elimination. Being a philosopher, for example, is a life-forming desire of mine. It is, moreover, a *satisfied* desire – I am satisfying it at this very moment. But that doesn't mean I have been *deprived* of the goal of being a philosopher. It is one which – so far as I know – I shall retain for the rest of my life. Some desires, in short, can be satisfied without being extinguished.

(Why does the satisfaction of desires such as the desire to be a philosopher not entail its elimination? In a nutshell, I think, because becoming a philosopher (novelist, poet, physicist, doctor, mother, and so on) is a beginning, not an end. To satisfy one's desire to become a philosopher is to take possession of an (almost certainly inexhaustible) range of further desires – desires to communicate with the great minds of the past, to understand the nature of knowledge, truth, being, the human being, the good life and so on. It is to enter, in Heidegger's language, a 'path of thinking' which is almost certainly endless.)

For numerous reasons, then, the 'stress or boredom' argument fails to constitute a compelling argument for pessimism. (This, however, should not be allowed to disguise the considerable insight it contains. Human beings *do* – typically, though not, I suggest, inevitably – fall into the trap of sacrificing their present lives on the altar of some future goal, only to find boredom awaiting them when they achieve that goal. That allowing one's life to be formed by a desire whose satisfaction does not entail its extinction escapes this trap is a point to which I shall return.)

One final criticism of Schopenhauer. According to his metaphysical philosophy, his inference to the nature of the thing in itself as that hypothesis which best 'deciphers' the character of the phenomenal world, the thing in itself is will. And the will is absolutely evil, 'devilish' not divine. According, however, to his practical philosophy, his account of what we are to do about the truth of pessimism, 'salvation' lies in transcendence of the *principium individuationis* and unification with the thing in itself. Yet how can unification with absolute evil be regarded with anything but horror? How could it be regarded as *salvation*? How could a vision of absolute evil be the object of the mystics' 'ocean-like calmness of spirit'? There seems, in short, a serious inconsistency between Schopenhauer's metaphysics and his practical philosophy. In the next chapter we will see how his ardent disciple, the youthful Nietzsche, perceived this inconsistency and proposed a solution to it.[8]

A final comment. Schopenhauer does not, I have argued, establish the truth of pessimism; that the character of life is overwhelmingly one of suffering. On the other hand, by having the clear-eyed independence of mind to point out the very great deal of suffering that undoubtedly exists in the world, he surely does show the theist's assertion that this is 'the best of all possible worlds' to be, as he claims, a shallow 'sophism'. That a totally powerful, all-knowing, wholly benevolent deity could not have ameliorated the fate of the turtles *even a little*, consistent with the aim of preserving the species *canis rutilans*, beggars belief.

This, as the Frankfurt philosopher Max Horkheimer calls it, 'stripping the gold foil from the absolute' is, perhaps, Schopenhauer's principal significance in the history of philosophy. What he shows, specifically, is the pointlessness of Kant's strategy for preserving traditional Christian belief. For, even if it can survive the challenge from science, it cannot survive the 'candid' use of our own eyes.

4

Early Nietzsche

Friedrich Nietzsche was born in 1844, the son of a Lutheran pastor who died – probably of a degenerative brain disease – when Nietzsche was 5 years old. In 1869 he discovered Schopenhauer's *The World as Will and Representation* in a second-hand bookshop, a book he found to be written 'especially for me'. Mutual reverence for Schopenhauer – mutual conviction that Schopenhauer had courageously told the *truth* about life and the world – led to his close friendship with the composer Richard Wagner which began about three years later. Four years after that, however, claiming to have discovered them both to be 'sick', Nietzsche broke with both Schopenhauer and Wagner. Though an honoured and invited guest at the First Bayreuth Festival of Wagner's operas in 1876, he walked out, in disgust, half-way through.

In 1869, Nietzsche became professor of Greek at the Swiss university of Basle, where, in 1872, he published his first book, *The Birth of Tragedy* – the topic of this chapter. In 1879 he resigned the chair at Basle and took up the life of a wanderer, living in cheap boarding-houses in Germany, Switzerland, Austria and Italy. In 1882 he pronounced for the first time that 'God is dead' (in *The Gay Science*), and between 1883 and 1885 produced his most famous book, *Thus Spake Zarathustra*. In 1889 his rapidly deteriorating mental condition tipped clearly into madness. (In a letter to Jacob Burckhardt he claimed to be God, and to the patients in the sanatorium to which he was, for a time, confined he apologised for the bad weather they had been having, promising to 'prepare the loveliest weather for tomorrow'. Clearly he had forgotten, by this time, that God had 'died'.) The cause of his madness is uncertain. Many – keen to preserve his philosophy from any taint of madness – suggest it to have been syphilis. Others, however, among them his friend Franz Overbeck, think that the cause really is to be found in his philosophy. Nietzsche died in 1900 without ever regaining sanity.

Nietzsche wrote *The Birth of Tragedy* under the influence of his intense admiration for Schopenhauer. The book's alternative title, *Hellenism and Pessimism*, indicates how much Schopenhauer was on his mind. The argument of the work is, in outline, the following.

The Greeks, a 'hypersensitive' people, 'emotionally intense', exquisitely 'equipped for suffering', knew full well the 'terror and horror' of existence. Their myths reveal it: for example, 'the vulture which fed upon the great philanthropist, Prometheus, the terrible lot drawn by the wise Oedipus; the curse on the house of Atreus which brought Orestes to the murder of his mother' (BT 3).[1] The Greeks knew the horrendous 'cruelty of nature' (Schopenhauer's 'war, all against all') and the 'terrible destructiveness of so-called world history' (BT 7) (a rejection of what we will see to be Hegel's view that history is an inevitable progress towards perfection). The Greeks, in a word, knew the truth of Schopenhauerian pessimism, they knew that life is suffering. And, as their myths also reveal, they knew the powerful inclination to move from pessimism to nihilism, to the conviction that life, human life, is not worth living: the story, for example, of the demi-god Silenus who, captured by king Midas and forced to disclose his wisdom, spoke as follows: 'the best for you is . . . not to have been born, not to *be*, to be *nothing*. But the second best is – to die soon' (BT 3).

The Greeks knew, then, the experience of action-paralysing 'nausea', and the temptation to lapse into a 'Buddhistic negation of the will' (BT 7), the ultimate expression of which is suicide (BT 15). But, in fact, they did not lapse into denial of the will. They acted. They defeated the Persians and, *en passant*, as it were, created Western civilisation. They survived and thrived. How so? Through, according to Nietzsche, their art. More specifically, through their two main types of art, the 'Apollonian' art of Homer and the 'Dionysian' art of the great tragedians, Aeschylus and Sophocles.

Formally speaking, this argument is offered as a piece of classical scholarship – as already noted, Nietzsche was a professor of Greek literature when he wrote *The Birth*. His fundamental interest, however, is in *us*, in understanding ourselves in the 'polished mirror' provided by the Greeks. If, Nietzsche holds, we can understand how the Greeks overcame 'nausea' and 'negation of the will', we shall understand how *we* can overcome nihilism. (Nietzsche's answer to the question 'how can *we* overcome nihilism?' is: 'through the rebirth of Greek tragedy that is happening in the music dramas of Richard Wagner'. His basic motive in writing *The Birth* was to support Wagner's attempt to build the opera house at Bayreuth – which is why his walking out of the first Bayreuth Festival represented such a dramatic change in his thinking.)

Since they had two types of nihilism-overcoming art, the Apollonian art of Homer in the ninth century BC and the Dionysian art of the fifth-century tragedians, the Greeks had, in fact, Nietzsche notes, two 'solutions' to the problem of nihilism. I shall begin with the former.

'Apollonian', as Nietzsche uses it, is ambiguous: sometimes it merely describes a type of consciousness, and sometimes the enhancement of that consciousness through art. In the first sense, 'Apollonian' applies to consciousness which is of the mundane, everyday variety. In this sense, Apollonian consciousness is consciousness of oneself as one individual in the midst of a plurality of individuals located in space and time. It is consciousness which, says Nietzsche, is subject to the *principium individuationis* (BT 1, 2). (This use of Schopenhauer's terminology suggests, what is in fact the truth, that the metaphysics of *The Birth* is identical with the metaphysics of *The World as Will*. As we shall shortly see, for Nietzsche, too, the world of individuals is ideal and the reality behind it, the 'thing in itself', is 'beyond plurality'.) The essence of the Apollonian mind is, says Nietzsche, plurality, division, 'boundary setting' (BT 9). It is the Apollonian mind that distinguishes between you and me, but also between yours and mine. Legality, justice, is essentially the product of the Apollonian side of the mind (BT 2, 9).

Apollonian art is the aesthetic transformation of consciousness subject to the *principium individuationis*. In the *Iliad* and the *Odyssey*, Homer produced the 'radiant dream-birth of the Olympians' through which the Greeks 'overcame . . . or at any rate veiled' (BT 3) the terror and horror of existence. In their tales of gods and heroes, says Nietzsche, the Homeric Greeks erected, not a non- or anti-human ideal like that of Christianity (Jesus never has, for example, sex), but rather a 'transfigured' (BT 18) *self*-portrait, a glorification of *human* existence. In this way they 'seduced' (ibid.) themselves into continued existence. 'Existence under the bright sunshine of such gods is regarded as desirable in itself' (BT 3).

What, exactly, is transfiguration? Frequently, Nietzsche says it is a matter of 'illusion' and 'lies' (BT 3, 7, 16, 18), which suggests that, in Nietzsche's view, what Homer produced is (like the television advertisement for cornflakes, or the 'spun' image of the presidential candidate) a picture of life with all the nasty bits airbrushed out. Yet Homer is full of death and destruction – most of his stories are *war* stories – and Nietzsche, in any case, says that, in Homer, 'all things whether good *or evil* are deified' (BT 3; my emphasis). So censoring out the nasty bits cannot, in fact, be his account of transfiguration.

Nietzsche speaks of Apollonian art as 'transform[ing] the most terrible things by joy in mere appearance and redemption through mere appearance' (BT 12). And he speaks of the Apollonian artist as – unlike the scientist, who always wants to get to the bottom of, to 'uncover', things – one who 'cling[s] with rapt gaze on what remains covering even after such uncovering' (BT 15). Even after the uncovering of unpleasant truth, the Apollonian artist takes delight in the 'beautiful', delight, that is, in 'beautiful forms' (BT 16).

This suggests that the art of the Homeric epic – and the corresponding attitude to life – is a matter not of elimination, but rather of focus. It suggests an attitude in which one is inclined to describe life as 'terrible but magnificent'. In the Renaissance painter Uccello's *Battle of San Romano*, for example, the ground is littered with bodies and body parts, but what captures one's attention is the magnificence of the horses, the exhilarating athleticism of the combatants, the sheen on the armour and the vibrant colour of the proudly flying pennants. (This is an apposite comparison since, at one point, Nietzsche says that human existence is like the existence of a soldier in an oil-painting of a battle scene (BT 5).) Were one to look for a modern instance of Apollonian art, what might come to mind is the Western: death and destruction are all about, but what one focuses on is the beauty, courage and sheer 'style' of its heroes. To some extent the same phenomenon occurs in the world of the 'woman's magazine'. Terrible things – drunkenness, disease, divorce and death – happen to the gods and goddesses who inhabit this world (film and rock stars, royals and football players), but through it all their glamour remains, their stardom shines on. (Homer was, of course, the *popular* culture of ninth-century Greece, so this comparison is not as wide of the mark as it might seem.)

The Apollonian attitude to life – in later works Nietzsche calls it 'superficiality out of profundity' – requires a strongly external approach to both others and ourselves. It requires that death be, as it is in the Western, bloodless and painless. It requires a kind of inner anaesthesia. This, I think, is why Nietzsche associates it with 'illusion': it, as it were, represents a three-dimensional object as two-dimensional. Though there is no censorship of *facts*, there is, none-the-less, censorship; censorship of *perspectives*. The inner perspective, how it feels to be on the *inside* of loss, injury and mortality, is not allowed to be shown. But the Greeks *knew* about the inside of things. They had an exquisite sensitivity to the 'terror and horror' of existence. This is why Nietzsche calls the Apollonian attitude (in an entirely non-judgemental way) a 'lie'. It is a form of self-deception.

This makes the Apollonian outlook seem a somewhat fragile 'prophylactic' (BT 11) against nihilism, against 'nausea' and despair. The pain of things has a way of forcing itself on one, no matter how 'superficially' one lives. One thinks, perhaps, of the tragic imprisonment, decay and death of the brilliant Oscar Wilde, Nietzsche's contemporary, and in many ways someone who attempted to personify the Apollonian stance. Or one thinks of the impossibility or maintaining such a stance in the face of the death of one's child.

It is on account of this fragility, I think, that, while giving the Apollonian solution to nihilism honourable mention, Nietzsche's preferred solution, in *The Birth*, is the Dionysian one embodied in Greek tragedy, a solution which he describes as the 'more profound' (BT 10) of the two. With Greek tragedy, he says, art attains 'the highest goal . . . of all art' (BT 21, 24), is, that is to say, of the highest service to life (BT 2, 5).

Nietzsche's key word for the Apollonian is 'dream'. This does double duty, indicating, first, that the world of the *principium individuationis* is ideal, ultimately a mere 'dream', and, second, that, in Apollonian art, that world has been raised to a state of beauty. It serves the latter function because, for Nietzsche, beauty consists in the economy of 'essential' or 'significant' form, and because 'in our dreams we delight in immediate understanding of figures; all forms speak to us; there is nothing unimportant or superfluous' (BT 1).

By contrast, his key word for the Dionysian is *Rausch* – intoxication, ecstasy, rapture, frenzy. (Dionysus, Bacchus, is of course the god of wine.) Dionysian consciousness is a state of metaphysical intoxication in which we overcome the 'sobriety' of ordinary

Apollonian consciousness which presents the world of the *principium individuationis* as absolute and ultimate reality. In Dionysian rapture, one penetrates the 'veil of Mâyâ' (BT 1) (notice, once again, the reappearance of Schopenhauer's Indian terminology) to realise that, in fact, reality is beyond plurality, is the 'universal will' (BT 17), a 'primordial unity' (BT 1).

Dionysian consciousness is (like literal intoxication) a double-edged phenomenon. On the one hand it can have a benign expression: 'under the charm of the Dionysian' it can happen that the 'rigid hostile barriers' which the Apollonian mind sets between man and man, and between man and nature, are broken down. In the Dionysian festivals of the ancient world those barriers are replaced by a 'gospel of universal harmony' in which everyone 'feels himself not only united, reconciled, and fused with his neighbour, but as one with him, as if the veil of Mâyâ had been torn aside and were now merely fluttering in tatters before the mysterious primordial being' (BT 1). (Nietzsche adds that it is this 'gospel' that receives expression in the final movement of Beethoven's ninth symphony.)

On the other hand, Dionysian consciousness can lead to a 'horrible witches brew' of 'sensuality and cruelty' (BT 2). It can have this consequence because if we are all, in reality, one, then the individual is without value. In the death of an individual, nothing at all is lost. Human sacrifice may even occur as an affirmation of the transindividual nature of our true identity. (Deer hunters sometimes speak of the mystic bond between hunter and prey, even of the deer as 'willing' its own death. Underlying such talk is, I think, the metaphysics of Dionysianism, the identity of all things in the primordial unity.)

The 'barbarians' of the ancient world had no protection against the possibility of a horrible manifestation of Dionysianism. It was the achievement of the Greeks, however, to divert Dionysian consciousness into art, specifically into tragedy. Instead of actual human sacrifice, we have, in tragedy, the symbolic sacrifice of the hero. Without eliminating Dionysian intoxication, the Greeks made it safe.

The question Nietzsche focuses on with regard to Greek tragedy is the nature of the 'tragic effect', a question that has puzzled philosophers since Aristotle. Why is it that we willingly subject ourselves to – and therefore, presumably derive some kind of satisfaction from – the sight of the catastrophic, the destruction of not just human beings, but in many respects the finest examples of itself that humanity has to offer? Nietzsche's answer is that, whereas Apollonian art teaches us to take delight in the phenomenal world, Dionysian art 'teaches us that we are to seek joy not in the phenomena but behind them' (BT 17). The destruction of the tragic hero is presented in such a way that we do not become 'rigid with fear'. (Greek tragedy is different from a horror movie.) Rather, 'a metaphysical comfort tears us momentarily from the bustle of changing figures. We really are, for a brief moment, the primordial being itself' (ibid.).

Schopenhauer, following Kant (and, ultimately, the eighteenth-century English philosopher-politician Edmund Burke), distinguished between the 'beautiful' and the 'sublime'. Experience of the beautiful is experience of significant form in the phenomena; the feeling of the sublime is becoming alive to one's supra-phenomenal nature – to, in Kant's words, 'the supersensible side of our being'. Tragedy is the highest form of the 'feeling of the sublime' (WR I p. 253, WR II p. 433). Nietzsche's account of the tragic effect is almost exactly the same; indeed, he uses the same word: the 'artistic taming of the horrible' is, he says, 'the sublime' (BT 7). Tragic joy consists in an at least momentary escape from the terrors of existence as an individual human being and is, therefore, an intimation of our 'higher', supra-human destiny: tragedy

> in the person of the tragic hero . . . knows how to redeem us from the greedy thirst for existence, and with an admonishing gesture . . . reminds us of another existence and a higher pleasure for which the tragic hero prepared himself by means of his destruction, not by means of his triumphs.
>
> (BT 21)

What enables Greek tragedy to produce this 'metaphysical comfort' is the chorus. Tragedy, that is to say, grew out of the Dionysian festivals of archaic Greece, festivals of ecstatic chanting in which everyone took part. Even after the addition of actors and the formal division between chorus and audience, the audience still felt itself to be part of the chorus. Thus, though partially identifying with the tragic hero and experiencing, therefore, his or her suffering, the primary identification of the audience is with the chorus whose dithyrambic singing draws it into a primal oneness (the football crowd feeling). Thus, whereas the 'barbarians', in an exuberant affirmation of their supra-individual and inexhaustible identity, sacrificed people in reality, the Greeks sacrificed them in art.

Nietzsche says that tragedy offers 'a profound and pessimistic view of the world'. It offers 'the conception of individuation [membership of the world of the *principium individuationis*] as the primal cause of evil' but also 'the joyous hope that the spell of individuation may be broken in augury of a restored oneness' (BT 10). And he speaks of the yearning of Dionysian initiates for a 'rebirth of Dionysus which we must now dimly conceive as the end of individuation' (ibid.). But, if *this* is the nature of the tragic effect, why did the Greeks not lapse into 'nausea' and 'Buddhistic negation of the will'? Why did they *act*? Because, Nietzsche answers, they were subject to the 'noble deception' (BT 21) that their tragedies concerned only individuals in a world of individuality, concerned only the Apollonian realm. Even the authors of these works could not understand their true import. In this way, they gained 'metaphysical comfort' while, at the same time, being 'relieved of the burden' of explicit metaphysical insight. The effectiveness of Dionysian art, therefore, is that, while affirming to us our ultimate deliverance from the pain and anxiety of individuation, at the same time – recognising, as it were, that 'action requires the veil of illusion' (BT 7) – it acts like a fairy godmother and draws a veil of forgetfulness over what we have experienced. In this way, we are returned to the world, strangely comforted yet able to act.

What has early Nietzsche to tell us about the meaning of life? Here, we have to confront a difficulty in his methodology. Nietzsche assumes that by studying the Greeks we are studying ourselves and our own situation. The task of the classicist, he writes in an unpublished essay, is that of 'understanding *his own* age better by means of the classical world'. The Greeks overcame nausea and nihilism through tragedy, and so can we – through the rebirth of Greek tragedy in the music dramas of Richard Wagner. But what he forgets is the effect of his own discussion of tragedy: *we*, his readers, can't be subject to the 'noble deception' because he, Nietzsche, has, as it were, spilled the beans. If, that is, we are convinced by his metaphysics, then we *know* about our supra-individual identity; and if we are convinced by his pessimism, then we know that life in the world of the *principium individuationis* is, inescapably and unalterably, suffering. Why, then, should we engage with that world, why should we act? If 'action requires the veil of illusion', if action requires false belief about life and metaphysics, then knowing the truth entails that we should *abandon* action. Unlike the Greeks, *Nietzsche*, and any reader he manages to convince, is, in fact, himself committed to 'Buddhistic negation of the will'. In a word, though he is somewhat confused about it, early Nietzsche's response to pessimism is essentially the same as that of his master, Schopenhauer. Like Schopenhauer, he is a 'European Buddhist'.

Later Nietzsche knows this perfectly well, referring to his youthful self as suffering from a bad case of 'romanticism', by which he means pessimism about this world combined with 'metaphysical comfort', the offering of a fuzzy kind of other-worldly salvation. In the 1886 'Attempt at a self-criticism' which he added as a kind of introduction to later editions of *The Birth*, he advises 'young romantics' such as himself to abandon metaphysics and seek rather a '*this-worldly* comfort'.

Is there nothing Nietzsche has to add to Schopenhauer's solution to nihilism? One thing, I think. Schopenhauer says, it will be remembered, (*a*) that 'salvation' consists in reunion with the absolute, transcendence of the *principium individuationis*, but also that (*b*) the absolute is absolutely evil. As we observed, however, these propositions are incompatible. Union with evil cannot be regarded as salvation, but can only be viewed with horror and revulsion.

Schopenhauer's view of the absolute as absolute evil is simply the reversal of the Christian view of it as absolute good. Nietzsche, however, suggests a third view. The source of all existence is to be conceived neither as saint nor as sadist, but rather as 'an entirely reckless and amoral artist-god' (BT 'Attempt at a self-criticism' 5), a 'world-building force' which 'the dark Heraclitus compares to a playing child that places stones here and there and builds sand hills only to overthrow them again' (BT 24). This child-artist creates the world of the *principium individuationis* for its own entertainment. That is its sole point and justification: 'only as an *aesthetic phenomenon* is existence and the world . . . justified' (BT 5, 24). The world is a kind of gigantic movie the point of which is to occupy and entertain its 'sole author and spectator'. Or rather, it is a series of movies – to view the same movie all the time would become boring. From time to time the creative force destroys the sandcastle-worlds it has built and constructs new ones. (This corresponds to what *we* regard as 'the terrible destructiveness of . . . world history' (see p. 45 above).)

How does this Nietzschean anthropomorphisation of the absolute bear on the inconsistency in Schopenhauer's philosophy? Very much later, in the *Will to Power* (section 1005), Nietzsche says:

> Against the theory that the 'in-itself' must necessarily be good, blessed, true, and one, Schopenhauer's interpretation of the 'in-itself' as will was an essential step; but he did not understand how to *deify* this will; he remained entangled in the moral-Christian ideal ... see[ing] it as bad, stupid, and absolutely reprehensible.

This is completely correct. Schopenhauer judges the Christian God by the standards of Christian morality and finds it absolutely wanting. This moralism, Nietzsche suggests, is what creates the inconsistency in Schopenhauer's position. If, on the other hand, we view the primordial unity as a 'child' – as, that is, 'innocent', an inappropriate object of moral judgement – then the barrier to regarding unification with it as 'salvation' is removed.

This, it seems to me, is Nietzsche's contribution to the Schopenhauerian solution to the perceived worthlessness of our existence. It is not merely the child-artist who must be regarded as 'amoral'. *We* must become amoral – 'beyond good and evil' (BT 'Attempt at a self-criticism' 5) – in order to escape the pain of life as an individual through identification with the author-creator of the world-movie. The main significance of *The Birth* is as a kind of footnote to Schopenhauer, a footnote that removes an inconsistency in 'European Buddhism'.[2]

European Buddhism is an exotic version of true-worldism. According to it, the meaning of life is the attainment of *nirvana*, passage from this world of pain to a place (or 'place') that is 'beyond suffering'. Should we become European Buddhists?

The answer, surely, is that we should if and only if there really is (or we have reason to think there might well be) a place beyond suffering, a paradise or utopia. Why should we believe this?

According to Schopenhauer, the serenity of the mystics, their 'ocean-like calmness of spirit', is 'complete and certain gospel' (WR I p. 411). But this is silly. There are people who are serene because they think they are about to be teleported away by beings from another planet. Others are serene because they think Christ's Second Coming is about to happen. Are we to believe in salvation by aliens or salvation by Christ? What is important for serenity is belief, not knowledge. Delusions can produce serenity at least as well as truth. ('We possess art lest we perish of the truth,' says later Nietzsche.) And, in any case, mystic serenity may well be caused not by any particular vision, but by the endorphin bursts produced by ascetic practices.

The real argument that beyond the phenomenal world there really is a painless place, only implicit in Schopenhauer, is first made explicit by Nietzsche. It goes like this.

We know from Kant that the world of space-time is ideal, appearance merely, not reality 'in itself'. And we know from Schopenhauer that plurality and individuality can only exist within space and time. It follows that ultimate reality is 'beyond plurality', beyond individuality. But 'individuality [is] . . . the source of all suffering' (BT 10). Hence ultimate reality must be beyond suffering.

The reason individuality is taken to be the source of suffering is, I think, this. At the most general level of analysis, as we know from Schopenhauer, suffering is a disjunction between subject and object, between the way I want the world to be and the way it is. So suffering presupposes a distinction between subject and object, presupposes division, difference, plurality, individuality. Hence, beyond space and time, beyond plurality, there can be no suffering.

The trouble with this argument is that, actually, we *don't* know from Kant that reality itself is beyond space and time.

Let us return to the sunglasses analogy (p. 26 above). Everything looks green through green sunglasses. So we suppose that the image of reality that appears through the glasses fails to correspond to the way reality actually is. But maybe, in fact, everything *is* green. The same is true with respect to Kant. From the fact that the human mind constructs its own story of the world, nothing at all actually follows about whether or not that story corresponds to the way it really is. Maybe it just so happens that the world we construct exactly corresponds to the way the 'in itself' really is.

René Magritte, the brilliant surrealist painter, made this point in a witty critique of Kant's style of true-world thinking. One of his hyper-realistic painting shows, from the inside, a window on which has been painted a landscape of meadow and hills. The window has a jagged hole in it, evidently broken by a projectile coming, perhaps, from the inside. Through the hole one can see a portion of the real landscape beyond the window. It exactly fits the painted landscape, the contours of the two are completely continuous. The painting seems to be aimed directly at European Buddhism: *Free at Last* is its ironic title.

What follows from this is that Kantians – those who accept the broad (and surely correct) thesis that the mind (or language) constructs our image of reality – must take absolutely seriously, more seriously than Kant himself took it, the thesis that there is *nothing at all* we can know about that which lies beyond that image – *including* the claim that it is different in character from the world that is presented within the image.[3]

Moreover, even if reality does not, in fact, possess the spatio-temporal ordering of our constructed world, it by no means follows that it is 'beyond plurality'. For it might still be spatio-temporal, its space-time differing from ours only in having different mathematical properties. (This seems to be the case with respect to the difference between common-sense space and Einsteinian space. The former is Euclidean – the angles of a triangle equal 180 degrees – but the latter is not. Since gravity 'bends' light, a triangle in Einsteinian space, defined as the intersection of three light rays, actually has angles greater than 180 degrees.)

In Chapter 3 we saw Schopenhauer providing us with a powerful reason for rejecting the Christian account of ultimate reality. Since our world is evidently *not* the best of all possible worlds, it cannot be the creation of an all-powerful, wholly benevolent God. That left the field open for an alternative account of the 'thing in itself', specifically, for the account provided by European Buddhism. We now see, however, that we have no good reason to believe in a domain beyond plurality and hence beyond pain. Belief in *nirvana*, while not *as* irrational as belief in the heaven of traditional Christianity, is still irrational.

Another, quite different kind of objection to European Buddhism – and, in fact, to the Platonic and Christian versions of true-world philosophy as well – is one that is raised by Nietzsche himself, in a later phase of his thinking. Discussing 'romantic pessimism', he raises the question as to why anyone should *need* a 'metaphysical comfort' for life in this world? Why should they be attracted to a doctrine – *this*-worldly nihilism – that represents life in this world as worthless? Because, it seems plausible to conclude, such people represent life's *failures*, those lacking in the spiritual energy, the spiritual *health*, to cope with its complexities (see, for example, *The Gay Science* section 370). They are, to put it unkindly, 'losers', life's cripples.

The upshot of the reflections of this and the previous two chapters is, then, that neither the Christian nor the European Buddhist version of the true-world answer to the question of the meaning of life is any good. As thinking beings we have no grounds for believing in any kind of supra-natural paradise. And if we find ourselves, in spite of this, drawn towards such belief, then we should question our state of psychological health.

This, however, is not the end of the true world. For, as we shall see in the next chapter, its extraordinary adaptability enables it to survive the death of the supernatural.

5

Hegel

Georg Wilhelm Friedrich Hegel (1770–1831) was born, wrote and died. Nothing else interesting happened in his life. (Actually, this is not strictly true. He had an illegitimate child and was intimate friends with the great romantic poet Friedrich Hölderlin.)

Readers disagree as to where, in his massive output, the 'real' Hegel is to be found. Following Marx and Sartre, I take the view that he is to be found in the relatively early work, the *Phenomenology of Spirit*, which he completed in 1806, in Jena, to the sound of the guns of Napoleon's advancing army.

Hegel was sharply critical of the, as he called it, 'bourgeois (*bürgerlich*)' society of his own day (a society, as we shall see, he saw as prefigured in the 'citizen (*bürgerlich*)' society of the Roman Republic). He characterised it as a society in which individuals think of themselves as ultimate 'subjects', giving meaning to their lives by an arbitrary choice of ends, and in which they are guaranteed the personal space, the freedom to pursue those ends, by the state. The trouble with such social atomism (or 'liberalism' as we would now call it), in Hegel's view, is that it gives rise to what, in the preface to the *Phenomenology*, he calls 'alienation' (PS 19),[1] a loss of integration with one's fellows, of community, which leads to the replacement of co-operation by competition. His primary aim, he says, is to address the problem of alienation. The means of doing so is his philosophy of, as he calls it, 'absolute idealism'.

What is absolute idealism? Writing only twenty-five years after the publication of Kant's *Critique of Pure Reason* and only two years after Kant's death, one would naturally assume 'idealism' to indicate that Hegel is operating within Kant's dichotomy between mind-dependent, mind-constructed 'phenomena' and the mind-independent 'thing in itself'. This assumption is, however, I believe, false. In spite of the name, Hegel is not an idealist about the world of space and time at all but, rather, a *realist*. The natural world, for Hegel, is in no sense a dream or figment of the human mind. (As we will shortly see, the transition from 'scepticism' about the reality of the natural world to acknowledging that reality constitutes, for Hegel, epistemological *progress*.) Contemporaries, and near-contemporaries such as Schopenhauer, were quite clear that Hegel is actually a realist (as a Kantian, Schopenhauer took this to be a crushing *objection* to Hegel). Hegel, he says, 'regards the *phenomenon* as the *being in itself* of the world' (WR II p. 442), in other words draws no distinction between the natural world and ultimate reality.

Hegel is, then, I suggest, no Kantian. This is why, though he is their chronological predecessor, I have chosen to discuss him after Schopenhauer and the younger Nietzsche: whereas, so far as their metaphysics are concerned, they are Kant's true followers, Hegel represents a radical rejection of Kantianism. 'Absolute idealism' is, indeed, a thesis about 'the absolute', about ultimate reality. But, for Hegel, we shall see, the absolute is not 'beyond' but rather *within* space and time. That Hegel joined with Fichte, Schelling and others in calling himself an idealist is a tribute to Kant's mana: Kant cast such a long shadow that everyone, in the age of so-called 'German idealism', *had* at least to appear to be some sort of idealist. I shall continue to talk about Hegel's 'absolute idealism', but it should be borne in mind that, in many respects, 'absolute realism' would be a less misleading label.

What, then, does 'absolute idealism' have to say about the absolute? The doctrine can, I think, be represented in terms of the following five propositions.

(1) The absolute is a 'subject', an 'I' (PS 233). It is a person-like entity in that it reasons and has intentions and goals. (Hegel's designation of it as *Geist*, 'mind' or, better, 'spirit', is indicative of this person-like character.)

(2) 'The true is the whole. But the whole is nothing other than the essence consummating itself through its development' (PS 20). The absolute is not a thing, but a process, an 'organic' (PS 2) process of self-development. As with a plant, the goal of this process, and the path to it, is in the absolute from the beginning as a kind of blueprint or 'essence'.

(3) Individuals are merely parts of the process, the parts in and through which it happens. They stand to the whole (so one might

elucidate Hegel's view) as the constituent molecules which make up my body stand to that body which exists in and through the constantly changing flux of molecules.

(4) As *mere* parts, individuals are not genuine 'subjects'. They have 'no being in themselves' (PS 171). The absolute is, then, not just *a* subject: it is the *only* genuine subject. It follows that the everyday distinction between self and others is superficial, not ontologically speaking, of ultimate validity. (Consider, by way of elucidation, David Beckham. As is well known, Beckham has a life outside football. But suppose that he didn't. Then he would be *nothing but* a football player, his entire being or nature would be defined by his role in the team. In this situation Beckham's desires, ambitions, goals, in general his 'will', would be identical with the will of Manchester United. Manchester United would, we could say, constitute his *true self* and the same for everyone else similarly devoted to the team. In this case, the distinction between self and others would ultimately be invalid.)

(5) The *telos*, or goal, of the absolute is simply the knowledge that it is the ultimate and sole subject, and that consequently it is 'all reality' (PS 233), everything is (part of) itself. Hegel calls possession of such knowledge 'absolute knowing' (PS 788–808). The process of the absolute's self-development is the process of its moving ever closer to absolute knowing. Absolute knowing comes into being when all (or nearly all) individuals recognise the truth of (1)–(4), when absolute knowing becomes, as we say, the *Zeitgeist*, the 'spirit of the age'.

How does Hegel argue for this mind-boggling metaphysical doctrine? He does so by actually *presenting* the history of the 'world' to date (actually the history of the West) as a process of development towards absolute knowing, and by arguing that 'history comes to an end' with and only with spirit's attainment of absolute knowing. The *Phenomenology*, that is to say, is a telling of 'world history' as a kind of *Bildungsroman*. (A *Bildungsroman* is a 'novel of education' in which, through a series of 'learning experiences', the hero progresses from naïveté to wisdom.) For Hegel, history is made up of sharply different, epoch-defining 'shapes (*Gestalten*) of consciousness', 'world-views' or fundamental modes of world-understanding. The transition from a given 'shape' to its successor represents an 'advance' in the education of the West; from the point of view of absolute idealism itself, that is to say, an advance in the education of spirit towards absolute knowing, towards the knowledge that it is 'all reality' (PS 233).

Hegel's 'biography' of the West differs, however, from the typical *Bildungsroman* in that there is a strict *logic* to history, a logically necessary relation between the character of one shape of conscious and the character of its successor. The inadequacies of a given 'shape', that is to say, as revealed by rational criticism, lead, as a matter of necessity, to the modification that transforms it into its successor. The driving force of history is, then, constructive criticism (or 'negation', as Hegel calls it). History is essentially 'dialectical' (from the Greek *dialectos*, conversation). It is spirit's critical dialogue with itself. History finishes when there is nothing left to criticise, when 'absolute knowing' becomes the shape of consciousness that defines an epoch – the epoch with which history, understood as the dialectical succession of shapes of consciousness, comes to an end.

This, at least, is the theory of how things are supposed to work, as set out in the preface. Unfortunately, it is not always easy to match what actually happens in the work with what is supposed to happen. Partly this is because of the extraordinary mud-like obscurity of Hegel's prose (Schopenhauer claims that reading Hegel rots the brain (WR II p. 40)). But mainly it is because, rather than the neatly organised, linear development promised by the preface, what we actually get is a fragment of history here, another disconnected fragment there, and, in between, something that doesn't look like history at all. Hegel appears to swerve arbitrarily from topic to unrelated topic in a way that has led some readers to compare the *Phenomenology* to the works of James Joyce – to view it as the product of an unmediated 'stream of consciousness'.

In fact, however, things are not that bad. There is a structure, a principle of organisation, to the work, one which more or less fits the structure we have been led to expect. It is, I think, as follows.

Hegel's intention, I suggest, is to provide three different histories of the West, each of which is concerned with a different aspect of human existence, a different aspect of the 'shapes of consciousness' which define the epochs of world history. (Shapes of consciousness are, therefore, *complex*, multi-aspected.) These histories are the following. (1) The history of humanity's knowledge of nature. (2) The history of personal relations, of the individual's relationship with 'the other' in the form of persons. Central to this history is the history of the individual's relation to the 'highest' of all persons, namely, God. (3) The history of the state, of, in other words, politics. Each history is intended to exhibit Western humanity's progressive development towards 'absolute knowing' within its own domain. With some over-simplification, the three histories may be called the histories of science, of personal relations and of politics.

First, then, the history of *science*. The form of consciousness which Hegel represents as the beginning of humanity's knowledge of nature is what he calls 'sense-certainty' (PS 90–110). In this form, knowledge of nature is considered to consist in immediate sensory consciousness devoid of any interpretation whatsoever. That is – as far as, for example, vision is concerned – coloured shapes.[2] Hegel argues that sense-certainty is riddled with contradictions and so inevitably collapses into a new shape of consciousness.

Consider what the subject of sense-certainty knows. (I have slightly modified Hegel's example, here.) Perhaps 'This is red (all over)'. Moments later, however, she knows 'This is green'. So she knows 'This is red and this is green (all over)'. But that is impossible. One might object that there is no paradox here since the 'this' refers to a different object on each occasion. But that is precisely Hegel's point. In order to avoid the contradiction one needs a whole lot of conceptual postulation that goes far beyond the deliverances of immediate experience: oneself as a subject in space and time along with a variety of objects some of which one sees at one time and others at a later time. The contradiction disappears only when consciousness goes beyond the immediately given, when it allows itself conceptual interpretation of the given. Sense-certainty, therefore, necessitates a new shape of consciousness, one which Hegel calls 'perception'.

Perception (PS 111–31) is distinguished by the fact that it has developed the concept of a thing – a 'substance' – something that 'has' properties. (We are still, presumably, at a very primitive stage in human history.) Consciousness, however, cannot work out whether a substance – say, a cube of sugar – is something over and above all its properties (as a pin-cushion is something over and above the pins sticking in it) or merely the collection of those properties: of sweetness, whiteness, cubicalness and so on. Neither alternative is satisfactory. If it is the latter, Hegel seems to argue, there is no principle to explain why contradictory properties like 'red all over' and 'green all over' cannot belong to the same collection, and if the former – if the essence of a thing is a 'bare' something completely devoid of properties – then there is nothing to distinguish it from any other thing and hence nothing to explain the *plurality* of things in the natural world. (Hegel's argument, here, doesn't make a lot of sense – the conclusion rather than the details of how to get there seems to be all that really interests him.)

So 'perception' collapses, too. Knowing the true nature of physical reality isn't a matter of even interpreted *looking* at things, but essentially involves *reasoning*. With this step we make the transition from common sense to natural *science*.

What Hegel means by 'science' is the enterprise that started in the sixteenth and seventeenth centuries with the likes of Copernicus, Galileo and Newton. The main discussion, under the title 'Observing reason', runs from section 240 to section 346. The principal point Hegel wants to make is this: what science looks for is patterns, laws, exceptionless laws that hold throughout the universe. But laws have to be laws *of* something, have to describe the behaviour of some set of entities. Everyday entities, however – pen-knives or snuff-boxes (PS 244) – are unsuitable since they do not behave in properly lawful ways. One snuff-box dropped into water may float, another sink. Hence science deals, not in ordinary, everyday, middle-sized objects but rather in 'matters'. (An earlier discussion of science at sections 132–65 identifies these 'matters' as, at bottom, 'forces'.) 'Matters' are distinguished by the fact that their behaviour is completely determined by their 'essence'. Given you know something is a water molecule, you know *exactly* how it is going to behave. Every water molecule behaves exactly like every other water molecule; its behaviour is completely lawful.

Science *thinks* that it *discovers* these 'matters'. In fact, however, they are constructed rather than discovered, posited as part of 'reason's' project (the project, that is, of spirit in its aspect as reasoner) of exhibiting the whole of nature as patterned through and through.[3]

Why does it do this? Because, claims Hegel, the highest – though 'secret' – impulse of reason is the desire to discover *itself* in nature. It 'digs into the very entrails of things and opens every vein in them so that it may gush forth and meet itself' (PS 241). In a word, according to Hegel's, as it were, psychoanalysis of science, reason unconsciously knows, is 'dimly aware' (ibid.) of, the truth of absolute idealism and, in its practice, seeks to confirm this presentiment.

What has exhibiting nature as, beneath the superficial chaos, completely lawful, regularly patterned, got to do with reason's meeting itself in nature? The great sixteenth-century astronomer Johannes Kepler thought that the planets must have souls in order to preserve their perfectly spherical orbits. Order, we assume, is the mark of intelligence, disorder the mark of the non-intelligent. If you discover a perfect octagon on the sandy beach, you assume it has been *drawn* on the beach, that you are not alone in the universe.

(Of course – a point Kepler missed – the discovery of pattern in nature does not prove that *it* is an intelligence. The pattern may have been imposed by a creating but entirely distant God. Remember, however, that Hegel represents science as seeking merely to *confirm* the truth of absolute idealism, not to prove it. Given that one starts with the hypothesis that nature is an intelligence – indeed, the very same intelligence as one's essential self – the discovery of pattern does tend to confirm it.)

However, when it comes to inorganic and particularly human nature, claims Hegel, reason can discover at best tendencies, not laws. Hence reason's desire to discover itself in nature is ultimately frustrated.[4] This shows that scientific thinking must ultimately turn to another kind of thinking in order to 'experience the consummation of itself' (PS 241). This other kind of thinking manifests itself in Hegel's second history of the West, his *history of personal relations*, to which I now turn.

Hegel's history of personal relations is a history of the individual's relationship with other persons – above all, with God. It begins with what he calls 'animal' consciousness.

Life (in other words, spirit), says Hegel, is an infinite whole. It exists in, and only in, the generation and destruction of individuals which themselves, however, are not genuine entities, 'have no being in themselves' (PS 171). But the individual animal does not wish to be a mere part of a universal whole. It desires existence that is independent of anything else, and the knowledge of such independence, which Hegel calls 'self-certainty' (*Selbstbewusstsein*, which could also be translated as 'self-confidence'). Consequently its basic approach to other manifestations of life is to 'consume' it (ibid.).

To grasp the basic idea here, consider a fire. A fire is made up of flames, none of which is anything more than a momentary part of the fire. But imagine (we might call this 'the revolt of the flame') a flame that possessed self-consciousness and wished to establish its own status as an independent entity. The sure way of doing this would be to 'kill' the rest of the fire. If the flame saw that the rest of the fire was dead while it itself still existed, it would have proved to itself, beyond doubt, its own independence.

Hegel did not, of course, really intend his account of 'animal' consciousness to be an essay in animal psychology. Far more likely is that what he means by 'animal' is pre-social, pre-cultural, pre-linguistic *humanity*. In any case, the point of the account becomes clear in the discussion of what he calls 'the-life-and-death-struggle' (PS 187–8), a discussion which clearly does concern human beings. This phrase describes a world in which the human individual sees its 'essential being' in the form of another human individual and, in the quest for certainty concerning its own independence, seeks to kill it. (Notice that even at this early stage the human being intuits the truth of absolute idealism. What leads him to react with horror to this intuition is, as we shall see, a mistaken idea of independence. True independence (or 'freedom'), Hegel will argue, is not in conflict with, but is rather guaranteed by, the truth of absolute idealism.)

Pretty clearly, the life-and-death struggle corresponds to what the seventeenth-century English philosopher Thomas Hobbes called the 'state of nature': the condition of humanity before the coming into being of the state. Like Hobbes, Hegel pictures this as a condition of 'war, all against all'.

The flaw in the strategy of one engaged in the life-and-death struggle is that 'self-consciousness exists in and for itself [only] when it is recognised by another' (PS 188). 'Self-certainty', in other words, *entails* 'recognition (*Anerkennung*)', and cannot exist without it. The combatant, therefore, requires that the 'other' should remain alive. A corpse cannot provide 'recognition'.

Sartre, as we shall see in Chapter 11, provides what I take to be the best explanation of this passage. Hegel says, 'The real is essentially what it is for another' (PS 390). Sartre, rephrasing the thought, says that the other 'holds the secret of my being' (see p. 145 below). I want to exist as a genuinely independent entity. But any genuine entity exists as a *kind* of thing. It has an 'essence' or nature. So I want to be confident of my independent existence as, let us say, a loving husband and kind father. But I can only be confident of possessing that nature if my wife and children accord me the 'recognition', in this case love and gratitude, appropriate to my possessing that nature. If, however, I have killed them all, I have removed every possibility of receiving such 'recognition'.

This flaw in the shape of consciousness which sees every other human as an enemy is the motivating force for its collapse into a new shape which Hegel calls 'the master–slave relation' (PS

178–96). Since it is presented as immediately following the state of nature, this represents Hegel's account of the first social order.

One fine day (as it were) the victor in the life-and-death struggle, reflecting on his need for recognition, has a brilliant idea: a slave is better than a corpse. Since he knows he can kill the slave at any moment his independent existence remains assured. But since the slave is a living human being he is available to accord his master 'recognition'.

But actually, observes Hegel, the strategy of enslavement is not a brilliant idea at all. Since, for the master, the slave is nothing more than an *instrument* for the satisfaction of his desires, he can no more receive genuine recognition from a slave than from a washing machine or a vacuum cleaner (my examples, not Hegel's). Having made this point, and having pointed out that the master is a mere consumer, living in idle decadence (we seem now to find ourselves in the declining days of the Roman Empire), Hegel's attention abruptly switches from the master's perspective to that of the slave. The future history of the West, it seems, consists in evolutions within the slave's perspective on the world, evolutions within slave consciousness.

Hegel claims that, right from the start, the slave has, in fact, a more evolved consciousness than the master. The point has to do with *work*. In work, the slave imposes form on materials, 'humanises' them, and thereby has at least an intimation of discovering himself in the 'other', discovering the truth of absolute idealism. The master has no such intimation. For him, rather, everything 'other' is a mere instrument (or 'object', as in 'sex object') for satisfying his desires. It is something *completely* 'other', completely different from, and alien to, himself. The master lives in a kind of empirical solipsism (possessing the consciousness sometimes ascribed to new-born babies): nothing exists for him except his own ego as a locus of desires, and a world entirely made up of instruments for satisfying those desires. He is alone.

Though superior to the master's consciousness, slave consciousness is, none the less, far from ideal. For it exists in bondage, pain, and fear of sudden and arbitrary death. It is out of these conditions that 'Stoicism' (PS 197–201) appears.

As a 'manifestation of world spirit', as the defining philosophy of an entire historical epoch, Stoicism requires, says Hegel, a highly developed intellectual culture[5] and 'universal fear and bondage'. It is, therefore, 'the philosophy of the cultured slave' (PS 199), though of course it can, and did, spread from the slave to other classes. Stoicism flourished from about 300 BC to 200 AD, but Hegel later makes it clear (see p. 67) below) that he thinks of it in particular connection with the Roman Republic (509–31 BC).

As Hegel observes, Stoicism is about freedom. It is, in a nutshell, the doctrine that 'stone walls do not a prison make'. Since one's true being consists in one's thoughts, and since these remain free even if one's body is imprisoned, Stoicism is a guarantee of absolute freedom.

This looks to be an obviously compensatory strategy – like the lonely child's imaginary friend. Hegel's main criticism, however, is that Stoicism misunderstands the nature of freedom, fails to grasp its 'living reality'. What is required for that is 'grasping the living world as a system of thought' (PS 200), in other words, grasping that spirit, and hence one's true self, is 'all reality', grasping the truth of absolute idealism.

Stoicism is a doctrine that *contracts*. The 'I' that is alleged to possess absolute freedom is contracted to a tiny point of empirical self-consciousness (the 'I' of Descartes' 'I think, therefore I am'). For Hegel, however, true freedom is a matter of infinite *expansion*: the 'I' of absolute idealism is the inner reality of absolutely everything. As, therefore, 'all reality', it is such that outside it there is absolutely nothing. There is no 'other' of the 'I' of absolute Spirit, and nothing, therefore, that can restrict its freedom. Hence, as the 'I', not of Stoicism, but of absolute idealism, we are all absolutely free.

Stoicism, as we have said, is about freedom. This looks to be an abrupt change of topic from the quest for 'self-certainty', certainty of one's 'independence', that seemed to motivate 'animal' consciousness, the life-and-death struggle, and the master's side of the master–slave relation. In fact, however, since 'freedom' as Hegel conceives it, just *is* 'independence', being dependent on nothing outside oneself, freedom is what we have been talking about all along. The quest for 'self-certainty' as displayed to date, we now see, is the misguided quest for that which, according to Hegel, can only be properly achieved in 'absolute knowing', knowledge of the truth of absolute idealism.[6]

A natural progression from Stoicism is 'Scepticism' (PS 202–6), another school of philosophy that flourished in the Roman world. (Sometimes it is called 'Pyrrhonism' after its Greek founder Pyrrho of Elis who lived in the third century BC.) Scepticism is, says Hegel, the 'realization of that of which Stoicism is only the notion, and is the actual experience of what freedom of thought is' (PS 202). Whereas Stoicism achieves only an incomplete 'negation' of natural existence, Scepticism achieves its 'absolute negation'.

To understand this, it is important to see that Scepticism in the ancient world was not, as it became with Descartes and Hume, a kind of philosopher's tool that one left behind when one left the study and went off, as Hume put it, to 'consort with modest women and play backgammon'. Rather, it was a way of life appropriate to an age of 'universal fear and bondage'. One deployed Zeno's paradoxes,[7] arguments from perceptual relativity,[8] dream argument[9] and so on, not as philosophical arguments designed to bring out the nature and limits of human knowledge, but rather as kinds of mantras, meditative techniques designed, through repetition, to induce a practical suspension of belief in external reality. The point of that was to produce a state of 'ataraxia', equanimity or peace of mind, based on a realisation of the phantasmagoric character of the objects of all one's hopes and fears.

This is why Hegel views Roman Scepticism as the 'completion' of Stoicism. Both seek absolute indifference to events in the natural world. But Stoicism alone, since it does not deny the reality of the locomotive hurtling along the railway tracks to which one is tied, cannot, in fact, maintain such indifference. Only if, through prolonged meditation, one can convince oneself of the illusory nature of things like locomotives can one truly achieve indifference.

But even with the transition from Stoicism to Scepticism this slave's view of things, Hegel asserts, doesn't really work. Instead of ataraxia, what actually occurs is a kind of oscillation between 'master' consciousness and 'slave' consciousness.

Sometimes, probably immediately after a particularly focused set of sceptical meditations, the devotee achieves genuine equanimity. There is nothing there, nothing that can threaten or limit his freedom – he is as much a 'master' of the situation as the master he envies and covertly seeks to emulate. But sometimes, too, the would-be sceptic finds himself gripped by practical lusts (sex, food) and fears (pain, death) and is, *a fortiori*, gripped by a vivid sense of the reality of the objects of those lusts and fears. So he needs more meditation. And thus, in this oscillating manner, his life continues.

What terminates the oscillations of Scepticism is the arrival of a new shape of consciousness which Hegel calls 'the unhappy consciousness' (PS 206–30). Since the discussion of this is evidently a (wildly brilliant) interpretation of medieval Christianity, we have moved, now, out of Roman antiquity and into the Middle Ages.

Scepticism, we saw, oscillates between two states, a 'master' state in which it feels completely 'independent', completely 'free' of the changing and uncertain flow of events in the natural world, and a 'slave' state in which it feels utterly dependent on that flow of events. The unhappy consciousness stops this oscillation by bringing the two states into a unity, albeit a 'disrupted', 'unhappy' unity. It does this by giving up trying to pretend that the natural world is unreal. It acknowledges itself as an empirical individual inhabiting a natural world. Its consciousness of something that is entirely independent of nature it projects on to an 'alien . . . beyond' (PS 208) and refers to as 'the unchanging' – in other words, 'God'. What happens, therefore, with the emergence of medieval Christianity is the replacement of the two *states* of Scepticism with two *worlds*, the natural world and, in Nietzsche's language, the 'true' world.[10]

Why is the unhappy consciousness unhappy? Because, in experiencing its separation from the unchanging, it experiences its natural existence as a state of exile, cast-outness, 'thrownness' (Heidegger's term actually has its origin in the Middle Ages). The myth of the fall from paradise, Hegel points out, expresses this sense of alienation, a sense that must have been particularly strong in the violent and chaotic times of the 'Dark Ages' that succeeded the fall of the Roman Empire.

Because it feels this way, the unhappy consciousness indulges in worship, 'devotion'. This is a kind of thinking, 'a chaotic jingling of bells or a mist of warm incense, a musical thinking which does not get as far as the concept' (PS 217). (This looks like a Protestant reaction to what Protestants tend to experience as the 'cheap theatre' of Catholicism.) What worship expresses is, first, the worshipper's sense of alienation and, second, her yearning for reunification with the unchanging. The unhappy consciousness expresses its hope of reunification by postulating the incarnation of God in the person of Christ, a symbolic expression of the hope of overcoming the schism between the two worlds.

Why does the unhappy consciousness yearn for unity with the unchanging? As we have seen, the unhappy consciousness originates in Scepticism and in the two states of consciousness between which it oscillated. But both of these states were states of the self. So what gets called 'the unchanging' continues, deep down, to be thought of as the self. The longing for unity with God is the longing to overcome, as Hegel calls it, a *self*-alienation. Of course, the 'self' that is the unchanging is a self that is completely 'independent', absolutely 'free'. So, in the end, medieval Christianity represents yet another attempt at 'self-certainty'.

Why does medieval Christianity represent a dialectical advance over preceding shapes of consciousness? The answer, it seems, has to do with the priesthood, which Hegel regards as a dialectical development within Christianity itself (PS 226–30). The commands of the priest are thought of as the direct expression of the will of God. In submitting to the priest, the unhappy consciousness affirms its own 'nothingness': it divests itself of existence as a 'for itself' (a self-conscious being) and becomes a mere 'thing' to be disposed of by the priest.

Hegel, as we shall shortly see, does not approve of abject submission to the will of one individual or class of individuals. None the less he finds something positive in medieval Christian community. In submitting to the priest one at least takes a step away from the solipsistic individualism of Stoicism and Scepticism and towards the realisation that one's 'essence' lies in the universal rather than the individual, in the 'spirit' of absolute idealism. (Notice that, in Hegel's representation, the unhappy consciousness is confused. On the one hand, it places its essential being in a supernatural 'true world'. On the other, in Christian practice, it senses its essential being to be immanent in the here and now. It is this latter strand of thinking, which, as we will see, points, for Hegel, towards the proper nature of Christianity.)

What happens next? Quite arbitrarily, the story of humanity's relation to God breaks off at this point, and continues only two hundred pages later in a discussion of the eighteenth-century Enlightenment and its attempt to eliminate what it regards as 'superstition' (PS 538–73).

Enlightenment, for Hegel, is the drive to reduce everything to conceptual clarity and order. As such, it appears identical with what, in Hegel's history of science, is called scientific 'reason' (see pp. 61–3 above). The fundamental aim of 'reason', remember, was, by discovering a rational patterning of things in nature, to discover *itself* in nature, and thereby confirm its 'secret' intimation of the truth of absolute idealism. Reason, then, seeks integration. Its attitude to (medieval) 'faith' is correspondingly hostile, for it sees it as something which harms its victims by alienating them from the (one and only) real world. Its weapon for destroying superstition is simply reason itself. If people will only give up their irrational belief in the word of the priests and learn that the only source of knowledge is reason based on sense experience, they will be liberated from the shackles of superstition.

Hegel makes two criticisms of Enlightenment. First, it has its own account of the absolute, 'material substance', as that which underlies all sensible properties of things. As such, however, it turns out to be merely a 'vacuum to which no determinations, no predicates can be attributed' (PS 577).[11] In other words, Enlightenment turns out *itself* to be deeply alienating, since this featureless absolute is something with which we have no chance of identifying ourselves. Second, in its excessively negative attitude to Christianity, it fails to see how, in the individual's submissive membership of Christian community, there is an important anticipation of the integrating truth of absolute idealism. In short, in condemning faith, Enlightenment condemns what is, in fact, 'its own thought' (PS 565).

Religion, then, needs a radical, post-Enlightenment reappraisal. Above all, Christianity, whose doctrine of the unity of the universal and individual in the figure of Christ makes it the most advanced of all religions (PS 684), needs to be taken very seriously. Not, of course, the Christianity which subscribes to the theology of the unhappy consciousness, but rather a religion in which God and the essential, universal self of every individual, in other words spirit, are understood to be one and the same. This is the true meaning of the allegories of the Incarnation, Crucifixion, and Resurrection. In the Incarnation, God, the universal self, becomes an individual. But he becomes only *one* individual. Jesus must, therefore, die in order to return as the Holy Spirit, the universal spirit that is the inner reality of Christian community (PS 759–63).

Thus the second of Hegel's journeys through the history of the West. In the following chapter I shall turn to the third.

6

Hegel (continued), with a postscript on Marx

Hegel's third history of the West is concerned with politics, with the individual's relation to the state. It begins (and almost ends) with what he calls the 'ethical' or 'happy' state (PS 444–83). Hegel indicates that the reference, here, is to the ancient world (PS 390). Fairly clearly, I think, it is to the tribal society of Homeric and pre-Homeric Greece.

The happy state is a state of harmonious co-operation, grounded in the fact that every individual recognises his or her true self in the 'ethical substance' of a people. This ethical substance, the 'living spirit' of a society, is constituted by the *ethos*, the customs or ethical tradition of a people. It is constituted, as one might put it, by an intuitive, shared sense of how 'we' do things. Since everyone accepts the same set of fundamental ethical standards, it would seem that there can be no fundamental ethical clashes within the ethical state. Moreover, since custom is something independent of the will of any individual or élite, there can, Hegel thinks, be no question of anyone finding the conventions of custom oppressive. The harmonious order of custom-based society is something entirely different from the kind of order created by a dictator or his secret police. It is not an order that is imposed, but one that freely flows from the individual's own essential will.[1]

This 'ethical' state looks very much like the practical realisation of absolute idealism and, as such, from Hegel's point of view, the ideal state. But though it is very close to that – shared custom (*Sittlichkeit*) *is*, for Hegel, the true basis of both morality and the state – it is not quite the ideal state: its collapse and the rise of 'individualism' was, Hegel says, a 'necessary', dialectical outcome since the ethical state contained within it the seeds of its own collapse (PS 354–5).

What are 'customs'? Following Sophocles, Hegel divides them

into 'divine' and 'human laws' (PS 445). The former, he claims, are the laws of the family, the latter the laws of the state. The former are generally intuitively felt rather than verbally articulated (in *Antigone* Sophocles refers to 'the unwritten law divine'), the latter conceptually articulated. Otherwise put – since, says Hegel, men generally have clear, conceptually articulate intelligences focused on the universal, while women have dark, intuitive intelligences focused on the particular – 'family values' are the primary values of women, state values the primary values of men. The two sets of values are always in tension, and sometimes, as in *Antigone*, come into outright conflict. (The king, Creon, orders that, as a traitor, Polynices' body is to be left unburied. Antigone, however, sees it as her duty to bury her brother, does so, and is condemned to death.)

This tension between men and woman – 'sexual politics' – caused the downfall of the Greek state. The woman make fun of the grave universalism of the men and encourage the natural tendency to anarchic individualism (teenage rebellion) among the youth. Eventually anarchy takes over and the state collapses.

With the collapse of the ethical state – of tribal society – a world of atomic individualism came into being. Eventually – Hegel is referring, here, to the Roman Republic (509–31 BC) – there came into being the shape of consciousness he calls 'legal status' (PS 477–83).

The world of 'legal status' is a world of isolated individuals, a world, as I pointed out earlier, which for Hegel prefigures the alienated world of modernity. The reason is that no one any longer experiences any 'continuity' with anyone else.[2] The foundation of the 'ethical' state, the 'universal substance', a 'universally dominating will of all' to which the individual owes 'service and obedience' since it is his own true will, has entirely disappeared (PS 479).[3] There is, Hegel points out, a profound ontological shift involved in the transition to the world of legal status. In the ethical state, personhood is a fundamentally non-individual phenomenon. But in the Roman world the universal has entirely disappeared: individuality become ontologically ultimate. This ontology is embodied in the concept of the person as citizen – a bearer of rights that are equal to the rights of every other citizen.

Hegel makes a comparison with Stoicism. The world of Roman legality is the concrete, living expression of that of which Stoic philosophy is the abstract expression: the ontological ultimacy of the 'I' of individual self-consciousness (PS 479).

The world of atomic individualism is a world of competition between rival egos, of covert 'war, all against all'. (It differs from the 'state of nature' in that the rights of citizens – so long as the state has the power to enforce them – constitute, as it were, 'rules of warfare' which must not be breached.) Since, in the end, there has to be a winner of this war, it is inevitable that someone will emerge as 'top dog', dictator, someone who sets rather than observes the rules. The transition from the legalism of the Roman Republic to the tyranny of the Roman Empire is therefore inevitable.

In the Empire, the character of social life is determined by the will of just one – necessarily oppressive – individual, the emperor. Consequently, the ordinary individual can find no 'continuity' between himself and the state and experiences it as a hostile, alien phenomenon. This condition of alienation Hegel regards as characterising Western relations to the state from the early Roman Empire (31 BC) until the French Revolution (1789).

In the feudal state of the Middle Ages (PS 488–526) there exist two sorts of people: the 'base' whose interest lies in creating and acquiring wealth (the bourgeoisie of the cities, the forefathers of the capitalism into which feudalism would one day collapse), and the 'noble' whose ideal is public service.[4] The base, says Hegel, of course see the state as oppressive (since, presumably, it taxes their wealth in order to prosecute the king's interests – usually war and conquest.) But, beneath the veneer of a morality which extols the virtue of public service, the nobles, too, are alienated from the state. Because, rather than embodying the spirit and will of a whole people, the state embodies the will of just one man, the king, service to the king is a matter of 'haughty honour' (PS 505) rather than the personal fulfilment of finding one's own will, oneself, in the state. The noble may die heroically for king and country. But he cannot die the right sort of death. His heroism is a simple renunciation of existence. 'True' self-sacrifice, on the other hand, is a 'renunciation [of self which] no less preserves itself' (PS 507) – the self which is identical with communal spirit.

Given, then, that even its apparent supporters, the military nobility, were inwardly alienated from it, the feudal state was bound to collapse. Power was bound to be transferred to the overtly rebellious bourgeoisie. A value reversal takes place. (We are now, perhaps, in the fifteenth century.) Whereas the value system of the Middle Ages[5] valued public service and despised the self-seeking production of wealth, capitalist values now become triumphant. It now becomes the case that, as the movie *Wall Street* succinctly put it, greed is good.

For the next significant transition in Hegel's history of politics, we visit, once again, the Enlightenment.

As we saw, the Enlightenment is strongly committed to rejecting entities (God) believed in only on the basis of 'superstition'. At the level of everyday consciousness this expresses itself as a crude empiricism, as the principle that nothing exists unless you can see it. Since everyday consciousness is practical, instrumental consciousness – things show up not as abstract arrangements of steel or plastic but as hammers or pens – this leads to 'utility' (PS 574–81) becoming the criterion of existence: nothing exists unless it has utility. In effect, the 'being-in-itself' of things becomes their 'being-for-us' (PS 580).

Unlike Heidegger (as we shall see in Chapter 15), Hegel does not view this as a regressive phenomenon. For, in taking utility as the criterion of existence, consciousness overcomes alienation, overcomes the subject–object distinction. If, that is, Hegel argues, the world is made up of equipment, things useful to 'the will', then it is the product and expression of that will. Clearly, however, this world-creating will is not the will of any individual – a hammer is usable by *anyone*. It is, therefore, as Jean-Jacques Rousseau put it, a 'general will', a will that belongs, equally, to everyone (PS 584).

Rousseau's metaphysics of the 'general will' provides, says Hegel, the foundation of the French Revolution.[6] The general will, evidently, is something that is fully and equally present in all individuals. It is a universal essence of humanity equally present in all social classes. But this means that the old class structure, the legacy of feudalism, is unjust: if all men are the same in essence, then they are the same in worth. If Jack is the same as his master, then he is as good as his master. Hence the old class system is seen to be oppressive and is overthrown by the new, revolutionary consciousness. A period of 'absolute freedom' (anarchy) now sets in.

Absolute freedom, however, cannot provide the basis of a social order, since that requires the assigning of particular individuals to particular roles within it. Society, that is, cannot exist without a specialisation of function which includes, significantly, a division between leaders and followers – a division which is by no means necessarily the same as a division between oppressors and the oppressed. Since, however, absolute freedom seeks to overthrow any government, regarding it as oppressive and in the service of factional interests,[7] it follows that social order can only be maintained by fear. Hence the 'terror' which followed the French Revolution.

Since he has now reached what was, for him, the present, Hegel's history of politics stops at this point. It is unclear what he has to say about places other than France, save that 'alienation' is the order of the day. He does, however, indicate how the history of politics will end. Rather than a regress to a pre-revolutionary shape of consciousness, individuals will preserve the insight of the Revolution that their essence is universal will, i.e. spirit. Spirit will, however, now understand that, though it is the universal essence of things, it must express itself through the differing forms of individuality (PS 594). It will take, in other words, the dialectical step of realising that, though it is a unitary entity, the unity it possesses resembles that of a *team*. As the activity of a successful football team consists not in everyone being captain, but in everyone contributing to the success of the whole by fulfilling their own, individual role, so *my* fulfilling *our* will consists in my fulfilling my own special function, whatever that may be.

Thus the last of Hegel's three histories of the West.

What is the point of absolute idealism? There might, of course, be no point other than the quest for disinterested metaphysical truth. But this, as we saw, is not the case. The point of the doctrine is to deal with the alienation Hegel perceives as – in spite of the momentary insight of the French Revolution – the pervasive condition of Western modernity. How, however, does it do that? Not by giving a set of practical instructions for the overcoming of alienation. There is, in the *Phenomenology*, no programme of action. Rather, what Hegel offers is the promise – indeed, guarantee – that, as the inexorable laws of history unfold, alienation will one day be overcome and everyone will live in peace and harmony. This means that – in Nietzsche's language – what Hegel offers is a kind of 'metaphysical comfort' (BT 17) for the alienation of the present.

Not, of course, an *other-worldly* metaphysical comfort – other-worldliness, as we now know, intensifying rather than overcoming alienation, produces the unhappiness of the 'unhappy consciousness' – but, rather, a metaphysical comfort located in the future of *this* world. This tells us how Hegel is related to the theme of this book. Even though he is a thoroughgoing realist, even though he naturalises metaphysics, he is, in fact, yet another true-world philosopher. The meaning of life consists in the attainment of a 'true world', a kind of utopia located at the end of history, a state of apocalyptic peace and harmony. Hegel is quite explicit about this. With the arrival of the epoch of absolute knowing, he says, 'time' is 'annulled' (PS 801), where by 'time' he understands 'history', the dialectical sequence of different shapes of consciousness through which spirit reaches its final goal (PS 802). As with Christianity, the meaning of life, in Hegelianism, is the attainment of the 'city of God'. The only difference is that it is located not in the sky but on the (future) earth. Hegelianism is, then, not the abandonment, but simply the relocation, of the 'true world'.[8]

Hegel would not, I think, object to this characterisation. For he is quite explicit that his reinterpretation of the doctrines of the Incarnation and Resurrection are intended to preserve the essence of Christianity for an age that neither can nor should accept any longer the 'picture thinking' of the medieval theology (PS 374–787). What I am suggesting, in short, is that Hegel is, first and foremost, a Christian theologian who seeks to naturalise theology, to overcome the alienating dualism of the Middle Ages with an integrating monism.

There is, however, a basic flaw in Hegel's philosophy, one that is, I believe, relatively obvious. It was first stated by Schopenhauer, who had the temerity, at a time at which Hegel exercised an almost God-like ascendancy over European philosophers, to point out that, actually, the emperor had no clothes.

Schopenhauer's criticism of Hegel is simple: 'history', he claims, does not exist. Nothing happens. And, even if it did, its representation as inexorable progression towards a state of final perfection is as tasteless a joke as the idea of the Christian God of love (an idea with which, of course, if my argument is correct, it is fundamentally identical) (WR II pp. 442–3). Of course, Schopenhauer admits, lots of things happen. But nothing 'essential'. History is simply the repetition of the same dreary truths – life is suffering, life swings like a pendulum between pain and boredom, man is a wolf to man and so on – over and over again. It is an endless performance of the same play merely with, from time to time, a change of cast.

The first part of Schopenhauer's criticism is, I think, wrong. The Hegelian insight that history falls into epochs distinguished by sharply separate 'shapes of consciousness' is by now widely accepted. Our more pluralistic, less 'Eurocentric', understanding of things has made us more open than was Schopenhauer to the idea of our own past as made up of radically different modes of world-understanding.

But the second part of Schopenhauer's criticism is, I believe, correct. The idea of history as an inexorably rational progression towards utopia is a grand and seductive idea. To the optimistic, self-confident nineteenth century it may even have seemed true. But to us in bewildered postmodernity, us who live in the shadow of the century of mega-crimes, the shadow of two world wars, of Auschwitz, Stalin, Mao, Hiroshima, the Twin Towers and the poisoning of our earth and sky, it is, I think, clearly – even obviously – false. At the beginning of the chapter I suggested that what Hegel offers is the history of the West as a *Bildungsroman* (novel of education). It is now time to emphasise that what he offers is a ***Bildungsroman*** – a novel, a romance, a work, that is, of *fiction*. This, of course, is why (though one admires its ingenuity and the many insights that occur *en passant*) Hegel's history is fragmented, massively selective, and the interpretations often patently forced. Throughout, there is a constant tension between what Hegel's grand idea says *should* have happened and what he knows *actually* to have happened.

A further objection to the idea of history as a 'dialectical' or logical progression is this. The most fundamental point about Hegel's 'spirit' is, I have suggested, that it is his account of God. (And also, of course, of the essential self.) But a god worth believing in is one whose might, majesty and power exceed human comprehension. A god that is truly godly must be one before whom we can bow down in awe. But we are awed only by mystery. In particular, therefore, a true God it is not to be comprehended, predicted or controlled by the humanising parameters of narrow rationality. If, therefore, there is a god that in some sense is, as Hegel suggests, present in history, then the attempt to limit it within the laws of Hegelian dialectic is a kind of blasphemy. In spite of the friendship of his youth with the lyrical and often mystical poet Friedrich Hölderlin, Hegel totally opposes the, as he calls it, 'rapturous haziness' (PS 10) of poetic thinking.[9] His attempt, however, to encompass everything within the limits of 'reason' produces a kind of spiritual claustrophobia. A true God, as opposed to what Heidegger calls 'the god of the philosophers', is, I would argue (see further, Chapter 15), one that is ultimately accessible *only* to poetic thinking.

A Postscript on Marx. Undoubtedly the greatest ideological change in the intellectual life of the West in the last fifty years is the death of Marxism. Whereas in the 1960s and 1970s it was, in universities, *de rigueur* to be some kind of at least neo-Marxist (to be at least 'Marxoid', as I heard someone say recently), to be a Marxist in the current climate would be on a par with being an alchemist. Apart from scholars, historians and dinosaurs, no one is interested in Marxism any more. Hence, his relegation to a postscript to Hegel, to whom, in any case, he has, from our point of view, nothing essential to add.[10]

Like Hegel, Karl Marx (1818–83) has a 'dialectical' view of history. Like Hegel, that is, his famous book *Capital*[11] tells the history of the West (on the basis of which it predicts its future) as a *Bildungsroman*, divided up into clearly separate chapters. As with Hegel, history is divided into sharply separate epochs, the developmental sequence of which works itself out according to an inexorable logic. Marx's major difference from Hegel, however, is that, whereas Hegel sees the shapes of consciousness that constitute history as embodied in human activity in general, for Marx, history is embodied in just one kind of activity: economic activity, activity concerned with the production and ownership of material wealth. This has the consequence that, for Marx, fundamental history is a history of economic structures. Economics provides the foundation of history; everything else – art, religion, politics, law – is mere 'superstructure', the foam on top of the beer.

Like Hegel, the centre of Marx's concern is 'alienation', the alienation of one human individual and social class from another. The origin of alienation, he holds, stems from the coming into being of private property. His narrative then traces the history of the West through various modes of production – slavery, feudalism, capitalism, socialism, communism – where each member of this sequence either has collapsed, or will collapse, into its successor.

The predicted arrival of communism rests on the disappearance of private property. Since it is private property that has alienated one human being from another, with its replacement by communal ownership, the human being's natural tendency (as Marx sees it) towards co-operation, to pursue the private good only to the extent that it is also the general good, will reassert itself. The state, together with all its means of coercion will thus become superfluous and, in the end, will simply 'wither away'. Utopia will have arrived.

Marx purports to be a complete naturalist – his version of Hegelian dialectic he calls 'dialectical *materialism*' – and claims to scorn all forms of supernaturalism. Religion, he famously said, is the 'opium of the masses'. The point to notice, however, is that, just like Hegel, Marx posits a paradise, a 'true world', whose arrival will herald the 'end of history'. Like Hegel, therefore, he, too, is a covert theologian, a true-world philosopher in disguise.[12] For, like Hegel, what Marx does it to translate the duality between nature and supernature into a duality between present and future, to reproduce the meaning-giving structure of Platonism and Christianity within the one world of nature. Like Hegel, therefore, he is subject to the fatal objection that history, in his sense, does not exist.

Marxism, like Hegelianism and all other versions of the true-world account of the meaning of life, is, then, a myth. It does not merit serious belief; it deserves to 'die'. And it has died, visibly and finally, with the fall of the Berlin Wall in 1989. Since Marxism represents the final effort at a true-world philosophy, we may therefore conclude that the deserved, but lingering, 'death of God' finally completed itself in 1989.

Part II

After the death of God

7

Later Nietzsche

'Continental philosophy', I suggested in the Introduction, is philosophy which responds to the death of the Christian God. 'Conservative' Continental philosophy – the principal topic of Part I of this study – I suggested, seeks to resurrect him in different forms. 'Radical' Continental philosophy – the topic of Part II – on the other hand, accepts that resurrection is impossible, that if anything helpful can be said about the meaning of life it must take some form other than that of the grand – true-world/end-of-history – narrative.

When Nietzsche announced, in 1882, that 'God is dead' (GS 125)[1] he did not mean merely the God of traditional Christianity. He meant, rather, anything that performs the function in human life that was once performed by the God of traditional Christianity. A 'religion', in other words, is anything that postulates or promises a true world. Hence 'European Buddhism' counts as a religion, as do both Hegelianism and Marxism. Nietzsche explicitly includes the latter pair among the doctrines that can no longer be believed:

> The total character of the world is . . . in all eternity chaos – in the sense not of a lack of necessity but of a lack of order, arrangement, form, beauty, wisdom, and whatever other names there are for our aesthetic anthropomorphisms.
>
> (GS 109)

In one sense, Nietzsche is saying, the world is far from chaotic: it exhibits the 'necessities', the lawful regularities, discovered by science. But in another sense it is: it lacks the historical 'arrangement, form, beauty' and ever-increasing 'wisdom' attributed to it by the Hegelian or Marxist *Bildungsroman*.

This is the beginning of radical Continental philosophy, as I call it. Radical Continental philosophy begins with the recognition that not only the Christian God but also all these 'shadows of God' (GS

108) are mirages, 'anthropomorphic' projections, wishful thoughts that have no basis in reality. It begins with the recognition that reality is, in Nietzsche's sense 'chaos'.[2] How (if at all), it then asks, can life be worth living – be, that is, meaningful (see pp. 4–5 above) – in such a 'chaotic' universe?

Notice that while Nietzsche is the first radical Continental philosopher – the first to announce the death of all true worlds and ask what we are to do about it – he was also (among major figures) the last of the conservatives. For, as we saw in Chapter 4, in his youthful Schopenhauerian/Wagnerian days, he himself offered the 'metaphysical comfort' of a supernatural world accessible through art. Thus the line between conservative and radical Continental philosophy cuts through Nietzsche's work, separating earlier from later Nietzsche, the topic of this chapter.

As I mentioned at the beginning of Chapter 4, the decisive mark of Nietzsche's break with Wagner, and with Schopenhauerian–Kantian metaphysics, was his abandonment of the first Bayreuth Festival in 1876. His first book thereafter, *Human, All-too-human* (1878), I count as the beginning of 'later Nietzsche', and his last published work, *Ecce Homo* (1888), I count as the end. I shall, however, focus mainly on two works: *Thus Spoke Zarathustra* (1883–5), which Nietzsche considered his greatest book (indeed, the greatest book ever written by anyone), and *The Gay Science* (1882–7), which I consider to be his greatest book.

Think back, for a moment, to all the attempts to answer the question of the meaning of life we have so far considered; to true-world philosophy in all its forms, whether supernaturalistic, as in traditional Christianity, or naturalistic, as in Marxism. One thing to notice about all of them is that life's meaning is taken to be, first, *universal*, the same for everyone, and, second, *independent of choice*. Whether we are talking, with Plato, about a return to 'the rim of the heavens', with Christianity about the attainment of eternal bliss, with Schopenhauer about absorption into the 'nothingness' of *nirvana*, with Hegel about the coming into being of 'absolute knowing', or with Marx about the 'withering away of the state', that which makes life meaningful for me is exactly the same as that which makes it meaningful for you. Moreover, this meaning has nothing to do with anyone's choice. For the Christian, for example, what gives life meaning (that we are in transit to an afterlife in which, depending on how we have lived, we will suffer either eternal damnation or eternal bliss) is simply *given* to us as something written into the metaphysical structure of reality, given in the same way as is the height of Mount Everest, the second law of thermodynamics or the structure of DNA. For traditional thinkers, that is to say, the meaning of life is something we *discover*: we do not *choose* or *make* it to be the case. These two features – universality and givenness – characterise every grand-narrative philosophy. All true-world philosophers, of whatever shape or hue, presuppose that these two features must characterise any genuine answer to the question of the meaning of life.

Suppose, however, that we now reject both of them. Suppose we acknowledge that there are no true worlds, that every grand narrative is a fiction, that reality is, in Nietzsche's sense, 'chaos'. And suppose we further conclude (at least, for the time being) that there is no such thing as *the* – universal – meaning of life, that no meaning is written into the metaphysical structure of reality. Still, one might reflect, that doesn't mean that *my* life can't have meaning. It doesn't mean that I can't *create* meaning in my life, my own *individual* meaning.

> Gunvald Larsson didn't want to become any older. He was almost fifty, and asked himself, ever more frequently, what meaning his life had had. He had enjoyed squandering the greater part of his inheritance as quickly as possible. He had quite liked it in the navy and even more in the merchant navy, but . . .[3]

What is it that bothers Gunvald Larsson? Not, I think (at least, not explicitly) the death of God. Rather, two things about his own life. First, that it has been an accidental life, a matter of *drift*, reactive rather than proactive – the life, as he would perhaps put it, of a rat in a maze rather than of a human being. And, second, that it has no overall point to it. These features are, of course, connected. It is because there is no overall purpose to which his life is dedicated that Gunvald must react rather than proact. What should he do about his life?

As we have seen throughout Part I of this book, an insight grasped by every grand-narrative philosopher is that *stories create meaning*. Every true-world philosopher is, in one way or another, a story-teller. Every true-world philosophy from Plato onwards, in one way or another, tells a story of 'the soul's journey'. Perhaps, then, when one complains that one's life is meaningless, what one is complaining about is the lack of a story. If I look back on my past, all I see is a series of episodes connected by nothing more than 'and then's – I was born, and then I went to school, and then I became a loving wife and mother, and then the kids left home, and then . . . and if I look forward into the future all I see are many options – to stay married, get divorced, become a feminist, travel the world, start a career, take up knitting – which are all equally possible and appropriate and yet, for that very reason, all equally pointless. Maybe, in short, what I need to do to overcome my sense of meaninglessness is to construct the story of my life, to construct my 'personal narrative'. Notice that even in the absence of a *grand* narrative there seems no reason why one should not be able to construct a *personal* narrative.

The above reflections occurred, I believe, to the later Nietzsche. In order to create meaning in our lives we must, he says, become the 'heroes' of those lives. 'Hero', here, does not mean 'performer of heroic deeds' (though, of course, heroism *might* turn out to be the character of my particular story). It simply means what it means in 'the hero of the novel': central character.

To become the hero of our lives we must, first of all, be able to *see* the hero that we are, 'see the hero that is concealed in everyday characters' (GS 78). And to do this we must 'learn from artists while being wiser than they are in other matters. For with them [their] . . . subtle power usually comes to an end where art ends and life begins; but we want to be poets *of our life*' (GS 299; my emphasis).

Stereotypically, that is to say, artists produce great art but messy lives. (Wagner was an anti-Semitic egomaniac, Dostoyevsky a compulsive gambler, Coleridge a drug addict, Dylan Thomas drank himself to death, Beethoven drove his nephew to suicide, Van Gogh, Sylvia Plath and Virginia Woolf all committed suicide, Philip Larkin was given to fascist opinions and kinky sex, and so on.) What 'we' want to do, however, is to devote their organisational powers to life, to make life itself the primary 'artwork'.

To become 'heroes' we need to learn from artists

> the art of viewing ourselves . . . from a distance and, as it were, simplified and transfigured – the art of staging and watching ourselves . . . Without this we would be nothing but foreground and live entirely in the spell of that perspective which

> makes what is closest at hand . . . appear as if it were vast, and reality itself.
>
> (GS 78)

Nietzsche observes that, once, we had no need of this art since an understanding of the 'heroes' that we were was provided for us, ready-made, by Christianity; that grand narrative which, 'by surrounding man with the eternal [true-world] perspective, taught him to see himself as something past and whole' (ibid.). Now, however, in our post-death-of-God age, it is up to each of us to construct our own, 'heroic' selves. To do this we must learn the art of 'simplifying' our view of ourselves: the art, that is, of viewing our life as if from its end – grasping ourselves as a completed totality, as 'something past and whole'.

Nietzsche wants us to think visually here. If one is very close up to something – say, a mountain – all one sees are its details. Everything is, as Nietzsche puts it, 'foreground'. To see its overall shape, to allow the mountain to resolve into figure and background, what one needs is 'distance'. The same is true with regard to our lives. Normally, we are so, as it were, close up to them that all we see are the details: the next essay to be written for our university course, the five o'clock bus to catch for which we will already have to run, the shopping to be done, the dinner to be cooked, this morning's squabble with one's partner over the proper positioning of the loo seat to be patched up somehow, and so on. In daily life we are so involved in its details that we miss the wood on account of the trees. We fail to ask ourselves, for example, whether and why it is important to finish our university essay, whether and why it is really important to be at university at all, whether and why it is important to patch up the quarrel with our partner.

If, on the other hand, perhaps on a tramping holiday in the Southern Alps of New Zealand, we do achieve distance from (or, as we say, 'perspective on') our lives, then, with luck, suggests Nietzsche, we may be able to see ourselves as if we were the hero of a well-constructed novel. He calls this becoming a 'poet of one's life' to draw attention to the idea that living a meaningful life is living it as though in the process of constructing a fine work of literature.

What does one achieve if one achieves 'artistic distance'? What happens if one takes 'time out' from the hurried and harried business of everyday living to reflect upon its overall character? With luck, what happens is that one grasps the overall script, the 'big picture', the personal narrative of one's life. This narrative – in *this* respect it is just like the Platonic or Christian grand narrative – tells one three things: first, one's history up to now; second, one's present condition; and, third, in virtue of these two together, the outline of the *proper continuation* of one's life into the future. To know the story of one's past and present, that is to say, is to know who one is, to know one's 'identity'. And to know one's identity gives purpose and meaning to one's life. It is to know *how to go on*, to know, in elevated language, one's 'destiny'.

To make Nietzsche's idea as clear as possible, let me try to give you a concrete illustration of the process he has in mind, which I have simplified to the point of banality. (To give a fully realised example of seeing one's life as a work of literature one would have to produce – a work of literature.)

Suppose I have studied for years and have eventually become an accountant. All this time, however, I have written poetry. I feel miserable and find my life meaningless. One day, tramping through the Southern Alps, I attempt to grasp my life as a totality, as a story with a past, a present and a future which I am in the process of living out. What is the story? There are at least two (in real life, indefinitely many) decisions I may make as to an answer.

First decision: I'm an untalented poet about to become a partner in an exciting multinational accountancy firm with many opportunities for lateral movement and foreign experience, who is making himself miserable through sentimental yearnings (generated by the frustrated poetic ambitions of his father) for a lifestyle to which he is, in fact, completely unsuited. I must burn my sonnets.

Second decision: I'm a talented, passionate poet who is making himself miserable by living a life that is secure but fundamentally at odds with his deepest desires and needs. I need to make the act of courage that I have so far evaded.

Notice two things about this example. First, each story tells me who I am – poet or accountant – and by doing so gives meaning to my life, tells me how to go on. Second, which story I tell is *absolutely up to me*. I do not discover but rather *create* the character that I am. Nietzsche emphasises this point: 'we want', he says, to become 'creators', 'beings who create themselves' (GS 335) through their 'practical and theoretical skill in interpreting and arranging events' (GS 277).[4] (This emphasis on self-creation, the idea that we are not born into but rather choose our identities – that we have 'existence before essence' – is, as we shall see when we come to Sartre, the central principle of existentialism. It is for this reason that Nietzsche is often regarded as the first existentialist.)

In 1881, in Sils Maria in the Swiss Alps, 'six thousand feet above man and time', as he put it, there came to Nietzsche what he regarded as his most important idea, the idea of 'eternal recurrence'.[5] Here is his first statement of it (a statement which, in *Ecce Homo*, he describes as expressing 'the basic idea of *Zarathustra*'):

> What, if some day or night a demon were to steal after you into your loneliest loneliness and say to you: 'this life as you now live it and have lived it, you will have to live innumerable times more; and there will be nothing new in it, but every pain and every joy and every thought and sigh and everything unutterably small or great in your life will have to return to you, all in the same succession and sequence – even this spider and this moonlight between the trees, and even this moment and I myself. . . . Would you not throw yourself down and gnash your teeth and curse the demon who spoke thus? Or have you once experienced a tremendous moment when you would have answered him: 'You are a god and never have I heard anything more divine' . . . how well disposed would you have to become to yourself and to life *to crave nothing more fervently* than this ultimate eternal confirmation and seal?
>
> (GS 341)

As presented here, the idea of the 'eternal recurrence' of one's life and world,[6] exactly as it is down to the very last detail, is clearly not a metaphysical thesis about the nature of time. It is, indeed, not a thesis at all, for the question of its truth or otherwise is, here, irrelevant. Its status, rather, is that of a 'what if'. It is a thought-experiment, the point of which is to provide a test to determine whether one is living as successfully as possible.

Nietzsche, who describes the philosopher as 'the doctor of culture', is much given to medical metaphors. Human types are classified as either 'sick', 'convalescent' or 'healthy'. One's degree of health or otherwise is measured according to one's ability to 'affirm life', to be a 'Yes-sayer' (GS 276). Someone like Schopenhauer or the Christian ascetic (or the youthful Nietzsche), for whom this life is nothing but a veil of tears from which he yearns for the quickest possible release, is completely sick. Such people are, in Nietzsche's judgement sick because they are full of 'resentment' against life. Someone (like Zarathustra) who has overcome the disposition to believe in a true world but finds the eternal recurrence an 'abysmal thought' (Z III 13) is convalescent, but not yet properly healthy. That they cannot will the recurrence shows that they are still full of resentment and guilt (i.e. resentment against oneself.) To count as a fully healthy, fully thriving human being, to possess 'the great health' (GS 382), one must be entirely free of resentment. One must experience one's life as being of such perfection that one can say to the demon 'never have I heard anything more divine'; in other words accept, embrace, 'crave nothing more fervently' than the eternal return of one's exact life. (Of course, since I am unaware in this life of having lived it before, if it recurs *exactly* as it is, I will continue to be unaware of having lived it before. Boredom, therefore, is not an issue.)

How does the test of the eternal recurrence fit together with the idea of living one's life as if it were a well-constructed work of literature?

An essential element in all grand-narrative philosophy is redemption. The final state that brings history to an end is always a redemptive state, one that makes sense of, and makes up for, the suffering and imperfections that have preceded it. 'Redemption' is a notion that is at least as important to Nietzsche as it was to his grand-narrative predecessors. It is just as important, that is to say, that a personal narrative should be redemptive as that a grand narrative should be so (Z II 20).

But not all personal narratives *are* redemptive. For it is perfectly possible to use one's novelist's art to construct a story of one's life in which one figures, in one's own eyes, as a victim or villain. (I'm told that delinquent adolescents often do this: construct an account of their lives in which they are victims of their upbringing and are consequently thoroughly bad in themselves.) That way, however, lies self-loathing and despair. Hence, Nietzsche emphasises, the story one tells must be one which constructs a self that one 'desires' and 'esteems' (GS 78, 290). It must, that is, be a story one *likes* being the 'hero' of. One must like the life one has decided to have.

There are, however, degrees of liking. I may tell the story of my life (as I presented them, my poet-accountant stories were of this character) in such a way that, while on the whole I like the life I have led, there are some things which I wish hadn't happened to me, and some things I regret having done. Though this qualified affirmation of life might seem to be the best we could hope for, for Nietzsche, for Nietzschean 'health', it is not enough.

One of Nietzsche's central mottoes is '*amor fati*', love of fate or necessity, the ability to 'see as beautiful what is necessary in things' (GS 276). Since the whole of the past is 'necessary' – it cannot be altered – to 'love fate' is (not just to tolerate but rather) to love the *whole* of the past, *everything* that has happened. In other words, it is to will, to 'crave nothing more fervently', than the eternal recurrence of *everything* that has happened. That we should be able to 'love fate' and 'will the eternal recurrence' are the same idea in different language.

How can I 'write' my life so that I not merely like it, but like it so much that I can will its recurrence for ever and ever, down to every last detail? To do so, says Nietzsche, we must be able to see a 'personal providence' in things, reach a 'high point' in which we see

> how palpably always everything that happens to us turns out for the best. Every day and every hour, life seems to have no other wish than to prove this proposition again and again. Whatever it is, bad weather or good, the loss of a friend, sickness, slander, the failure of some letter to arrive, the spraining of an ankle, a glance into a shop, a counter-argument, the opening of a book, a dream, a fraud – either immediately or very soon after it proves to be something that 'must not be missing'; it has a profound significance and use precisely for *us*.
>
> (GS 277)

So, for example, to return to my poet-accountant example, in the *Bildungsroman* which is my story of my life, the misery and frustration I suffered in my years as an accountant must find their place and justification as something necessary to point me in the direction of my true vocation as a poet. ('What doesn't poison me makes me stronger' is one of Nietzsche's most celebrated aphorisms.)

Nietzsche thinks it is very difficult to will the eternal recurrence, and he is right. To see this, it is vital to bear in mind that willing the eternal recurrence is to 'crave *nothing* more fervently' than the *exact* return of one's life down to the very last detail. Many people would be prepared, in general terms, to live their life again, but few, if any, would *prefer* to relive their exact life to living a judiciously expurgated version in which certain traumatic events – the failed second marriage, the death of a child, the destruction of the World Trade Center, the Holocaust (as noted in note 6 above, my knowledge of those events is part of my life) – were simply omitted. The reason, of course, is that, in practice, it is doubtful whether anyone can fit everything that has happened into the *Bildungsroman* that is the story of their life. And even when events can be thus 'redeemed', even when one finds justification for an incident in terms of some subsequent effect that it causes, one cannot but be conscious of much less painful ways in which the same effect could have been achieved. Instead of seven years of misery as an accountant, for example, a week.

Certainly Nietzsche himself couldn't will the eternal recurrence, though he constantly told himself to try. After, for example, the rejection of his proposal of marriage by Lou Salomé in which he saw his friend Paul Rée, also in love with Lou, as having played a treacherous hand, he wrote to another friend,

> If I do not discover the alchemist's trick of turning even this – filth into *gold*, I am lost. Thus I have the *most beautiful* opportunity to prove that for me [here Nietzsche quotes the American Ralph Waldo Emerson, whom he had admired since boyhood] 'all experiences are profitable, all days holy, and all human beings divine'!!!
>
> (GS p. 8)

Nietzsche expresses the difficulty of willing the eternal recurrence by saying that only the '*Übermensch*' (Z I 4) – 'overman' or, in older translations, 'superman' – can do so. Only, that is, someone who transcends the present state of humanity, only a type of human being of which as yet history offers 'no certain examples' (GS 288) possesses 'the great health'. Who, then, is the overman? What has he got that we lack?

The answer in a word is 'frenzy', intoxication, ecstasy, 'Dionysian' (GS 370) ecstasy. (Though it has lost its interpretation in terms of Kantian metaphysics, Dionysian 'intoxication' is as important to later Nietzsche as it is to earlier.) 'What is essential about frenzy', says Nietzsche, is

> the feeling of increased strength and fullness. Out of this feeling one lends to things, one *forces* them to accept from us, one violates them – this process is called *idealising*. Let us get rid of a prejudice here: idealising does not consist, as is commonly held, in subtracting or discounting the petty and inconsequential. What is decisive is rather a tremendous drive to

> bring out the main features, so that the others disappear in the process.
>
> (TI IX 8)

In other words, the difference between the overman and us is that he does not have a problem about turning 'filth into gold'. He does not have a problem because he simply *does not see* the details of his life that are irrelevant to, or cannot be justified in terms of, his life-story; not because, being too weak to face up to them, he represses them, but rather because, passionately committed to the creative task determined for him by his life-story and full of the urgency of the creator, full of 'an overflowing energy that is pregnant with future' (GS 370), he is too busy getting on with things to spare them the time of day:

> to be incapable of taking one's enemies, one's accidents, even one's misdeeds seriously for very long – that is a sign of strong, full natures in which there is an excess of power to form, to mould, to recuperate, and to forget (a good example is Mirabeau[7] who had no memory for insults and vile actions done him and was unable to forgive simply because he forgot).
>
> (GM I 10)

The reason, then, that the overman does not have a problem with willing the eternal recurrence is that he suffers from what one might call creative amnesia. (This is the background to Nietzsche's remark: 'that a philosopher sees a problem in life is an objection to him'.)

The section from which the quotation about 'idealising' on page 92 is taken is actually entitled 'Towards a psychology of the artist'. The fact, though, that it also tells us how the overman is able to will the eternal recurrence reveals something very significant. Far from the Nazi storm-trooper of popular repute,[8] Nietzsche's overman is, in fact, the consummation of *the artist*. The mark, that is to say, of the hero of a work of literature is indeterminacy: since Shakespeare doesn't discuss the matter, it is neither the case that Hamlet has a small mole on the back of his neck nor that he does not. The *only* details we are given about the hero of a well-constructed work of literature are ones that, more or less obviously, contribute to the construction of the narrative as a whole. A well-constructed work of literature (anything Nietzsche would have recognised as such, at least) is, in other language, an *organic* whole: every one of its parts contributes to the existence of the whole.[9] It is the same with the overman: as he views himself, nothing but that which helps constitute its 'main features' is visible. The story of his life that he tells to himself has become a *complete* work of art.

Later Nietzsche's ideas are thought-provoking, deep, 'relevant' and exciting. Important truth, surely, is to be found in what he says. Questions, none-the-less, remain.

Nietzsche's response to the question of how one is to render one's life meaningful seems, as we have seen, to be the following. One is to construct one's life as if it were a well-constructed work of literature with oneself as its 'hero'. (Sometimes he expresses this as the injunction to 'become who you are' (GS 270): become, that is, whoever you have *chosen* that you are – one's life, remember, is one's own creation.) If one happens to be endowed with *übermenschlich* energy, the intoxicated 'fullness of life' (GS 370) of the overman, then one will be able to take the further step of willing the eternal recurrence. Passionately committed to the urgency of one's chosen life – 'am I concerned with *happiness*? I am concerned with my *work*' (Z IV 20), says Zarathustra impatiently – one will simply 'forget' details that do not fit into the organic whole of one's life-narrative. (*Ecce Homo*, Nietzsche's quasi-autobiography which is subtitled 'How one becomes what one is', is full of 'forgetting': that he was a German – he claims to be Polish; that he was related to his horrible (fascist) sister; that he had never adopted an 'arrogant or pathetic pose'; that no trace of 'fanaticism' is to be found in his nature; and so on.[10]) If, on the other hand, one constructs oneself as a hero but cannot will the eternal recurrence – if, that is, one's life-story is less well constructed, a less perfect work of art, than that of the overman, if there are parts that will not fit, organically, into the whole – then one is, presumably, what Nietzsche refers to as a 'higher' type (Z IV 13): one does not possess the 'great health' of the overman, but, on the other hand, one lives a more thriving existence than someone like Gunvald Larsson, who has no life-narrative at all.

One thing, however, that is common to the lives of both the overman and the higher type is the fact that their life-stories, together with the 'futures' with which they are 'pregnant' (GS 370), are, as we have seen, *chosen* rather than *discovered*. In neither case is one's life-story and task given to one as part of the furniture of the world in which one finds oneself. Rather, it is always the product of 'our own practical and theoretical skill in interpreting and arranging events' (GS 277). In no case, that is, is one's life-story determined by 'the given'. It is always, rather, an act of free 'interpretation'. Whether overman or mere higher type, one chooses one's interpretation of oneself and chooses, therefore, 'who one is'.

This generates two problems. The first, which I shall call 'the problem of the immoral script', is this. If all that matters is that I *like* the person I have chosen to be, does it not follow that it doesn't matter whether that person is a saint or a sinner, that the flourishing life is, in Nietzsche's own language, 'beyond good and evil'? Granted that to like myself I must show up as an admirable person in my own eyes, still mustn't there be some external check on what counts as an admirable person? The Mafia chief may well count, in his own eyes, as a fine fellow (good family man, generous to his wife, children, friends and dog), but do we really want to allow him to be able to count as a leading example of flourishing humanity?

The second problem I shall call 'the problem of authority'. A life that is chosen by me can always be unchosen by me. For if the sole ground of my task is my own choice, then that task, it would seem, cannot have *authority* over me. (Authority, that is to say, seems to presuppose 'otherness' – even if it is only the otherness of my so-called 'higher' self with respect to my 'lower' self.) And if a task has no authority over me, then it cannot be an object of my *commitment*. Thus, to go back to my poet-accountant example, suppose I reject accountancy in favour of the life of a poet but then none of my poems get published, my bank balance looks bleak and my wife begins to complain. If this happens, I will find myself with no ground at all for resisting the thought: 'Well, I chose poetry; it hasn't worked. Let's go back to accountancy.'

Nietzsche says that we must learn from artists, 'and especially those of the theatre, . . . the art of staging and watching ourselves' (GS 78). But isn't it in fact the case that, in living the life he recommends, we actually learn *too much* from artists of the theatre: that we become, not passionate and committed human beings capable of pursuing our projects through hardship and disappointment, but rather *actors*, ironically detached from the roles we play at any one time, ready to swap roles if and when the whim takes us? Isn't a life that is, in Nietzsche's sense, chosen, not meaningful but rather meaningless?

Nietzsche's account of the artistic – more generally, creative – psyche as one gifted with a superabundance of energy is, it seems to me, deeply insightful. Iris Murdoch, for example, in a letter to a friend, wrote: 'I feel, even at the lowest moment, such endless vitality within me', a vitality she referred to as 'joy'.[11] But Murdoch, I feel sure, did not, in Nietzsche's sense, *choose* to become a novelist. Having found herself unable to communicate the nature of the good in the language of Oxford philosophy (she was, for a time, a tutor in philosophy at St Anne's College, Oxford) she *had no choice but* to become a novelist. She did not 'create' but rather *discovered* her vocation. 'Discovery' is, indeed, the language we use to talk about vocation: 'created vocation' is an oxymoron. The reason is that a vocation is a 'calling' and a call must come from somewhere *else*, somewhere outside of oneself.

To allow for the idea of a genuine calling, it seems to me, one has to view the self as essentially embedded in a larger context of morality and society. One has to allow that the individual is *born into* a set of ends or values which have ultimate authority for her and which, in conjunction with her particular, concrete situation – her talents, tastes, social and historical location, and so on – *determine* a vocation for her, a vocation which, if she looks hard and long enough, she can discover.

But all this is missing from Nietzsche's philosophy. Though he rejects Descartes' 'soul hypothesis'[12] – 'soul is only a word for something about the body' (Z I 4) – he none the less retains the Cartesian view of the self as a disconnected, self-sufficient, atomic individual: an individual who is, in Nietzsche's own language 'beyond good and evil', one with 'free' 'horizons' (GS 343), a blank sheet characterised by nothing but the power of free choice. This is why he cannot make sense of discovered vocation, of a discovered – and therefore genuine – meaning to one's life.

In sum, Nietzsche's recommendation that we should become the 'heroes' of our lives is an excellent and indispensable idea. But the notion that we should *choose* the hero we are to become is not. In Chapter 8 we shall see how Heidegger seeks to improve on Nietzschean thinking: how he retains the former idea but integrates it into an account of things which seems to make discovered rather than merely chosen meaning possible.

8

Posthumous Nietzsche

Nietzsche's notebooks, along with remarks like 'I have forgotten my umbrella', contain various sketches for the contents page of a prospective book to be called *The Will to Power*. In some sketches the subtitle *Attempt at a Revaluation of All Values* is suggested. After Nietzsche's death, his sister, Elizabeth Förster-Nietzsche (a dyed-in-the-wool Nazi and friend of Hitler), gathered together a bunch of jottings from Nietzsche's *Nachlass* (unpublished papers) written between 1883 and 1888 and published them as *The Will to Power*. Thanks in no small measure to Heidegger, this posthumous collection came to be viewed as Nietzsche's masterwork. The view became established that, as Heidegger puts it in his massive, four-volume Nietzsche study produced during the 1930s and early 1940s,

> Nietzsche's philosophy proper, the fundamental position on the basis of which he speaks in . . . all the writings he himself published, did not assume a final form and was not itself published in any book. . . . What Nietzsche himself published during his creative life was always foreground. . . . His philosophy proper was left behind as posthumous, unpublished work.[1]

We now know, however, not only that Nietzsche abandoned the *Will to Power* project in 1888, but also that over three-quarters of the 1,067 entries that appear in what now presents itself as *The Will to Power*[2] were never intended for publication in any shape or form.[3] (As the chapter progresses I shall suggest that Nietzsche had extremely good reasons for wishing not to publish these musings – good reasons, indeed, for abandoning the entire project.) What follows from this is that for Nietzsche's final word we must look to the works published during his lifetime that were discussed in the last chapter rather than to that trash-bin of thought, the doodles, day-dreams and (usually failed) thought-experiments of *The Will to Power*.

In spite of this, 'posthumous Nietzsche' as I shall call him (I might equally well have spoken of 'Heidegger's Nietzsche' or 'the Nietzsche that never was') is interesting, important (particularly for his influence on postmodern French philosophy), and relevant to the theme of this book. He deserves, therefore, a chapter to himself.

The 'true world', posthumous Nietzsche of course holds, is a 'mere fiction' (WP 568). But he also holds that the world of our everyday experience, the 'manifest' or 'life world' as some philosophers call it, is a fiction – a construct moulded by considerations of utility, by our needs and desires as practical agents. What, then, putting aside all fictions, both useless and useful, is the world really like?

One thing philosophers have always observed about the manifest world (usually downgrading it on that account) is that it is a world of 'change, becoming, multiplicity, opposition, contradiction' and, Nietzsche adds, 'war' (WP 584). The world's 'becoming' is, moreover, he claims, entirely devoid of any 'goal or end' (WP 12 A). Since the world is uncreated (there is no God to create it), it has, Nietzsche reasons, existed for an infinite period of time. Since every possibility is realised over infinite time, if the world had a goal, if there could be an 'end of history', it would already have been reached. But once history stops it can never start again. QED (WP 1062). This argument is obviously suspect (one reason for doubting that Nietzsche was doing anything more than playing around with it, for resisting the idea that he was convinced by the argument).

What are the elements that figure in this endless flux of becoming? Not 'beings', not the ordinary middle-sized objects of everyday experience. These are just the useful fictions by which human beings conceive of the world in action-friendly ways (WP 517). Rather, the ultimate constituents of reality are 'quanta', quanta of, in the first instance, 'force', force-fields. 'Force', however, as the ultimate concept of science, is inadequate. Inadequate in two ways. First – Nietzsche exactly follows, here, Schopenhauer's line of reasoning (see p. 33 above) – the word has no meaning for us unless we specify its meaning in terms of the only force of which we have experience, namely 'will': 'a force we cannot imagine is an empty word and should be allowed no rights of citizenship in science' (WP 621), from which it follows that 'the victorious concept "force" by means of which our physicists have created . . . the world, still needs to be completed: an inner will must be assigned to it' (WP 619). Second, since mere force-fields might exist in harmonious equilibrium with each other, the idea of reality as force will not explain the observable fact of, metaphorically expressed, 'contradiction', 'war'. From this it follows that the nature of the world-constituting quanta must be characterised not merely as will, but more specifically as 'will to power' (ibid.). This is what reality ultimately is: '*This world is the will to power – and nothing besides!* And you yourselves are also this will to power – and nothing besides' (WP 1067).

Why 'will to power' rather than Schopenhauer's will to survive, his 'will to live'? Since the most enduring things are always the simplest, the mere will to live cannot explain the existence of complex systems (WP 684). Of course, survival is necessary to power. The point, however, is that it is willed as a means, never as an end. (The premiss of this argument is, in its universality, so obviously questionable that one doubts, once again, that Nietzsche took it very seriously.)

Will to power is will to 'mastery' (WP 636), to 'domination' (WP 715). Every 'quantum of will to power' (ibid.) strives to dominate every other quantum, to incorporate it, to take it over. (Political and possibly commercial models of domination, imperialism and colonisation are surely at the root of Nietzsche's thinking here.) But it encounters resistance. The outcome of such power-struggles is that organised systems of quanta come into being – 'bodies', from our everyday point of view – which then try to dominate other organised systems (WP 636). Hence the power-struggles visible on the macroscopic level, the fact that life, whether on the animal or human level, is nothing but 'lunging at the weaker' and 'defending against the stronger' (WP 655), 'a will to violate and defend oneself against violation' (WP 634).

Two further points. First, the will to power is always the will to more power (WP 689). The will to power is always 'insatiable' (WP 619). Second, as a system of quanta becomes larger and larger it becomes potentially more and more unstable. This is because power is a function of the organisation as well as the quantity of force, and because increased size puts increased strain on the organisation of a system. (The Roman Empire provides one example of this; the business that turns from a small, focused, efficient organisation into a shambles as it takes over more and more companies is another.) What follows from this is not indeed the eternal recurrence as we met it in the last chapter, but at least a *vague* version of it: that systems go on getting larger and larger until, one day, they implode and everything goes back more or less to the beginning (WP 1067).

The fact that the idea of the world as will to power entails the vague version of eternal recurrence leads posthumous Nietzsche to wonder whether the *precise* version discussed in the last chapter – the infinite recurrence of the world's history *down to the very last detail* – is not just a useful test of psychological health but also a metaphysical truth. He suggests that it is. Since every possibility is realised over infinite time it follows that the return of the *exact* present state of affairs is guaranteed (WP 1066). (As we saw (p. 32 above), exactly the same argument is used by Schopenhauer to refute the 'oft-repeated doctrine of a progressive development of mankind to an ever higher perfection', i.e. Hegelianism. History, Schopenhauer and posthumous Nietzsche agree, is circular, not linear.) In fact, however, the argument is unsound since, as Georg Simmel showed in 1907 (in a book called *Schopenhauer und Nietzsche*), the idea that every possibility must be realised over infinite time can be mathematically disproved.

Given Nietzsche's (naturalistic) metaphysics, given that the world is, and we ourselves are, 'will to power and nothing besides', what follows about the meaning of life? 'Assuming that life is the will to power', Nietzsche answers, 'there is nothing in life that has value except the degree of power' (WP 55). The meaning of life is, therefore, *power* – the power to 'violate' (WP 634) other things, both human and non-human; in other words, to exploit them. To what end? To the end, presumably, of more power.

Power, one must hasten to add, comes in many forms. There are more or less subtle ways in which it may be exercised. Though it may be the power of the general, it may also be the 'transfigured' power of the artist (WP 1051). I shall return to this point shortly.

The death of God, Nietzsche holds, results in the 'devaluation' of the hitherto 'highest values' (WP 2). They no longer grip us, are no longer able to give direction and meaning to our lives. A value vacuum – Nietzsche calls it 'nihilism' (ibid.) – comes into being. What is needed is a 'revaluation of all values', a new and fundamental principle of value. This is the will to power: 'The standpoint of value is the standpoint of conditions of preservation and enhancement for complex forms of relative life-duration', complex 'forms', that is to say, 'of domination' (WP 715). The highest value, in other words, the only thing that is valuable in itself, is increase in power. Everything else is valuable to, and only to, the extent that it promotes the growth of power.

Although I have called the will to power a 'new' principle of valuation, it is, for Nietzsche, only relatively new. Throughout the Christian era, he says, values (compassion, selflessness, turning the other cheek) were 'denaturalised' values. All his revaluation of values does, therefore, is to 'again set free' 'the value feelings that hitherto have been squandered on the world of ["true'] being' (WP 585 C). The 'naturalisation of morality' (WP 462), in other words, merely restored us to the values we used to have before we fell under the spell of that strange, 'sick'-making thought-construction called Christianity.

The goal of this process of liberation and restoration is the creation of a new 'species', a 'higher type', of humanity – 'my metaphor for this type is, as one knows, the word "overman" ' (WP 866). (Another way, therefore, of expressing posthumous Nietzsche's account of the meaning of life is to say that it is the overman.) The goal, that is, of the revaluation of values is, in Hegelian language, a new (but also old) 'shape of consciousness' in which human beings fully accept and affirm the propositions that 'This world is the will to power – and nothing besides! And you yourself are also this will to power – and nothing besides!' The goal is human beings who say an unqualified 'yes' to life in the full and explicit knowledge that 'life is will to power' (WP 254), and nothing besides.

What are we to say about this strong and in many ways repellent portrait of being and value? The first thing to say, I think, is that there is something uncomfortably familiar about the portrait. We seem, somehow, to recognise who it is a portrait of. In his commentary on Nietzsche, Heidegger explains this familiarity in terms of his general thesis that great metaphysicians, 'essential thinkers', articulate, in their metaphysics, the shape of consciousness definitive of the historical epoch they inhabit.[4] (The history of Western metaphysics is thus the history of the West.) Nietzsche's metaphysics of will to power, Heidegger holds, articulates the metaphysics of modernity. Generalising about the dominant character of our culture as a whole, it is in fact true, Heidegger suggests, that more or less explicitly and more or less wholeheartedly we accept the will to power as the principle of valuation, regard things as valuable only to the extent that they enhance power. That modernity is the struggle for unconditional power over man and nature shows that, as a species, *we* are the overman.

More exactly, since the overman is one who does not merely accept but *ecstatically affirms* life as the will to power, the overmen are those among us who glory in the fact that they are 'will to power and nothing else'. Writing in 1943, it was obvious to Heidegger who were the glorifiers of the will to power *par excellence*: the Nazi SS.[5]

Scholars who object to this reading of Nietzsche as a proto-Nazi as an utterly crude misunderstanding point to Nietzsche's admiration for artists and his emphasis on sublimation. All passions, says *Twilight of the Idols*, have a 'stupid' phase. That is why the Church tried to 'castrate' them. What we should do, however, since we need the energy and drive they constitute, is to 'spiritualise' them (TI V 1). And again, in *Zarathustra*, 'once you suffered passions and called them evil'. The trick, however, is to turn these 'wild dogs in your cellar' into 'birds and lovely singers' (Z I 5). And they point to Nietzsche's unequivocal condemnation of the 'uncaged beast of prey', 'the blond . . . beast' (GM I 11).

The overman, then, seems to possess a passionate heart but a cool, self-disciplining head. The will to power seems to be the will to a kind of power over *oneself* rather than over others, the power to channel the energy of one's raw impulses into productive, cultural achievements – very much as the Greeks, according to *The Birth of Tragedy*, channelled raw Dionysianism into the art of Greek tragedy (see pp. 48–9 above).

Yet as the metaphysics of will to power is developed in *The Will to Power* there is no question but that power, as we have seen, is specified in terms of 'violation', 'lunging', 'domination' – domination of others (other 'systems of quanta'). If we are unlimited 'will to power and nothing else', then wholehearted self-affirmation *is* seeking as much power over others as possible. Though we may find ourselves more adept at gaining power by spiritual rather than by physical techniques – we may seek to control others through their minds and wills rather than their bodies, to 'manufacture' rather than compel assent, in the language of Noam Chomsky – it is, so far as I can see, impossible to rule out the 'blond beast' as one genuine example of the overman, as conceived in the philosophy of posthumous Nietzsche. This is an especially strong reason for reiterating that *Nietzsche* is a different person from posthumous Nietzsche.

The Nietzsche who wrote *Twilight of the Idols* and *Zarathustra*, the real later Nietzsche, is a different Nietzsche from the one who thinks that life is the will to dominate others – and nothing else. The impossible task of integrating the metaphysics of will to power over others with the theme of sublimation is created not by Nietzsche, who never wanted anyone to see his musings, jottings, experiments, day-dreams and nightmares, but by those who pry indecently into his notes and then try to represent them as constituting his 'philosophy proper'.

Heidegger sums up his reading of Nietzsche by saying, with reference to the 'blond beast', that 'at the end of [his] metaphysics stands the statement: *Homo est brutum bestiale*' (*Nietzsche*, vol. IV, p. 148), man is brutal, a bestial brute. This, I have suggested, is not Nietzsche. But it might still be *true*. More exactly, two things might be true: (1) that the world really is will to power and nothing else, and (2) that, given (1), we have no option but to accept power as the highest value, the meaning of life. Is either of these two claims true? I shall start with the second.

Why does posthumous Nietzsche think that given that life is the will to power it *follows* that power is the highest value? Isn't this assumption, it might be said, a classic instance of the well-known fallacy of confusing the desired with the desir*able*, i.e. valuable? (Lying in bed until midday may be desired but is far from being desirable, *worthy* of desire.) I think not. Posthumous Nietzsche's move from (1) to (2) is based not on this elementary mistake but rather, I think, on the following piece of reasoning. Life is the will to power – not just here and now but in all places throughout all eternity. Power is, therefore, the only game in town, and will always remain so. There is no hope of ever overcoming the will to power. Hence the choice is a stark one: to affirm the will to power, to join in the game of power, or else to reject life as such. But the latter option is 'nihilism', the ultimate expression of which is 'nausea and suicide'.[6]

This, however, doesn't really answer the question. The all-embracingness of will to power on Nietzsche's picture indeed entails that *either* one embraces power as the highest value *or else* one rejects life and ought to commit suicide. But it does not tell us *which* of these alternatives to embrace. Given Camus' assertion that the question of suicide is the only truly serious question of philosophy, we have to conclude that this central question is one to which posthumous Nietzsche has, in fact, no answer. He *assumes* that suicide is a non-option but never actually tells us why. Even if life is the will to power, in short, Nietzsche fails to establish that power is the highest value – or that it has any value at all.

But, to turn to (1), *is* life the will to power?

What actually lies at the root of posthumous Nietzsche's vision of reality? Schopenhauer's world as will, of course, revised in the light of the pre-Socratic philosopher Heraclitus' assertion that 'war (*polemos*) is the father of all things' (fragment 53) and the view that history periodically comes to an 'end' and then starts again. These, however, are mere *sources* for Nietzsche's view. What supports it in the way of *evidence*?

Precious little. So far as I can see, all he has to go on is the claim that the manifest world is 'war' (WP 584), not just war but, specifically, imperialist war, war of conquest, colonisation. (As we shall see, this vision of things is shared by Foucault.) But why should we believe this?

One problem, internal to Nietzsche's own thinking, is that he claims that all beliefs about the manifest world are 'perspectival' (WP 567): useful fictions that serve the growth of power of the 'power centre' that has the belief. So why should *this* claim be supra-perspectival? Why should it be anything more than Nietzsche's personal 'take' on things? Setting this problem of consistency aside, however, why should we believe that life is more or less overt warfare?

If it is true that life is war, then it must be true, in particular, that non-human, animal life is war. And, as we have seen in discussing Schopenhauer, the idea of war, of 'war, all against all', can be applied quite successfully to the animal world. But is this 'war' generated by an impulse to empire or merely by the struggle to survive? Given there is a 'will in nature', is it Nietzsche's 'will to power' or Schopenhauer's 'will to live'?

Surely the latter. Surely the great and obvious contrast between some (but by no means all, I would suggest) human activity and that of the animals is that, whereas the former seek to dominate, the latter do not. Bees, ants, birds do not strive to take over the world. They strive, merely, to survive. (The nightmare quality of Hitchcock's *The Birds* is precisely that it imagines this not to be the case.) Nietzsche criticises Darwin as follows:

> The influence of 'external circumstances' is overestimated by Darwin to a ridiculous extent: the essential thing in the life

> process is precisely the tremendous shaping, form-creating force [i.e. the will to power] working from within which *utilises* and *exploits* 'external circumstances'.
>
> (WP 647)

Species, Nietzsche is suggesting, don't merely respond to their environments, for that would imply that life is merely a struggle for survival. Rather, they actively 'exploit' those environments in order to increase their power. But this, I think every contemporary biologist would agree, is pure fiction.

I conclude that (*a*) even if life were the will to power we would not have a conclusive reason to make the will to power the principle of valuation, but that (*b*) life is not, in fact, the will to power. To be sure, the will to power is a *prevalent* motive in human behaviour that *often* expresses itself in disguised ways which pre-posthumous Nietzsche is a master at exposing. But it is not the *only* motive on which human beings act, though it may be true, as Heidegger suggests, that it is the dominant motive for modern humanity. As I shall suggest in the last chapter, however, to the extent that this is true of it, the behaviour of modern humanity is *pathological*. The will to power, that is, represents, not a universal norm, but rather a pathology of human behaviour.

Since this is all really rather *obviously* the case we see, further, that Nietzsche had good reasons for abandoning the project of writing a book called *The Will to Power*, why he, in fact, *rejected* the metaphysics of will to power. (Though the published works often use 'will to power' as a diagnostic tool for discussing particular forms of human behaviour, in over eight thousand pages of text only two passages (GM II 12 and *Beyond Good and Evil* 36) even suggest the idea that 'the world is will to power – and nothing besides', and both have a strongly 'what if' character to them.)

Even though posthumous Nietzsche fails to prove it, could it not still be true that power, domination of others, is the meaning of life? No. Quite apart from what I propose to argue in the last chapter, we already know this, I think, from Hegel. What we know from Hegel, that is to say, is that a basic human need is for 'recognition' from others. But, as we saw (pp. 64–65 above), a slave cannot provide authentic recognition. It can be provided only by a free being, a being over whom we do not have – or refrain from having – power.

9

Early Heidegger

Heidegger is a tense topic. A recent history of Western philosophy contains the sentence 'Any subject that is responsible for producing Heidegger . . . owes the world an apology'.[1] The source of tension lies in Heidegger's biography.

Martin Heidegger was born, in 1889, into a peasant family in Messkirch in the Black Forest region of South-West Germany. (1889 was the year in which Nietzsche's productive life was terminated by the onset of madness.) He died, and was buried in the graveyard of the Catholic church in Messkirch where his father had been sexton, in 1976. Save for annual visits to Provence in the South of France in the 1950s and 1960s, which he came to regard as his 'second homeland', he spent almost his entire life in the region of his birth. His main teaching post was at the University of Freiburg where he remained in spite of repeated offers of more prestigious posts elsewhere.

Heidegger shared Nietzsche's analysis of the condition of the post-death-of-God West as one of 'nihilism'. In 1933 he joined the Nazi Party, believing it to represent the 'revaluation of all values' the West so desperately needed. In the same year he became Rector (vice-chancellor) of Freiburg University, seeking to make it, and the German universities in general, a vital force that would ensure that the Nazi movement became a movement of genuine spiritual renewal. As Plato had sought to make his philosophy the guiding force in the political life of the dictator of Syracuse (see p. 9 above), so Heidegger sought to make his philosophy the guiding force in the politics of the dictator of Germany. He made many compromising speeches in support of Hitler and National Socialism. Eighteen months later, realising that he had radically misjudged the character of the Nazi movement and had foolishly overestimated the possibility of his own influence over it, he resigned as Rector and returned to the duties of an ordinary professor. In his lectures from 1935 onwards – particularly in a series of lectures on Nietzsche that ran from 1936 until 1940 which became the *Nietzsche* work discussed in the last chapter (see p. 97) – he became an ever more bitter critic of the reality of Nazi Germany which he saw taking shape around him. This required a certain degree of courage given that from 1936 onwards, as already mentioned, his lectures were delivered under the observation of Gestapo spies.

In spite of the fact that Heidegger awoke relatively quickly from his initial euphoria to the real character of Nazism, his involvement with the movement, together with his stubborn refusal to provide a public *mea culpa*, has, as the sentence quoted at the beginning of this chapter illustrates, proved a disaster for his philosophical reputation. (Others who were also involved, Carl Gustav Jung, Hans-Georg Gadamer, the physicist Werner Heisenberg and the conductor Wilhelm Furtwängler, for example, have escaped virtually unscathed.) Since the end of the war there has been an enormous literature – a kind of feeding frenzy – devoted to proving that Heidegger was a Nazi *because of* his philosophy, in other words, that his philosophy is 'Nazi philosophy'. In 1997 I wrote a book, *Heidegger, Philosophy, Nazism* (see p. 214 below) which (though it has cost me a certain degree of abuse on the Internet and elsewhere) establishes, I believe, that none of the attempts to demonstrate this claim are successful. One can accept some, or all, of the central claims of Heidegger's philosophy while remaining committed to basic human rights and a democratic form of government.

Actually, 'Heidegger's philosophy' is a misnomer, for he spoke of a *Kehre*, a 'U-turn' or radical transformation in his thinking, as having occurred in the early 1930s. For this reason, one needs to distinguish between his 'early', pre-*Kehre* philosophy, which is the topic of this chapter, and his 'later' philosophy, which will be the topic of Chapter 15. The principal expression of the early philosophy is *Being and Time*,[2] which appeared in 1927.

So what is *Being and Time* about? The work starts by considering what it is to be a person, or, as Heidegger calls it, a 'Dasein'. (*Dasein* is the ordinary German word for 'existence', but literally it means 'being-here'. In asking what it is to be a Dasein, Heidegger is asking what it is to be here, in the world, in the manner that is distinctive of human beings.) Is, for example, being a person a matter of being a Platonic or Christian 'soul', a 'soul substance', as

Heidegger puts it: a non-physical entity temporarily housed in a body that is situated in a physical world but which might, and one day will, find itself existing in a non-physical world?

Not at all, says Heidegger. If we really want to understand what a person is (rather than fabricating a story to fit the requirements of Platonic–Christian metaphysics), the place to start is with the recognition that a person is essentially an *agent*, a being that does things, that *acts*. Moreover, the kind of person you are depends on the kind of acts you perform. To be kind, generous, truthful, polite or punctual is not a matter of something going on in some mysterious, invisible, inner entity called a 'soul' or 'mind', but simply to *act* – and act consistently – in certain specific ways. A punctual person simply *is* a person who regularly turns up on time, a polite person one who regularly says 'please' and 'thank you', a truthful person one who regularly speaks the truth. 'One is', says Heidegger, 'what one does' (BT 239).

Now, just as you can't have a (theatrical) actor without a stage to act on, so you can't have an agent without a world to act in. The idea of a person existing without a world to exist in makes no sense at all.

At this point, I need to introduce some background information. The great articulator of the Platonic–Christian view of the self in the modern era was the French philosopher-mathematician René Descartes (1596–1650). According to Descartes, the essential self is a 'thinking thing' or mind that is temporarily housed in a body – rather like a pea in a pod. (An invisible pea in a mechanical pod – like Newton, Descartes took the physical world to be a giant machine, to function according to mechanical laws that are universal and exceptionless. Hence the satirical account of Cartesianism as the view that a person is a 'ghost in the machine'.)

Descartes' quest is for absolute certainty. Accordingly, in his *Meditations on First Philosophy*, he sets out to doubt everything which can be doubted. His own existence and the fact that he thinks and experiences, however, he cannot doubt. Even if all his thoughts are wrong and his experiences deceptive, those thoughts and experiences must still exist to be wrong, and he must exist to have them. But what about the world outside his mind, the world of everyday things? Certainly he has *experiences* that seem to be of such a world. But he has experiences that seem to be of a world when he is dreaming. How, then (the old sceptical argument mentioned in discussing Hegel), does he know that he is not dreaming all the time?

Eventually Descartes decides that he does know, for certain, that the world exists: he 'proves' God's existence (with an exceptionally shonky argument), and then decides it would be inconsistent with God's goodness to give him such a powerful inclination to believe in a world outside his mind if, in fact, there was no such world. None of this is very convincing – one doubts that Descartes himself believed it. The result is that, on the Cartesian view, the existence of the 'external' world remains a permanent theoretical problem.

The primary negative ambition of *Being and Time* is the destruction of the Cartesian view of the self in all its aspects. With respect to the existence of the world, it would be wrong to say that Heidegger *refutes* the theoretical doubt raised by the dream argument. It's consistent with everything Heidegger says still to maintain that there *might* be an immaterial thing – one can call it 'I' if one likes – whose experiences as of a world are actually pure illusion. The mistake Heidegger points out is that of supposing this 'I' to be a *person* and of concluding that, since the 'I' can exist without a world, 'person' can be explained without reference to 'world', and personal characteristics – generosity, kindness, etc. – without reference to action. A person, to repeat, is a being that acts, and action requires a world. Person and world are inseparable, a point Heidegger makes by saying that Dasein is 'being-in-the-world' (BT 113) – the function of the hyphens is to emphasise this inseparability. What a person is can only be explained by reference to world and to action within it.

What, then, is a world? One thing it is not is chunks of matter floating around in physical space according to mechanical laws. (Once again, Heidegger has Descartes in his sights; here the 'machine' part of the 'ghost in the machine' story.) It is not that this is necessarily a *wrong* description of reality. On the contrary, it (or something like it) is a perfectly appropriate description if what we are doing is natural science. But if, on the other hand, we are trying to understand what a person is it is absolutely inappropriate.

What, then, is appropriate? Heidegger's central concept here is that of the 'ready-to-hand' (BT 69) or, in a very broad sense of the term, 'equipment' (BT 68).

What is 'equipment'? Cars are equipment, as are computers and hammers. Wind, too, is equipment when it is 'wind in the sails', when it is used, for example, to power a yacht. A river is equipment when it is used to generate electricity. Clouds are equipment when they are used to predict the weather.

Consider a hammer. What makes something to be *that* sort of equipment? Not, certainly, its physical appearance. Someone might construct something made out of papier mâché that *looked* just like a hammer. The inhabitants of a distant planet might manufacture things that looked just like hammers but were, in fact, religious symbols. Something might look just like a hammer – might in fact *be* an ex-hammer – but actually be an incredibly valuable piece of 'ready-made' art. What makes something a hammer is its use – that it is used for knocking in nails. By whom? By carpenters. What for? To build, for example, houses. Again, what for? For people – the purchasers of the houses – to live in. Dasein's world, therefore, essentially contains not just equipment but also other Dasein, other people.

Once again, a point is being made here against Descartes. One of the live possibilities, as we have seen, on a Cartesian view of things (on Descartes' view minus the world-guaranteeing God whose existence, of course, he cannot really prove) is that nothing exists outside my consciousness, that really there is no world at all. But supposing we have somehow been able to lay this first doubt to rest. Another doubt still remains. This consists in the possibility that, though there really is a world, I am *alone* in it. To be sure, says Descartes in the fourth of his *Meditations*, I'm surrounded by beings in hats and coats who look very like me and behave in remarkably similar ways – if I stick a pin in one of them it screws up its face, jumps and utters the sounds 'Ouch, that hurts' – but how do I know that they aren't all really just cleverly constructed robots completely devoid of consciousness and feeling? This kind of reflection – I know, for certain, that I exist, but whether anyone else does is open to doubt – makes it look as though one can and must explain what it is for me to be me, for a person to be a person, without any reference to the existence of other people. Once again, however, Heidegger points out Descartes' confusion between the idea of a solitary pinpoint of consciousness and the idea of a person. This confusion has serious consequences because it obscures the crucial fact that being-among-other-people is part of the *explanation* of what it is to be a person.

To see how deeply others are implicated in one's life as a person consider, says Heidegger, a boat or a field. Even though you want to cross the river, you do not touch the boat on the bank. To get to the other side of the field you walk round the edge rather than across the middle. Why is this? Because the boat and the field are *private property*; belong, that is, to *another person*. (Notice that we do not ascribe property rights to robots.) Far from being alone in it, our world is *saturated* with other-peopleness – even when they are not around. For Descartes, there is a serious problem in 'getting over' from the solitary 'I' to other people. But for Heidegger, as we shall see, the problem is precisely the opposite: getting away from them.

Dasein, then, essentially inhabits a world, a world that is a kind of interconnected network of equipment and other Dasein. Is this, then, all there is to be said about being a Dasein, being a person? Not so.

Another of Dasein's defining traits, says Heidegger, is that it is, essentially and uniquely, that being for which its own being is an 'issue' (BT 12). Dasein, that is to say, inescapably confronts a *choice* as to the fundamental quality of the life it is to lead. Neither dogs nor daffodils confront such a choice. Only beings that are persons do.

The key term in understanding this choice is *Eigentlichkeit*, usually translated as 'authenticity', though (since *eigen* means 'own', *lich* means 'ly' and *keit* means 'ness') a more revealing translation would be 'ownliness'. A person who has *Eigentlichkeit* is someone who is their *own* person.

To explain authenticity (since 'ownliness' isn't a proper word I'll stick to the standard translation) we need to start with the opposite – inauthenticity. What is that?

Go back to the carpenter. Being a carpenter is a *social role*. Social roles determine one's actions: Harry builds houses because he is a carpenter and because building houses is what carpenters do.

One's job description is one type of social role, but each of us inhabits an endless variety of others: being a Republican, being a Democrat, being a father, being a son, being a Protestant, being a Catholic, being a Manchester United supporter, being a Manchester City supporter, being gay, being straight, being middle class, being working class, being an intellectual, being a redneck and so on *ad infinitum*. Each role determines a range of actions that are appropriate to it.

Mostly, the way in which we inhabit the selection of social roles that defines who we are is, in a strong sense, *non-optional*. This is because we succumb to the pressure of 'public opinion' (BT 174–5,

403) to conform to the norms that are approved by the group or subculture to which we belong. We succumb to what Heidegger calls 'the dictatorship of the One' (*das Man*, which can also be translated as 'the They'), the pressure to do what 'one' does – the 'one' of 'one does not eat one's peas with a knife, Tommy'. This pressure 'levels us down' to the 'averageness' of the group. Typically, says Heidegger,

> we take pleasure and enjoy ourselves as *one* takes pleasure; we read, see and judge about literature and art as *one* sees and judges; likewise, we shrink back from the 'great mass' as *one* shrinks back; we find shocking what one finds shocking.
>
> (BT 126–7)

Typically, Heidegger suggests, individual lives are nothing more than functions of the One, functions of public opinion. Typically, individuals are nothing more than, as it were, a multiplicity of loud-speakers through which booms the single, self-confident voice of *das Man*, expressing the same opinions, the same tastes and the same judgements over and over again. Typically, that is to say, individuals are precisely *not* individual. They are, rather, endlessly repeated clones of each other, their lives tedious clichés concerning which, if you know a couple of features, you can predict all the rest. Nietzsche spotted this phenomenon and spoke, unkindly, of the great majority of people as 'herd animals'. (It is in contrast to these that he says that 'we, however' want to become beings who are 'new, unique, incomparable, who give themselves laws, who create themselves' (GS 335). As we shall see, however, Heidegger's conception of authenticity is more deeply thought out than this.)

Inauthentic life has a certain downside to it. There is, Heidegger suggests, a certain sense of something being amiss, a dim sense of self-betrayal. One senses that one has given over the running of one's life to someone else whereas, in fact, the only proper person to run it is oneself. One is troubled by the 'voice of conscience' (BT 268).

Heidegger, though brought up a Catholic and originally trained to be a Catholic priest, married a Protestant. He wrote *Being and Time* under the influence of a close friendship and collaboration with the Protestant theologian Rudolf Bultmann. This influence endows the work with a particular character that has led to its being described as 'Godless theology'. ('Godless' because, according to

Being and Time, that which underlies our this-worldly existence is the 'nothing' (BT 308); 'theology' because a plausible way of reading Heidegger's 'authenticity' is to see it as preserving the essence of a Christian life *in spite of* the death of God.) Heidegger's assertion that we all have a fundamental sense that the only proper person to run our life is ourself might well be seen as an articulation of the founding claim of the Protestant Reformation – Martin Luther's assertion that the ultimate authority which determines the right and the good is not the Pope but always, in the end, one's own conscience.

The downside of inauthenticity, then, is a sense of 'lostness' (BT 268), lack of self-ownership. On the other hand, there is a certain upside.

Inauthentic life, says Heidegger, can't exactly be called 'tranquil'. Because of the vague sense of self-betrayal there is an underlying restlessness which often expresses itself in a dabbling in Eastern religions or in 'the exaggerated self-dissection' (BT 178) of psychoanalysis. (Think of Woody Allen.) But, if not exactly tranquil, inauthentic life is, at least, 'tranquillised' (BT 177). As Prozac, alcohol and background music dull things down that we don't really want to think about, so inauthentic life has the advantage of covering over something that we are extremely reluctant to face up to.

What is this unpleasant something? What is it which, in the flight to conformism, we are seeking to evade? What are we running away *from*? At this point, Heidegger makes a startling and dramatic claim: what, in inauthenticity, we are seeking to evade is *death*.

Why, after all, asks Heidegger, do we succumb to the pressure to conform exerted on us by *das Man*? What makes the phenomenon surprising is that, unlike a real dictatorship, the 'dictatorship' of the One is not backed up by any obvious threat of punishment for those who fail to conform. No one, for example, actually gets tortured for wearing narrow jeans in an age of flares (unless they live under fundamentalist Islam).

Heidegger explains conformism in terms of what he calls 'distantiality' (BT 126). Human beings are so constituted that they begin to feel extremely uncomfortable if they find themselves more than a little distance from social norms.

At first, distantiality looks to be just a basic, brute fact about the human psyche, something incapable of explanation in terms of anything more basic. Later on, in *Being and Time*, however, Heidegger provides an explanation of our strong disposition to huddle up to social norms. The explanation is that it is, as it were, cold on the outside. In what does this coldness consist? It consists, says Heidegger, in *death*. Outside the group, what you feel is the chill wind of death.

Outsiders – individuals – that is to say, die. But the group, *das Man*, does not die. So to the extent that I identify myself with the group I seem to evade death. To the extent that I think of myself not as an individual for whom the question of what life one is to lead is an 'issue', but rather as a mere, as it were, vehicle for the One to drive around in, to the extent that I take the only 'self' in the picture to be the One, then I seem to rise above death. The flight from authenticity, the flight from owning one's own individuality is, then, the flight from owning – owning up to – one's own death.[3]

Given that 'average, everyday' Dasein is heavily committed to this self-deceiving evasion of death, it comes as no surprise that death – particularly 'my death' – is a topic we like to avoid. We – particularly we in the modern West – tuck dying and death out of sight in old people's homes and crematoria. We engage in euphemisms – 'passed away', 'gone to sleep' – and in nervous, Woody Allenish jokes ('It's not that I'm afraid of death; I'd just rather not be there when it happens'). Most importantly, as Heidegger points out (BT 258), we engage in evasive thought-patterns. I think, for example, of death as something that happens to *other* people (and even then only when there is some 'failure of the health system'). And, if I am forced to face up to the fact that death happens to me, I still, in effect, manage to make it someone else's problem. I tell myself: 'Of course I will die – but not yet.' The weasel clause here is the 'not yet'. What I am really thinking is: Death is something that happens to old people, to the old Young. But I am the young Young. So death is no concern of *mine* but only of some distant, as it were, 'descendant' of my present self about whom I am not concerned. (Students sometimes think about exams in the same way: the exam at the end of the term concerns only a remote successor of oneself, so one's present self has no need to do anything save smoke dope and go skiing.) Of course, when I get older I think of death as something that happens only to *very* old people, and so on. By strategies such as this we endow ourselves with, and live our lives under the influence of, an *illusion of immortality*, an illusion that enables us to escape the three, as Heidegger calls them, 'ontological' (defining) features of death: death is *mine* – it happens not just to other people but also to *me*; death is inevitable – it *must* happen; and, most importantly, it may happen *at any moment*. This last feature is of crucial significance because it is only its evasion which enables one to pass the buck of death from one's present self to a remote self of the future.

If the evasion of death is the real motive for living inauthentically, it follows that the key to getting out of inauthenticity, to becoming authentic, is genuinely to face up to the fact of one's own death, genuinely to face up to its three ontological features. Heidegger calls this owning up to one's own death 'authentic being-towards-death' and sometimes '*Vorlaufen*' – 'anticipation of' or, literally, 'running-forwards-into' – death (BT sections 52–3).

What happens if one does genuinely own one's own death; not just pay it lip-service, but live one's whole life in the light of one's mortality?

To make the question more vivid, imagine you have just been diagnosed as HIV positive. (Of course, metaphysically speaking, we are all, as it were, HIV positive: life, as someone wittily remarked, is a terminal condition that is sexually transmitted.)

Heidegger says that facing up to death 'wrenches Dasein away from *das Man*'. It does this because one realises that 'all being-with-others will fail us when [death] . . . is the issue' (BT 263). What he is pointing to here is the idea that inauthentic life is a kind of implicit *bargain*. The individual 'promises' to conform and, in return, *das Man* 'promises' to take away the awfulness – the endless nothingness – of death. In facing up to death (whether by choice or by necessity), however, one realises that *das Man* is a deceiver, that it won't, and in fact can't, take away death. Nothing can do that; death is inescapable.

This insight, of course, may only last a split second. One may hastily tuck it away under the usual cover-up. But suppose one holds on to it. Then, says Heidegger, Dasein becomes 'individualised down to itself' (BT 263). Understanding that entry into death is something I do alone, that my social group will betray me at the moment of death, I attain a vivid grasp of my own individuality. Understanding that, I understand that *I myself* have to make the choices that determine my life. I give up being a mindless conformist, become immune to the pressure to conform to the approved norms of public opinion. No longer 'dictated' to by *das Man* – no longer dictated to by 'the others' – one becomes, as I shall put it, 'autonomous', self-governing.

Autonomy, making your own life-choices, 'doing it *my* way', though a part, is not the totality of what makes up authenticity – being your own person. One might, after all – so, at least, it would seem on the surface of things – escape the clutches of the One only to lapse into a mind-blasted life of sex, drink and drugs; the last days of the ageing rock star, perhaps. If your choices add up to a meaningless chaos such as this, then Heidegger would say that, far from being an authentic person, you don't really count as being a person at all, only as a jumble of what might be called 'person-fragments'. Nietzsche says, as we saw in Chapter 7, that '*one thing is needful*' (GS 290) – that we become the 'heroes' of our lives so that 'it becomes evident how the constraint of a *single* . . . [narrative] govern[s] everything large and small' (ibid.). Heidegger believes this, too. To be any kind of a person, one's life must have a unity to it, the continuity and coherence which comes from constructing one's life as a work of art. The word I now want to use to designate the unity in question is 'focus'. So, using my own terminology, what I want to suggest is that Heidegger's notion of authenticity is really a *combination* of autonomy and focus. Authenticity is, as one might put it, focused autonomy.

But Heidegger thinks that facing up to death is the key, not only to autonomy, but also to focus. Facing and holding on to knowledge of our mortality (of death in the ontological richness of all of its three defining features) gives us autonomy and focus *at one and the same time*.

Why should facing up to death give our lives focus?

Go back to discovering yourself to be HIV positive. HIV may never kill you. Even if it becomes 'full-blown' AIDS, you may, with modern drugs, live a full life for a decade or more. None the less, in receiving the diagnosis you are unavoidably confronted with the fact you normally evade – your own mortality or finitude, the finiteness of your existence. If you hang on to this knowledge, if you make productive use of the occasion (I once heard a cancer patient refer to 'the privilege of having cancer'), then, says Heidegger, you become 'liberated' from 'lostness in those possibilities which may accidentally thrust themselves upon one', liberated 'in such a way that, for the first time, one can authentically understand and choose among the facticial possibilities lying ahead of ... [death]' (BT 264).

The thought here is neither particularly difficult nor particularly original. Dr Johnson had it in the eighteenth century when he remarked that there is nothing like the prospect of being hanged to concentrate the mind. The point is that to be properly aware of your finitude – to realise that death happens to *you*, that it *must* happen, and may happen *at any moment* – is to realise that you *do not have time* to explore all the multiplicity of options which life places before you. What one is compelled to do, therefore, is to determine which life-options are the important, 'essential' ones and which are the trivial distractions, the 'accidental' time-wasters, as Heidegger calls them, which life thrusts one's way.

Grasping one's finitude is more than simply realising that there is no time to lose. To be able to make the distinction between essential and irrelevant life-options one must, says Heidegger, grasp one's life as a 'totality', as a 'whole' (BT 232). (Nietzsche, remember, says exactly the same thing: to narrate one's life as a work of literature one must grasp it as if it were already something 'past and whole' (GS 78).) But to do that one must *vorlaufen*, 'anticipate' one's death, 'run forward', in imagination, to life's end. Only by positioning oneself at the end of life and grasping it as if it were completed and past, can one grasp it as a whole. The Christian notion of the Last Judgement is, in part, I think, an aid to this self-totalising, as is the injunction to write one's own obituary and then live in the light of what one has written. Another relevant phenomenon is the car-crash experience. 'My whole life flashed before my eyes,' survivors often say. Obviously in the split second before the crash there is not time to review every single incident in one's past. What presents itself, rather, in the moment before impact, is 'one's whole life' simplified down to its three or four defining moments or people. (Let me hasten to add that the car crash is just *a* way in which life can disclose its focus. One does not *need* to drive fast to become authentic.)

If, then, one 'anticipates' one's death, one grasps one's life as a simplified whole and sees which options are essential and which are trivial distractions. The poet-accountant of Chapter 7, for example, will see either that he is a poet or that he is an accountant.[4] Not only that, but – let's suppose that he sees he is a poet – he will see that he has wasted a great deal of precious time on irrelevancies and that, to be who he is, *there is no more time to lose*.

To sum up. Authentic life is autonomous. But it is also focused. As focused, it is marked by urgency, energy (becoming focused is a tremendous release of hitherto dissipated energy) and commitment. It is, in other words, intensely *meaningful*. Authenticity is Heidegger's account of what it is to live a meaningful life.

Notice, in passing, that on Heidegger's account, an immortal life would be a life without meaning. Since all life-possibilities can be realised over infinite time, there can be no choices that matter if I am condemned to eternal life. The poet, for example, does not have to *reject* being an accountant; he only has to reject it *for now*, knowing full well that it's an option he may well take up in the next hundred years. This means that his current life is no more than a role he is playing at the moment. It can't tell him who *he* is since he knows that he will soon be someone quite different. And, since it can't do that, it can't give meaning to his life.

I've been bringing Nietzsche into the discussion over the last few pages because it seems to me clear that Heidegger's notion of authenticity is very close to Nietzsche's notion of the meaningful life as a life lived as if it were a well-written work of literature. Now, however, I want to look at the differences between the two accounts of the meaningful life.

Nietzsche holds, we saw, that to live a meaningful life we are to narrate our lives into an organic whole in such a way as to disclose the 'hero' who we are. For him, however, it is absolutely *up to me* which of the many available stories I choose to be *my* story. Though superficially attractive (particularly to those dissatisfied with their current lives), this freedom to become whoever one wants is, on closer inspection, problematic. For two reasons (see pp. 95–6 above).

The first is that if all life-options are equally available, then the sole ground for my choice of one rather than another is my own free, and indeed arbitrary, choice. But that means that the life-option I have chosen possesses no genuine authority for me. It cannot therefore be an object of genuine commitment, cannot provide me with a ground for persevering through hardship and disappointment. And that, in turn, means that it can't render my life genuinely meaningful. This is what I called the 'problem of authority'.

The second problem we saw affecting Nietzsche's position is what I called 'the problem of the immoral script'. Given that all that matters is that I *like* the life I have scripted for myself, couldn't I just as easily script myself the life of a Mafia boss (who is kind to dogs and small children) as that of a research scientist seeking the cure for AIDS? Isn't Nietzsche committed to the view that the former life is just as valid a choice as the latter, isn't he guilty, that is, of elevating meaning over morality?

Now I want to return to Heidegger and see how he fares with respect to these two problematic features of Nietzschean thinking.

Authenticity, as thus far explained, is a purely *formal* concept. Its definition in terms of 'autonomy' and 'focus', that is to say, tells us about the form of the authentic life but nothing about its *content*. Put another way, authenticity, as thus far understood, is compatible with *any* life-content. You can be an autonomously focused communist, fascist, liberal democrat, terrorist, Mafia boss, AIDS-researcher, accountant or poet. This is the second of Nietzsche's problems.

Heidegger, however, thinks further than Nietzsche. Noting the purely formal character of autonomy-plus-focus, he explicitly raises the question of from 'whence . . . Dasein can draw those possibilities on which it facticially projects itself' (BT 383), from whence it can derive the content of its life. His answer is: 'from heritage' (BT sections 74–5).

Heritage – roughly speaking, the ethical tradition of one's community – is not written down in a big book of rules. Rather, it is embodied in certain 'hero' figures who are preserved – handed down from generation to generation – by the myths, folk-tales, artworks, sacred books and so on of the culture. Heroes (note that Heidegger's use of the term is different from the Nietzschean use with which we have been acquainted up to now) are, very roughly speaking, 'role models': exemplary figures which tell us how to live. For the Greeks, Hera embodied the virtue of homeliness, Zeus the virtue of leadership; for the Scots, the tale of Robert Bruce and the spider embodies the virtue of perseverance; for the Dutch, the little boy with his finger in the dike the virtue of social responsibility; for the English, Captain ('I am just going outside, and may be some time') Oates the virtue of quietly understated courage; for South

Africans, Nelson Mandela the value of freedom; for New Zealanders, Edmund Hilary the virtue of modesty in high achievement. Note that a 'hero' may be a living figure. If living, however, the figure in question will be, to one degree or another, mythologised. As he or she becomes part of the heritage of the culture, 'warts' will be removed, irrelevant features ignored.

Heidegger's crucial thought is that *heritage is not something we choose*. Rather, we are born into it. As we grow to adulthood – always, of course, within a particular culture – we find ourselves *already in possession of* a pantheon of hero-figures and the values they personify. It's part of mastering the language. We master our *native* language, that is, not in the classroom but in listening to the talk of our parents and peers into which are woven the value-laden, heritage-preserving tales and myths of our culture. By the time we have mastered the language – have become human beings in the full sense of the word – we have mastered our heritage, too.

The values embodied by our heroes, the commitments of heritage, it is important to see, *all belong to one's authentic self*. You are who you are, in a large part, because you have grown to adulthood – 'Daseinhood' – within a particular culture. The commitments of heritage, Heidegger holds, are *your* commitments, the deepest values that you have.[5] It follows that authenticity, and in particular autonomy – doing what *you* decide to do rather than what public opinion tells you to do – is acting out of the values of heritage. *Being true to heritage is being true to your own, deepest self.*

So how does heritage govern the choice of the content of the authentic life?

One finds oneself, says Heidegger, in a particular 'facticity'. (We will find this notion re-emerging in Sartre.) Facticity is made up of two things: one's personal circumstances and, as Heidegger puts it, one's 'historical' situation. By 'personal circumstances' is meant, here, the social context in which one finds oneself (that one is in a capitalist rather than a communist society, for example) together with the particular set of abilities and disabilities with which one is endowed. One may, for example, be an excellent writer but terrible mathematician. One's historical situation is constituted by the particular way in which current public opinion and practice fall short of the values of heritage.[6]

It is important to notice that there will almost always be such a discrepancy. There are at least two reasons for this. First, the way in which the values of heritage are applied in practice constantly needs updating in the light of new knowledge. If, for example, we become convinced that women are actually *capable* of doing those jobs it used to be thought only men could do – being a French horn player, being a conductor – then we may need to re-evaluate what, in practice, the value of equality comes to. Second, the meaning of the values of heritage – and that means the way we understand our hero figures – constantly need reinterpreting so as to make sense in the contemporary context. Freedom, for example, meant one thing in Nazi-occupied Europe, but to make sense in the age of the subtle herding of individuals into mass opinions by the media has to mean something else.

Dasein always finds itself, then, with a particular set of personal capacities and incapacities in a particular historical situation constituted by the salience of some gap between heritage and current opinion and practice. These two together, Heidegger holds, determine the content of the authentic life. Knowing equality to be a fundamental value enshrined in the heritage of your society, for example, you might be particularly struck by the discrepancy between heritage, on the one hand, and the actual treatment of women, as compared with men, on the other. This discrepancy, taken together with your exceptional talent for writing, might disclose to you that which defines and gives meaning to your life: being a feminist journalist.

It is important to emphasise that the content of the authentic – meaningful – life is not something you *choose*. Rather, you *discover* it in the conjunction of heritage and facticity. Certain elements of choice, of course, remain: which newspaper, for example, to write for. Even here, however, facticity is likely to suggest an answer.

Now I should like to return to the two problems that afflict Nietzsche's account of the meaningful life. Does Heidegger fare any better than Nietzsche with respect to these problems?

First, the problem of commitment. On Heidegger's account, this seems to disappear. Since the content of the authentic life is *discovered* in the conjunction of facticity and heritage rather than arbitrarily chosen, the problem that arbitrary choice can't provide a basis for commitment seems to disappear. Should, of course, one's feminist writings fail to get published, one might, in the end, have to reassess the question of one's talent as a writer. But all that means is that one might have made a *mistake* about one's facticity, not that there is anything wrong with the idea that the conjunction of heritage and facticity determines the content of the meaningful life. All it means is that one needs to look harder into that conjunction.

The problem of the immoral script. This problem also seems to disappear. Since the heritage of a culture *is* its morality, it follows that the authentic life, a life guided by the fundamental values of one's community, must also be a moral life.

And yet doubts about Heidegger remain. Concerning the problem of authority, he assumes that the values of heritage necessarily constitute one's own fundamental values, so that any questioning of the ethical (moral) tradition of one's culture is impossible. But is this, in fact, really so? Suppose, for example, one emigrates, and lives for a long time in a radically different culture – say, in Iran or China – so that one becomes aware that there are radically different ways of doing things, *fundamentally* different ethical traditions. If so, might this not reintroduce the arbitrariness of choice? Wouldn't it mean that one had to choose which fundamental heritage one is going to live within? And doesn't this suggest that something is missing from Heidegger's account, something that will put the fundamental values of one's life *genuinely* beyond question?

Concerning the problem of the immoral script, the truth of the matter is that Heidegger hasn't really solved it. True, it turns out that the authentic life must be not merely something pleasing to me, but rather something that accords with the fundamental values of my community. But what is there to say that those fundamental values aren't themselves immoral, or might, at least, be judged so from the perspective of the fundamental values of another moral community? It seems that what we need to *really* solve the problem of the immoral script is a *universal* set of values, values that hold for everyone regardless of the particular culture to which they belong.

This remark leads to another. With Nietzsche, as we may put it, the meaning of life is *individual*: there is the meaning of life for me – my chosen self-narration – and the meaning of life for you – yours. There is no linking or bond between the two; indeed, they may be in fundamental conflict with each other. (We grow up together in Sicily, but you choose to become a Mafia boss while I become a Mafia-busting policeman.) With Heidegger something different is the case: the meaning of life has become *communal*. There is, that is to say, a particular way or set of ways in which actual practice falls short of heritage. For everyone in the community their authentic life is the life dedicated to closing the gap between heritage and actual practice. Of course, I have my own particular way of closing that gap while other members of the community have theirs. Every authentic member of the community has, as we might put it, their own sub-meaning of life. Yet they are all linked together (like the members of a football team) by a commitment to the realisation of a common goal – Heidegger calls it the 'destiny' of a 'people' (BT 384–5). So, with Heidegger, we may speak of the meaning of life *for a community*. This, however, falls short of establishing *the* – community-independent – meaning of life. Early Heidegger, no less than Nietzsche, has given up on discovering *the* – universal – meaning of life.

Of course, there might be no such meaning. Suppose, however, that there were, that we could discover a *universal* set of fundamental values. Then we would have discovered a universal task to which *all* authentic human beings would, each in their own way, contribute. In this case we would have accomplished the Platonic task of discovering *the* human task, *the* meaning of life. These remarks are sketchy and probably hard to follow. They are intended, however, as a preview to the discussion of the later Heidegger in Chapter 15 where I shall try to make them clearer.

10

Sartre

Born into a middle-class background in Paris in 1905, Jean-Paul Sartre lived almost his entire life in the city of his birth. He never, he said, felt at home anywhere save in a fifth-floor Paris apartment and particularly disliked the countryside. An ugly, bug-eyed chain-smoker (rather like Socrates, in the eye and nature-hating departments), he was none the less highly attractive to women. Success as a novelist enabled him to give up university teaching and to spend most of his time in cafés, where many of his major insights occurred. In 1929 he met Simone de Beauvoir, who remained his companion in a sexually open partnership for the rest of his life. At the beginning of the 1950s Sartre engaged in a serious rereading of Marx and became a kind of free-thinking Marxist engaged in many political causes from a left-wing standpoint. In 1964 he was awarded the Nobel prize for literature, which, however, he declined on the grounds that he did not wish to become an institution: did not, that is, wish to become a member of the bourgeoisie, his life-long hatred. He died in 1980.

My interest in this chapter is entirely focused on one work, Sartre's philosophical classic, *Being and Nothingness*,[1] published in Nazi-occupied Paris in 1943. Since Marx is someone we have already discussed, I intend to ignore later Sartre's less original and, I think, less interesting thinking. My focus is entirely on his 'existentialism' and the comprehensive statement it receives in *Being and Nothingness*.

Being and Nothingness is a grandiose piece of elaborate philosophical architecture, clearly modelled on Heidegger's *Being and Time*, of which Sartre was a great, though not uncritical, admirer. Like *Being and Time*, it offers itself as a work that will describe the 'ontology' of human being (BN p. 625), an attempt to define the structures which human beings, as persons, necessarily inhabit; structures which define what it is to be human. Like Heidegger, however, Sartre has his own special term for 'human being'. Whereas Heidegger speaks of 'Dasein', Sartre speaks of 'being-for-itself (*être-pour-soi*)'.

Being-for-itself is contrasted with 'being-in-itself (*être-en-soi*)'. (The terminology comes from Hegel, who, together with Nietzsche and Husserl, represents the other major influence on Sartre's thinking. Behind every French thinker you can always find a German, someone unkindly remarked.) What the contrast is intended to be between is moderately clear: people, on the one hand, and 'things' on the other, 'things' in a very broad (and perhaps reprehensible) sense of the term which includes not just rocks, inkwells and robots, but also trees, worms and spiders. What, however, about cats, dogs, apes, chimpanzees, dolphins and whales? Are they beings-for-themselves or beings-in-themselves?

The rationale behind Sartre's choice of terminology has to do with self-consciousness. Beings-for-themselves come before – are 'for' – themselves in consciousness whereas beings-in-themselves do not. But what is it to be self-conscious?

Sartre makes a useful distinction between explicit ('reflective', 'thetic') and implicit ('non-reflective', 'non-thetic') self-consciousness. The first occurs when I make myself the direct target of consciousness, as when I monitor my thoughts, emotions, habits, character traits and actions ('Am I being paranoid?' 'Do I get angry too easily? 'Am I about to say "tu" when it ought to be "vous"?'). Sartre's example of the second sort of self-consciousness has to do with counting (actually of cigarettes (BN p. liii), but, this being a politically correct book, I have changed the example). A teacher anxiously counts the children getting back on the bus after a school outing to make sure none are missing. Her attention is entirely focused on the children. Yet if you interrupt her and ask what she is doing she will of course be able immediately to answer 'counting the children' – which indicates that as well as being explicitly conscious of the children she has implicit consciousness of herself and her own activity.

Sartre claims that all consciousness is self-consciousness (BN p. lii). Not, obviously, that all consciousness is explicitly self-conscious, but rather that it is always at least implicitly so. I think he is right about this (though not for the very poor reason he actually gives (ibid.).) The reason for this was given long ago by Schopenhauer.

How do I know where things are in the world? The mountain, for example? Well, the mountain, let us say, is behind the river. But where is the river? It runs down the easterly side of the wood. But where is the wood? Unless I can answer this question I don't know where anything else is. The answer is that the wood is about fifty metres and to the left of *here*. Where, in other words, *I* am. So what we see is that we can't locate anything in space unless the chain of references can be traced, ultimately, back to myself. All spatial locating is relative, ultimately, to the self as a kind of centre, a fixed point of reference in space. And the same with time. When did the Normans invade England? 1066. But when was that? 937 years before 2003. But when is 2003? 2003 is *now*, in other words, where, in time, I am. I can locate nothing in time unless I can relate it ultimately to myself as a centre, a fixed reference point in time.

It follows that, though cats, dogs, dolphins, etc., almost certainly do not have explicit self-consciousness, they – and any beings capable of using a conscious representation of their environment to guide their behaviour – must have implicit self-consciousness in order, for example, to know where their bowl of food is placed or where their bone is buried.

So it seems that Sartre ought to recognise many of the higher animals as beings-for-themselves. But he does not. As rigidly as his great French predecessor (and secret hero) Descartes – who thought that animals were all machines and only humans had consciousness – he uses the for-itself/in-itself dichotomy to divide off human beings from everything else.

The reason for this is that, though, formally, the dichotomy is supposed to turn on self-consciousness as such, it actually turns on a different property which Sartre attributes, uniquely, to human beings: freedom. 'In-itself' beings have fixed, immutable natures or, as Sartre calls them, 'essences'. 'For-itself' beings, on the other hand, have the power to decide what their essences are to be and, should they so wish, to change them.

This power, I think, the power to reflect upon and perhaps change one's 'essence', one's identity, Sartre plausibly takes to presuppose *explicit*, 'reflective' self-consciousness. So it is this capacity, it seems to me, that wears the trousers (or, as the French say, nickers) when it comes to distinguishing the for-itself from the in-itself.

But we have got a little ahead of ourselves. Let us return to the grand scheme of things, the fundamental aim of *Being and Nothingness*.

What the work seeks to discover, we have said, is the 'ontological' structure of human – the for-itself's – existence. Unfortunately, however, without ever being properly aware that this is what he is doing, what Sartre actually offers, it seems to me, is *two* – different and incompatible – accounts of that structure. The result, so I shall argue, is that what *Being and Nothingness* actually offers is two books inside one cover or, as it were, two buildings behind one façade. Aided by immense literary skills and the plasticity of key terms such as 'contingent', 'absurd' 'anguish', 'being-in-itself-for-itself', which play central roles in both accounts, Sartre is able to smooth over the join between the two buildings so that, even to him, they look like one. But in fact they are not, so that separating them becomes vital to an unmuddled understanding of *Being and Nothingness*. The first of the two accounts, whose author I shall call 'Sartre-One', is the account that tends to dominate in parts I and IV of the work, the second, whose author I shall call 'Sartre-Two', tends to dominate in parts II and III. Sartre-One will be the topic of this chapter, Sartre-Two of the next.

According to Sartre-One (hereafter and until further notice just 'Sartre'), the first and inescapable fact about human beings – the first ingredient in the 'ontological' structure which constitutes being-for-itself – is our 'facticity' (BN part II chapter I section II). At any moment in my life as a human being I find myself *already* in a given 'situation', a situation that is not of my making. The historical epoch I inhabit, my native language, my nationality, my social class, my sex, my biological capacities and incapacities (for example, that I can run a hundred metres in thirty seconds but not in ten) are facts about me that are completely independent of any desire or choice on my part. Other facts about me – that I am a member of the Labour Party and in training to become a professional football player – might seem to be different. Even these aspects of my facticity, however, Sartre wants to say, are not of my making. They depend, to be sure, on the decisions and commitments made by some *past* incarnation of myself. But if we use the word 'me' to designate *this here and now present being* – which is how Sartre always wants us to think of the 'me' – then even these aspects of my facticity are not of *my* making. My facticity is, then, the totality of the facts about me that are dependent on my *past*, whether that past consists in choices of my past self, or in factors that are entirely beyond my control. My facticity is the legacy of the past, the 'baggage' I carry around as a result of having had the particular past I have had.

A thesis Sartre calls 'psychological determinism' (BN p. 31) holds that how I choose to act now is a completely inevitable consequence of my facticity (together, presumably, with the particular circumstances in which I now find myself). Who I am, my 'essence', is an inevitable and unalterable function of my past. '*Wesen ist was gewesen ist*' (BN p. 35 *et passim*), 'essence is what has been'; Sartre regularly uses this quotation from Hegel to sum up psychological determinism.

Exactly what is psychological determinism? Notice that, since the thesis holds that *every* choice is determined by facticity, this must apply to the *first* choice I ever made. So, if we divide my present facticity into volitional (chosen) and non-volitional elements, what psychological determinism holds is that all my choices and actions are completely fore-ordained by the *non-volitional* part of my facticity. Psychological determinism is the thesis that the kind of person I am, and hence all my future choices and actions, are completely determined by the totality of physical and cultural facts about me. If someone – God, for example – knew all there is to know about my biological and cultural situation, he would be able to predict, with absolute certainty, all my future actions.

Sartre absolutely rejects psychological determinism. He points out, first of all, that we all have, as it is sometimes called, the 'feeling of freedom'. Often, this is an unpleasant feeling. The gambler, having yesterday firmly decided to give up his destructive habit, knows today, as soon as he wakes up, that he still has it all before him; that he is – unfortunately – still free to return to the tables should he now so choose. Nothing the gambler (let us call him Dostoyevsky) knows about the Dostoyevsky of yesterday can determine, take away the freedom, of the Dostoyevsky of today (BN p. 32). Another of Sartre's examples. Hiking along a mountain track I have a sudden feeling of psychological vertigo: I feel certain that, notwithstanding my eminently happy life and my exciting ambitions and hopes for the future, I *could*, at this very moment, decide to simply throw myself over the precipice (BN p. 31). The general point, so we feel, is that *nothing* that happened in the past can bind what one does now.

A deeper reason Sartre has for rejecting psychological

determinism has to do with the phenomenon of 'questioning' (BN pp. 33–4). What Sartre says here is greatly influenced by Descartes and by what he says about doubt.

Descartes suggests that, though, unlike God, my knowledge of the truth about the world is severely limited, I yet resemble God in one respect: my power to withhold assent from propositions which are open to doubt is absolutely unlimited. I have experiences as of a world of physical nature outside my mind. But maybe I am dreaming. Nothing can *force* me to believe in a world outside the mind in the absence of conclusive proof. Similarly, nothing can prevent me from believing something that is absolutely certain: 2+2=4.

Loyal to his French intellectual ancestry, Sartre thinks of the self in exactly the same way. What I, this present being, am is nothing but freedom, nothing but the power of assent or dissent. What I am, in particular, therefore, is the power to assent or dissent to my facticity or past self, the power either to choose that self to be *my* (present and future) self or to reject it in favour of something else. Crucially, I am the power of dissent. 'I am', says Sartre, 'the permanent possibility of negating what I am in the form of having been' (BN p. 439).

Since I always therefore stand outside, 'beyond', my essence, I am, says Sartre, 'transcendence' (BN p. 42) (a term which is, for him, synonymous with freedom). But since, on the other hand, this transcendent 'I' is not a thing – it has no intrinsic nature of its own – it is, says Sartre, a no-thing, a 'nothingness' (BN p. 34). In Sartre's technical yet dramatically paradoxical language, the for-itself is a nothingness that transcends its facticity.

At the end of the *Republic*, Plato presents what he calls 'the myth of Err'. What the myth offers is an account of reincarnation in which one's future life is determined by free choice. At the end of a life, the soul surveys a range of future lives (as one might survey a rack of suits) and chooses one that it likes best. Since, however, Plato announces, in the *Phaedrus*, the principle of 'karma' (see p. 15 above) – the general level of one's future life is determined by the degree of virtue displayed in the previous one – the range of options is, presumably, limited by karma. It is useful to keep this picture in mind, since it provides a vivid image that corresponds fairly closely to Sartre's account of the relation between the for-itself's freedom and its facticity. Like Plato, he believes that who we are, our identity or 'essence', is the result of an act of free choice, and like Plato he holds that that choice is limited – though limited not by karma but by facticity. I cannot (at present) choose to have three arms (BN

p. 481). If I live in the thirteenth century I cannot choose to fly (BN p. 522). Unless I am Japanese, I cannot choose to commit *hara-kiri* – though I can of course choose to commit suicide.

We are, then, free because we have the feeling of freedom. But on a deeper level we are free because of the nature of the self as a self-'questioning' being, a being with the absolute power to question and, should it so wish, reject the identity it has had up to now.

It may be objected that feelings are not proofs. That just because we *feel* free and able to change our identity at will doesn't mean we *are* free. Maybe our feeling of freedom reflects nothing but our ignorance of underlying causes. The business tycoon may feel he freely decided to build the hundred-storey skyscraper when in fact it is absolutely clear to the psychoanalyst that he is the victim of a bad case of penile anxiety. Or it may be clear to the physicist that he is nothing but a swirl of atoms the movements of which are completely determined by atomic events that happened millions of years ago. I think, however, that this objection misunderstands the nature of Sartre's project.

Being and Nothingness's sub-title calls it 'An essay on phenomenological ontology'. 'Phenomenology' is description; description of the world as it presents itself in immediate, natural, everyday human experience: the 'manifest world' as we might call it. Since, therefore, Sartre's self-appointed task is confined to describing the manifest world (and to doing so in such a way as to reveal its 'ontological', structural features) he would, I think, say that whether or not some scientific account of the world represents human beings as determined and hence unfree is entirely irrelevant to his interests. His task, he would say, is not to prove, against deterministic science, that humans are free, but simply to show that – however humans may appear in the 'scientific world' – freedom is a structural, central and inescapable feature of the manifest world. (He might also wish to suggest that science is just another story about reality, useful for practical purposes but with no unique claim to truth. This, however, remains peripheral to his task as a phenomenologist.)

Speaking from the perspective of a phenomenological ontologist, then, Sartre's claim is that I can, at any moment, 'negate' who I have been up to now, radically change my identity. Certainly, I may have lived the last thirty-five years as an insurance clerk, as did my father and grandfather before me. Certainly my life may seem, to others, as predictable as did Kant's to the citizens of Königsberg who corrected their clocks by his afternoon walks. Yet I *can*, should I so choose, this very moment, burn every bridge that connects me with my life to date. Like Reginald Perrin, no longer able to stand his tram-railed life with a bowler hat, a furled umbrella and a wife who's mother reminds him of a hippopotamus, I can simply vanish from my past life and re-emerge, let us say, as a dope-smoking hippie seeking enlightenment in far-off Benares. At every moment, that is, I have the inalienable power to choose to become a different kind of person, to choose for myself a new essence. When I reflect, moreover, I *know* that I have this power. Hence *not* abandoning my grey, insurance-clerk's life with a mother-in-law like a hippopotamus is a choice, too – the choice to prefer the boring yet familiar to the new and scary. The only choice I can't make is the choice not to choose. Choice is inescapable, freedom is something to which we are, says Sartre, 'condemned' (BN p. 439). (The reason behind this ominous choice of word will emerge shortly.)

Whereas I have been talking about the choice of one's 'essence' or identity (one's who-one-is-ness), Sartre often speaks in terms of 'values'. These are, however, two ways of talking about the same thing. The reason is the following.

Sartre says that who I am is my 'original projection of myself which stands as my choice of myself in the world' (BN p. 39). Elsewhere he calls this my 'fundamental project' (BN pp. 565, 479–80). One's fundamental project is that project which gives unity and meaning to all one's lesser projects. It consists in the set of things which one most fundamentally desires, aims at or, in other words, *values*. If, for example, the thread that runs through my life is the quest for love, then that defines who I am. If it is the quest for power or status, then I am someone else. (Notice the assumption that everyone *has* a fundamental project, has a kind of underlying consistency to their life. For Nietzsche or Heidegger, on the other hand, to acquire such consistency is a positive *achievement*.)

Put in terms of values, Sartre's point about freedom is as follows. I have, let us suppose, grown up in a small farming community in New Zealand. Though relatively young, I am talented and about to play first-grade 'football' (rugby union) for the local team coached by my father. Harriet and I have grown up together, and for some years now she has been wearing my ring. Our families have been friends for generations. I am expected to have as my fundamental project being-a-God-fearing-rugby-playing-loving-husband-and-father. And maybe I do. But – though there will be all hell to pay if I don't – none of this determines that I *will* play for the team or that I *will* marry Harriet. Only if I reaffirm the fundamental values of my community, the fundamental values I have had up to now, will these things happen. And maybe I won't do that. Maybe small-town rugby values will come to seem to me exclusionary and stultifying. Maybe I will launch myself into an 'identity crisis' and leave town.

Is *every* value something that is my present value only if I choose it to be such? Are there *no* values which are unchosen and which, moreover, I do not have the power to choose not to have? What, for example, about basic bodily desires for food, warmth and shelter? Are these not *unavoidably* mine?

Not so, according to Sartre. Values are always relative to goals, and goals only exist if they are chosen. Nineteenth-century industrial workers (those who figure, for example, in the novels of Dickens or Zola) suffered from desperately inadequate food and housing, but many found this to be *just the way things are* and so had no aspirations to a more adequate level of food or shelter. In general, claims Sartre, 'no factual state can determine consciousness to apprehend it as a lack' (BN pp. 435–6), to value, in other words, its removal. Other examples Sartre might have used to support this claim are asceticism and suicide. Religious penitents do not value food or shelter, and neither do those bent on suicide. To the extent, then, that I do value such things I choose to *reject* the life of the ascetic or would-be suicide in favour of some other form of life.

What about my emotions? Surely emotions are, first, conditions which introduce value into the world (if I'm in love with Harriet, then I place a high value on being near her, gazing into her eyes, etc.) but, second, things that *happen to* one rather than things one chooses, or could choose, to make happen. I *fall* in love, am *roused* to anger or to sympathy for the plight of another. I do not choose to be in love, choose to be angry or choose to be empathetic. This is why the traditional word for emotion is 'passion'. Emotions are things with respect to which one is 'passive' rather than active, a recipient rather than an agent.

Sartre simply denies this. Being in love, for example, *is* a choice – indeed, a stratagem by which we pursue various of our aims which have nothing in particular to do with the beloved. To be sure, we *talk* as if love were something that happens to, rather than being chosen by, us; but that is simply a way of disguising from ourselves its true nature. The argument for this account of love will have to wait until the discussion of Sartre-Two in the next chapter.

The determinists are, then, wrong. My facticity, my past, does not determine who I am. Only my free choice does. My past can never capture me (unless I let it); I am always 'beyond' its reach. But, if my identity does not come from my past, where does it come from? From my own free choice. What makes an identity, an 'essence', mine is my own choice. This is the point of the famous slogan which has come to sum up existentialism: 'existence precedes and commands essence' (BN p. 438); existence is prior to essence. I exist as nothing but – with no intrinsic nature other than – the power of free choice. Only *subsequent to* and dependent on an always revisable exercise of that power does an essence become *my* essence.[2]

One further point about the scope of freedom. In choosing ourselves – in choosing our identities – we also, says Sartre, choose our 'world', since the latter is just 'the image of my free choice of myself' (BN p. 554). Since we are the 'author' of our world, it follows that there are 'no excuses' (BN p. 36): 'I am without excuse; for from the instant of my upsurge into being, I carry the weight of the world by myself alone without anything or any person being able to lighten it' (BN p. 555).

What does Sartre mean in calling my world an 'image' of my own freely chosen self? And why does it follow from the fact that it is such an image that there are 'no excuses'?

Sartre's point is that the world or 'situation' in which I find myself isn't just made up of neutral, objective facts. It is, rather, created by the interpretation of those facts in terms of the values I hold. Since I choose my values – cannot but choose them – I create my world – out of, of course, the facts that are at my disposal. It follows that nothing in the world can ever provide an 'excuse', absolve me of responsibility for my actions, since the world is my very own creation.

Sartre's illustrative example – appropriately enough, given his situation in Nazi-occupied France – is the war (BN pp. 554–5). (In what follows, I have adapted the example since his own presentation is rather muddled.) My country (France) is at war, fighting for its survival. It seems that I have no moral alternative but to join in the defence of my country. In fact, however, there is always an alternative. Suppose, for example, in an act of fundamental choice, I adopt the values of pacifism. Then the war will present itself to me not as just and heroic resistance to brutal aggression, but as a crime against humanity for which blame is spread (though possibly not evenly) between two barbarous opponents. It follows that 'my country is at war' can never excuse me of responsibility for joining the fighting – making the war 'my war', as Sartre puts it – since it is entirely up to me, to my choice of fundamental values, whether 'my country is at war' is a reason for fighting.

This insistence on absolute responsibility looks to be an attractive doctrine – even to provide a philosophical foundation for the Nuremberg trials which would begin a mere three years after the publication of *Being and Nothingness*. But, to see how demanding Sartre's 'I create my world' doctrine in fact is, consider another example. Suppose I am attacked and raped in a night-time street. It seems that something indisputably damaging has happened, something objectively horrible. And it seems, therefore, that, contra Sartre, there is value in the world – in this case, negative value – that is entirely independent of any choice of mine. It seems that a misfortune has occurred of which I am clearly not the author and that I have a complete 'excuse' for the deep depression in which I now am.

Sartre, however, denies this: in this as in every case, 'I . . . decide the coefficient of adversity in things by deciding myself' (BN p. 554). The ultimate project by which I give shape to my life may, of course, be the masochist's one of 'being a victim' (BN pp. 471–5). I will then seize every opportunity to interpret events as life's thrusting yet another misfortune upon me. And, in line with this, the rape will be interpreted as yet another confirmation of my victimhood. On the other hand, however, the life-project I chose may be that of, as we might describe it, 'the builder', someone who realises, with Nietzsche, that 'whatever does not poison me makes my stronger', someone who turns every life-event, no matter how seemingly horrible, into a productive experience. If that is my fundamental choice, then perhaps the rape was not a misfortune at all, but rather the decisive moment in which I decided to found WAR (Women Against Rape), commitment to which subsequently became the meaning of my life.

The crucial point, for Sartre, is that, even in the rape case, I inescapably make the crucial choice. Even the rape, he is committed to saying, does not *have* to be assessed as possessing negative value, as being a misfortune. If it is so assessed, then I have *chosen* this to be the case. In every case, therefore, I am the author of my own misfortune and am solely responsible for the consequences. Since the world is my responsibility it can never excuse me from responsibility.

Sartre's doctrine of freedom and responsibility (which clearly owes a great deal to Nietzsche's ideas on self-creation and willing the eternal recurrence) looks, at least on the surface, extremely attractive. To be sure, the 'no excuses' aspect of his position is tough. But it is also bracing. And what seems positively exhilarating is the absolute freedom of self-creation that he offers us. All those 'bourgeois' values thrust on us by our parents and upbringing, Sartre seems to show, are nothing more than 'baggage' dumped on us by others. To live free, exciting and 'authentic' lives, all we have to do is to drop them. Sartre, it seems (and seemed to us in the 1960s), is the philosopher, the ultimate validator, of teenage revolt.

The surprising fact, however – at this point, the fundamental darkness of Sartre's existentialism begins to appear – is that, according to him, rather than embracing the seemingly joyful opportunity to create who we are, we do our level best to *evade* it. (It is, moreover, rather hard, in the end, to avoid the conclusion that what he is really committed to is that we are *right* in so doing.) According to Sartre, we do our level best to *deny* our 'transcendence' of facticity, to deny our freedom, to convince ourselves that we possess no such thing. We tell ourselves that *Wesen* really is *gewesen*, that who we are is absolutely fixed by our past, and that is the end of the matter. We tell ourselves, in other words, that 'psychological determinism' is true. Two questions now present themselves. First, *why* do we do this? And, second, *how*; how do we convince ourselves of something that is, actually, in Sartre's view, false? First, the 'why' question.

That freedom is not the joyous attribute it at first looked to be is indicated by Sartre's already noted remark that freedom is something to which we are 'condemned' (BN p. 439). Freedom, judging by the theological overtones of this word, is hell, a state of torment. To be conscious of one's freedom is not to celebrate but to be, rather, in a state of what Sartre calls 'anxiety' or 'anguish' (BN p. 29). Why should this be? Why is freedom not a blessing but rather a curse?

Sartre says that the gambler (see p. 129 above) who has resolved to give up is in anguish because he realises that yesterday's decision may be 'ineffectual' (BN p. 32). The hiker on the mountain path, though full of exciting plans and hopes for the future, is in anguish because he realises he *can* decide to throw himself over the precipice (BN p. 31). These examples make the claim that consciousness of freedom – consciousness that it can never be evaded, that fundamental choice can never be pushed into the past as something over and done with – is anguish. But they do not explain why it should be so.

A pointer towards answering this question is provided by the remark that 'everyday morality is exclusive of . . . anguish' (BN p. 38). Anguish is focused on *values*. But if we carry on in the morally sleepy, semi-conscious way of 'everyday' humanity, then we hardly notice it. But once we become explicitly aware of the fact that we are the source of our own values it appears. Yet why should *that* cause us anguish?

Sartre replies that since my freedom, my free choice, is 'the unique foundation of values', it follows that

> nothing justifies me in adopting this or that particular value, or this or that particular scale of values. As a being by whom values exist, I am unjustifiable. My freedom is anguished at being the foundation of values while itself without foundation.
>
> (BN p. 38)

What does this mean?

Normally, says Sartre, my life is one of 'engagement'. I am fully and busily engaged with the world that is shaped, coloured and created by the fundamental set of values, the fundamental 'project', that I am. In normal life I operate *within* this project. The result is that life is – or at least seems – meaningful. Alarm clocks, traffic lights, even tax forms show up as meaningful things demanding 'urgent' attention because they show up within my fundamental project. But sometimes engagement breaks down, I 'disengage' from the world (BN p. 39). Now, in reflective consciousness, I confront the fundamental project which defines my identity and gives my life urgency and meaning from *without*. I realise that I – that pinpoint of selfhood naked save for its power of choice – stand 'beyond' my (putative or hitherto) 'essence'.

But so what? What, exactly, is supposed to be so traumatic about one's standing-beyondness, one's 'transcendence', about the unavoidable necessity of having to say either 'yes' or 'no' to one's hitherto identity? Go back to Plato's myth of Err – which is really just a metaphorical picture of this moment of disengagement. I survey my current life and if I like what I see I say (à la Nietzsche): 'Yes, please; more of the same.' In other words, I simply rechoose, reaffirm my original choice. If, on the other hand, I don't like what I see, then I say, 'No, thank you,' and choose some new and different kind of life. So where, one might ask, is the anguish?

Sartre's answer is that in the disengaged, spectatorial stance I confront the fact that I, my free choice, am the foundation of my life. But I also confront the fact that this foundation is 'itself without foundation'. I confront the fact that I am the 'foundationless foundation' of my values, project or essence, that I create myself '*ex nihilo*' (BN p. 33). In a certain sense, I have an 'apprehension of nothingness' (BN p. 29).

Since my choice of values is groundless, I realise, says Sartre, that it is 'beyond all reasons', 'gratuitous' (BN p. 479). And realising this I realise 'the *absurdity* of my choice and consequently of my being' (BN p. 480).

What does 'absurd' mean here? Sartre says that to confront my life from the external, disengaged standpoint gives me 'a feeling of unjustifiability' (BN p. 480). I realise, that is, that whatever choice I have made or could make is no more justified (or unjustified) than any alternative choice. Consider the Spanish Civil War. Suppose I choose to fight for the communist left against the fascist right and that this is part of a life-defining act of fundamental choice. Then, if Sartre is right, I have no ground at all for saying that my choice is in any way more justified than – preferable to, better than – the equally life-defining choice made by the fascist. But that means that nothing can be said to show that it *matters* which choice I make, and hence, it seems, it *doesn't* matter which choice I make. It matters no more than, for example, choosing to make a habit of walking on the left-hand side of the pavement (sidewalk) as opposed to the right. Hence, my life as a communist doesn't matter, is utterly unimportant, trivial. This seems to tell us what 'absurd' means. Our lives are absurd in the way in which someone's devoting their life to always walking on the left-hand side of the pavement, or to never stepping on the cracks, is absurd. They are absurd because of the deadly seriousness with which we pursue goals that, in themselves, are utterly devoid of significance. Looked at from the spectatorial point of view, life is a tragi-comedy.

But just why, one might continue to ask, should this knowledge be a cause for anguish? Because, I think, to see the unimportance of your life-defining goal means that you cannot take it seriously, cannot be genuinely *committed* to it.[3] (I shall return to this point towards the end of the next chapter.) And if you are not committed to a goal, then you don't really *have* that goal. The result is that life discloses itself as meaningless. This is the reason knowledge of one's absurdity generates anguish. It frustrates, I take Sartre to hold, the human being's fundamental need for meaning; in Schopenhauerian language, it frustrates the 'will to will' (see pp. 37–8 above).

Given this, it is not surprising that we try to suppress the spectatorial knowledge we have of ourselves, the knowledge of the existence and nature of our freedom. We seek to 'veil' (BN p. 43) it from ourselves. We do this (here we come to the question raised earlier as to *how* we deny our freedom) by indulging in what Sartre calls 'bad faith (*mauvaise foi*)'. Instead of acknowledging that – absurdly – we choose our essences, we pretend that we *are* our essences. We pretend that the kind of people we are is laid down in our facticity, and that there is nothing we can do about it.

As mentioned at the beginning of the chapter, Sartre's great ontological divide is between the for-itself and the in-itself. Though a being-for-itself is always 'beyond', separate from, 'prior' to, its essence, a being-in-itself *is* its essence. For beings-in-themselves are, as we observed, in a broad sense of the term, just *things*. And the thing about things, the thing which *defines* them as things, is that they lack freedom, they simply *are* their essences. To be a daffodil, a worm or a tiger is to come into existence bound to a given nature which your life then simply unfolds. There is no question of choosing whether or not to live a daffodilish, wormish or tigerish kind of existence. (Children's books with titles like *The Tiger Who Became a Vegetarian* are either allegories or unfit for human consumption.)

It follows that the attempt to deny one's freedom is the attempt to cross from one ontological category to another, to convince oneself that one is a being-in-itself rather than a being-for-itself. In bad faith, says Sartre, we seek the 'impermeability and infinite density' of a mere thing (BN p. 566). (In Sartre's novel *The Age of Reason*, his hero Daniel 'wishes to be a pederast as an oak tree is an oak tree'.) We seek to convince ourselves we are beings who choose their natures as little as rocks choose theirs, and whose response to their environments is as inexorably the outcome of those natures as is the response of rocks. Hence Sartre's famous example of the Paris waiter whose waiterly gestures are always perfect – indeed, always a little too perfect – an over-the-top-ness which endows them with a robotic quality (BN pp. 59–60). This is what the waiter seeks to convince himself he is: a robot.

Sartre's explains that bad faith is always *self-deception*. (As he uses them, the terms are, in fact, synonyms.) In bad faith I am in flight from my 'transcendence'.[4] But to be in flight from something I have to have it constantly in mind: 'I must think of it constantly in order to take care not to think of it' (BN p. 43). So I really always know that my life is free – and hence absurd. Bad faith is lying to oneself.

As Sartre recognises, this raises the question as to whether bad faith – successfully lying to oneself – is really possible. What makes the possibility of lying to others unproblematic is the distinctness of the lie-teller and the lied-to. But when they are the same, one might think, the attempt can no more succeed than, when playing chess against oneself, one can succeed in luring oneself into a trap. How can I possibly convince myself of something, p, when I know perfectly well that not-p?

The most obvious way of explaining the possibility of self-deception is to suggest that lying to oneself *is* like lying to others; to invoke, that is, a plurality of subjects contained within the unity of the self. Though it goes back to Schopenhauer and even to Plato, this strategy is particularly associated, and is associated by Sartre, with Freud (BN pp. 50–4). As Sartre presents him, Freud postulates a conscious self or 'ego', an unconscious self or 'id' and a gateway between the two guarded by a 'censor'. Faced with unpleasant knowledge – for example, that life is free and absurd – the censor decides to 'repress' it, to extract it from consciousness and push it into the unconscious so as to keep it hidden from the conscious self.

Sartre, however, *rejects* this explanation of self-deception. He focuses on the censor. To do the repressing the censor, clearly, must be aware of the to-be-repressed truth. Yet he must be conscious of it 'precisely *in order not to be conscious of it*' (BN p. 53). So the censor both knows and does not know the truth in question and is, therefore, itself in bad faith. It follows that the problem of bad faith has not been solved but merely relocated (ibid.).

This criticism is a poor one. Why should the censor have to be unconscious of the unpleasant piece of knowledge? If Bill knows that Mary is cheating on Harry but decides, for Harry's own good, not to tell him, there is no paradoxical knowing and not knowing on Bill's part. He simply knows, period.

Since he offers no clear alternative, and seems to forget that he is committed to providing one, it is actually just as well that Sartre's critique of the Freudian strategy is no good. Given the centrality of bad faith to his account of human existence and the absence of a demonstration of his own that it is indeed possible, Sartre actually needs to adopt at least the broad outline of the Freudian strategy. He needs to take on board, that is, the general idea of repression: the idea that there is a distinction between clear and explicit consciousness, on the one hand, and fuzzy and indistinct consciousness, on the other, together with the idea that we often relegate knowledge to the latter region because we know that explicit knowledge of it would be an unpleasant experience. (Since Sartre already has the distinction between explicit and implicit self-consciousness (see p. 126 above), this should not be too much of a shock to his system.)

Sartre-One, to summarise, asserts the following. The fundamental, 'ontological' fact about us is our foundationless freedom. But to acknowledge this is anguish, the anguish of acknowledging the absurdity – that is to say, meaninglessness – of our lives. So our fundamental impulse is to deny, to escape knowledge of, our freedom. Our fundamental impulse is, like the waiter, to pretend – to indulge in the bad faith of pretending – that we are mere, unfree 'things', beings with fixed, unalterable identities. What is critical to Sartre-One's account of our lives is, then, anguish and absurdity. Our lives are governed by the attempt to escape the anguish of recognising our absurdity. In the next chapter I argue that, while absurdity and anguish are also central to Sartre-Two's account of our existence, it is, in fact, a radically different kind of anguish and absurdity that is involved.

11

Sartre (continued)

Anguish and absurdity lie at the heart of *Being and Nothingness*. They lie, too, at the heart of Sartre's novels of the same period, the title of one of which, *Nausea*, gives a pretty unambiguous indication of Sartre's assessment of the human condition. In the last chapter we saw one account of why a clear view of our condition should induce nausea. But, so I claimed, without being properly aware that this is what he is doing, Sartre in fact provides a second and incompatible account of the nauseating character of human existence. This is the account I attribute to, as I call him, 'Sartre-Two', and to which I now turn.

Like Sartre-One, Sartre-Two (until further notice, just 'Sartre') starts out from human facticity. We find ourselves in a facticial situation – in a particular historical epoch, a particular class, possessing a particular biology, and so on. This facticity is not, however, of our choosing. As we grow from babyhood into a properly self-conscious person, we find ourselves *already* in our facticity. (Heidegger, as we have seen, calls this our 'thrownness' (BT 135), in order to emphasise the point that we do not choose but rather – like the child of unkind parents on his first day at boarding school – find ourselves *thrown into* our facticial lot in life.) Not only do we find ourselves as a kind of person that is not of our own choosing; we are held responsible for maintaining ourselves as that kind of person. And if we do not behave in ways appropriate to being, for example, a white middle-class farmer, then we are subject to punishments of various more or less obvious kinds by the white middle-class farming community in which we find ourselves (Heidegger's 'the One').

All this is something we resent. We resent our 'contingency', our dependency on something other than ourselves, our not being 'the foundation of our own being'. We appear to ourselves as an 'unjustifiable fact' (BN p. 80). (Notice the reappearance of much of the same *language* that is used by Sartre-One. What it means, however, as will shortly appear, is now very different.) This means that our fundamental goal in life is to overcome our 'contingency', to become 'the foundation of our own being'. We want to *choose* our being, to make it the case that our being, nature, or essence is truly *our* being.

Sartre has a dramatic way of putting this account of every human being's fundamental goal: our goal is to become God (BN pp. 80–3).

One of the medievals' 'proofs' of God's existence was the so-called 'First Cause Argument'. Every event has a cause, as we know. But what got the whole historical sequence of causes and effects going in the first place? God. But what caused God? Nothing. If it had, then we would not have answered the question of what got the sequence of causes going in the first place. God is, then, by definition, the first cause. And that means that he caused himself, is, in the Latin tag used by Sartre, a *causa sui*. This is what, according to Sartre, we all want to become. To be in the world at all we must possess some kind of identity. As beings in the world we cannot but be beings of a particular kind, we cannot but have a particular nature or essence. But we do not want to be 'thrown' into this essence. Rather, we want to have *chosen* it. We want to be, like God, self-causing beings.

This, however, claims Sartre, we can never be. Our fundamental goal of becoming a *causa sui*, of having an identity we ourselves have freely chosen is, for reasons we shall come to shortly, one we can never achieve.[1] Hence, 'the being of human reality is suffering'. Human consciousness is 'by nature an unhappy consciousness with no possibility of surpassing its unhappy state' (BN p. 90). (Though Sartre gives it a different meaning, 'unhappy consciousness' is, of course, borrowed from Hegel (see pp. 68–9 above).) We are in the grips of a 'futile passion' to pursue a goal we can neither achieve nor abandon.

Before asking why this goal should be impossible to achieve, let me pause to take note of the huge difference between Sartre-One and Sartre-Two. According to Sartre-One, remember, our lives are absurd and therefore anguished because of our inescapable freedom – because we cannot escape being the 'foundationless foundation' of our being; because, in other words, we *cannot but* choose who we are. We feel 'unjustified' because there is nothing to justify making one choice rather than another. According to Sartre-Two, however, we feel unjustified for precisely the *opposite* reason: because we *cannot* become the 'foundation of our being', cannot choose who we are. Using the metaphor of 'becoming God', Sartre-One holds that we are anguished because we cannot but create ourselves '*ex nihilo*' (BN p. 33), in other words, *cannot but* be 'God', a *causa sui*. Sartre-Two, on the other hand, holds that we are anguished because we *can never* become 'God'.

Sartre-One and Sartre-Two are, then, not just different. They contradict each other. This is why one gets terribly confused if one does not distinguish them. To be sure, both Sartres picture human existence as absurd and therefore anguished. But the meaning of 'absurd' and hence the source of anguish is different depending on whether you read One or Two. According to Sartre-One our lives are absurd because their goal (whatever it may be) that we take so seriously is utterly unimportant. Here 'absurd' means *meaningless*. According to Sartre-Two, on the other hand, our lives are absurd in the way in which alchemy, trying to raise yourself off the ground by pulling at you own bootlaces or trying to trick yourself at chess is absurd. Here 'absurd' means *futile*. To be sure, as we shall see, Sartre-Two as well as Sartre-One pictures human beings as engaging in systematic bad faith in order to evade the absurdity of their lives. But what they are taken to be evading varies radically depending on which Sartre one reads.

Why, according to Sartre (Two), can't we choose our own nature, become who we want to be? What is the problem? Let us be clear, first of all, that the problem, for Sartre, is not a *practical* one. His point is not that the strength required to raise ourselves out of our facticity, and the self-discipline required to maintain ourselves in our chosen natures, is beyond us. Rather, the problem is a *logical or conceptual* one: the combination 'chosen' and 'essence' is, he claims (like the combination of 'square' and 'circle'), a combination of 'incompatible characteristics', an 'impossible synthesis' (BN p. 90). An oxymoron.

This is a claim that is far from obvious. It is far from obvious, that is, that the idea of (*a*) having an identity (or, as we might also say, character) which (*b*) one has chosen oneself is conceptually incoherent. Sartre-One seems to accept its coherence. And it is the basis of Nietzsche's idea of life as literature which didn't *seem*, when we looked at it, to be conceptually incoherent. It is also (if I may be allowed a small digression) the basis of Kant's reconciliation of freedom and determinism in the *Critique of Pure Reason* ('The antimony of pure reason', section 9).

For Kant, every action one performs in the phenomenal world of nature is completely determined by the combination of one's character and the circumstances one is in. It is only a matter of time before science achieves complete knowledge of the nature of each individual which, together with psychological laws, will enable it to predict, with absolute certainty, every action the individual performs. What one's character is, however, is determined by the free choice of one's real or 'intelligible' self[2] (essentially the pre-reincarnation choice made in Plato's Myth of Err), which makes it the case that, though determined, one's actions are free, and hence actions for which one is responsible. It's like catching a train. The timing and destination of the trains are determined by forces over which one has no control. Which train one catches, however, depends on one's free choice. Hence one is completely responsible for the destination one arrives at. Sartre realises that his discussion touches on Kantian territory, using Kant's distinctive terminology to refer to the matter under discussion as 'the "choice of intelligible character"' (BN p. 563).

So Sartre's claim is that something which *looks* perfectly intelligible and has a long history of apparently intelligible discussion by philosophers is, in fact, unintelligible, a completely impossible, self-contradictory idea. Clearly he is going to need a pretty formidable argument to establish this conclusion. Let us find out what it is.

The essence of the argument is the following. The goal, the fundamental aim, of all human striving, we have seen, is to be a *causi sui*, the cause of one's own nature or identity (to become an 'in-itself-for-itself' (BN p. 362) in Sartre's ambiguous terminology which I am not going to use). My identity is, however, claims Sartre (this is the crucial point in the argument), established, not by me, but by *others*. My identity *is*, indeed, my 'being-for-others'; it is the other who 'holds the secret of my being' (BN p. 363). I cannot, for example, be a waiter or an accountant unless others, people in general, take me to be a waiter or an accountant. I cannot take *myself* to be a waiter or an accountant unless others so take me. My essence is, then, how I look to others. It is, as one might put it, one's exteriority. 'Young is an X' means, 'Others take Young to be an X'. (It is, of course, somewhat tricky to specify *which* others are relevant here. 'Young is a spy' obviously doesn't mean 'People in general take Young to be a spy'. I'll return to this complication in a bit.)

But now, if it is the 'look' (BN p. 363) of the other that determines my being-in-itself, then it is obviously not me who determines it. What follows is that the goal of combining freedom and identity is impossible to achieve (BN p. 362). To the extent that I am free or (let me here introduce the term) autonomous, then I must be a *self*-choosing, *self*-determining being. But to the extent that I have a nature or essence, then I am *other*-determined.

We are, then, committed to a fundamentally self-contradictory goal. Sartre now interprets all human relations – and, in particular, sexual relations – as attempts to finesse this self-contradiction.

Take, for example, *love*. One of the points in the above argument for the impossibility of establishing one's own nature that might be challenged is the inference from the claim that it is the gaze of others that determines my being-in-itself to the conclusion that it can't be me that does so. According to Sartre, 'love' is, in effect, such a challenge.

The lover, perhaps an older, wiser, wittier man, makes himself so seductive, so 'fascinating' (BN p. 372) to the beloved – a young, impressionable girl, perhaps – that he becomes her 'whole world' (BN p. 367). (Notice that, if we fill in the details in this way, the lover begins to look very like Sartre himself. And, in fact, the entire discussion of sexual relations communicates an almost embarrassing sense of personal disclosure.[3]) So bedazzled is she that he becomes the 'foundation of all [her] values' (BN p. 369), with the result that the lover 'feels that . . . [his] existence is taken up and willed even in the tiniest details' (BN p. 371). In a word, though the lover's identity is indeed dependent on how he looks in the eyes of the beloved, since he has absolute control over those eyes he has squared the circle, has achieved his chosen nature even though that nature is dependent on her look.

Or so he thinks. In fact, like all the sexual stratagems detailed by Sartre, love is a dismal failure. First, because (BN p. 377) the more he is loved by her, the more totally she is absorbed into his outlook on the world and himself, the more he is deprived of a genuine exteriority. What I need to establish my status as, for example, a brilliant writer is for *you* to say: 'You're a very brilliant writer.' But if all I hear is, in effect, a tape-recording of my own voice, then I fail to obtain the confirmation of my chosen nature by another which I seek. In short, the more I succeed in the project of love the more I fail. (It should be obvious by now that Sartre's discussion of sex is, in essence, a rerun of Hegel's master–slave dialectic (see pp. 64–5 above) to which Sartre refers at BN p. 370.)

Sartre details two further deficiencies of the love stratagem (BN p. 377). First, love is fickle. Even if she sees things my way for now, since there is no guarantee she will go on doing so, my condition is one of perpetual 'insecurity'. Second, since the beloved is only one among many other others, that she sees me the way I want to be seen in no way guarantees that others in general do so. For the stratagem to succeed 'one would have to be alone in the world with the beloved'. (This may seem a very *obvious* flaw in the stratagem. Yet Sartre is right, I think, in suggesting that we do sometimes try to turn the beloved into the whole world of others. One thing I think he undoubtedly causes us to recognise – a theme he shares with Schopenhauer – is how *foolishly* we quite typically behave in sexual and other human relationships.)

Love, says Sartre, lasts just as long as bad faith lasts: just as long, that is, as I can deceive myself into thinking that the other's 'take' on my being is genuinely hers rather than, as is in fact the case, that which by subtle power I have forced upon her. But this means that the 'attitude' of love is inherently unstable, always liable to lapse into another kind of stance to others, another kind of stratagem for becoming a *causa sui*.

One attitude the disillusioned lover might lapse into is what Sartre calls 'indifference'. He describes this as a kind of 'blindness' (BN p. 381) in which I see and treat others not as people but as mere functional objects ('equipment', in Heidegger's sense of the word (see pp. 64–5 above)): everyone gets reduced to the merely functional status of ticket collectors, waiters and the like (BN pp. 380–1). In indifference, I lapse into 'a sort of facticial solipsism' (BN p. 380). I experience the world, that is to say, in terms of Descartes' nightmare: all those other hats and coats are *just* hats and coats. I am alone, the only genuine person in a world of robots.[4]

What the 'indifferent' person achieves – or seems to achieve – is the abolition of the other-determination which threatens his autonomy, his self-determination. But what he loses, of course, is the look of the other that is necessary to his achieving any kind of nature or identity. To the extent that he is alone – to the extent that not even God is there to witness his life – he has no exteriority, no identity. So indifference fails. Moreover, since he really *knows* that he is surrounded by people and not by mere mechanisms, and that they look at and judge him, he is perpetually 'anxious' (BN p. 382). He knows that there is something he is repressing (the rat in the bag). Though, if the repression is successful, he may not be explicitly conscious of what it is, he knows that there is *something* unpleasant there, and that it may jump out at any moment. The penalty for repression, for the bad faith on which indifference (and all the other attitudes to others Sartre discusses) is based, is anxiety, 'anguish'.

A specifically sexual version of 'indifference' would be to see the other as mere 'flesh', as a mere, as we say, 'sex object'. What Sartre actually discusses, however, is an interesting variation on this which he calls 'sexual desire'. Here the hidden strategy behind my *seemingly* simple attitude to women is not just that she appear as 'flesh' to me, but that, in the moment of ecstasy, she should appear so *in her own eyes*, too (BN p. 395). I want her to become nothing but her body – nothing but a kind of pleasure machine – so that she is incapable of the look that threatens my autonomy.

As a species of indifference the strategy must, of course, fail. For, since I need the look of the other to establish my identity, the project fails to the extent it succeeds. And again, since I really know she is looking and judging, the self-deception on which the strategy depends is liable, at any moment, to fail.

'Sadism', suggests Sartre (BN pp. 399ff.), represents one last throw of the dice by someone disillusioned with the stratagem of sexual desire. The – a – problem with sexual desire is that I really know that she has been looking all the time. In sadism, however, I try to *force* her to become pure flesh through pain.

What the sadist particularly hates is 'grace'; that unpredictable spontaneity of bodily movement which speaks unmistakably of the presence of another autonomous, looking, judging human being. What he seeks, therefore, through acts of torture, is to make the movements of the other 'obscene', that is to say, completely 'mechanical'.

Again, of course, the strategy must fail. If it succeeds, it fails. But, in fact, it is not very likely to succeed. The sadist is always liable (and is therefore anxious, on this account) to confront the look of the other in the tormented body – as when, in William Faulkner's *Light in August*, the white racist 'good citizens' cannot escape the piercing look of Christmas, the black they have just castrated (BN pp. 405–6). (The Christian name, of course, calls to mind, as another example of the unextinguished look, Jesus on the cross.)

The final 'attitude' Sartre considers is 'hate' (BN pp. 410–12). Here, as it were, the gloves are finally off. Realising the inadequacy of all the foregoing strategies – realising that the 'subjectivity' (personhood) of the other survives all my attempts to abolish it – I simply kill her. I kill the look which threatens my autonomy. Literal extinction of the other replaces the 'as-if' extinction of indifference, desire and sadism. But once again, of course, if I succeed I fail.

Sartre's ordering of the various stratagems – love, indifference, desire, sadism, hate – is not an order of decreasing preference. None of the strategies is any more successful (any less of a failure) than any other. The point is rather that since all the attitudes are based on bad faith – are attempts to achieve a goal which one really knows to be impossible – they are all inherently unstable; there is tendency to restless movement between them, we are 'indefinitely referred' (BN p. 408) from one to another. (Compare Schopenhauer's account of life as swinging 'like a pendulum' between stress and boredom (pp. 37–8 above).) Our ability to maintain any one attitude depends on how long we can maintain a particular form of bad faith (ibid.), something which, though it might last a lifetime, is almost certain to suffer, at the very least, relapses (BN p. 381).

In Sartre's 1944 play *No Exit* – appropriately titled since, according to his philosophy of the same period, as we have just seen, there is 'no exit' from the impossible goal of becoming a self-choosing being – there occurs the famous assertion that 'hell is other people'. In terms of *Being and Nothingness*'s analysis of human existence, one can see why. For, according to that analysis, while on the one hand I have an absolute need for other people to provide me with the identity that I seek, I also have an absolute need to be without them, since their existence takes away the self-determination, the autonomy which I also seek. Attempting to achieve both goals, I seek to dominate others, either by seeking to control their 'look' or else, more or less literally, by seeking to kill them. But the other seeks to do exactly the same to me. Hence human relations are always, under the surface at least, conflict, a power struggle, war. Sartre's lifelong relationship with Simone de Beauvoir may have had something monumental about it but, according to his philosophy (and, in fact, de Beauvoir's reports), it, too, was, in essence, conflict.

For Sartre-Two, then, other people are hell. Moreover, since life is other people – non-human nature no more figures in Sartre's thoroughly urban philosophy than it does in Socrates'[5] – *life* is hell. Since this conclusion is as devastating, as 'nihilistic' with respect to human life as anything in Schopenhauer, it becomes a matter of urgency to ask whether we should be convinced by Sartre-Two's account of the human condition. Should we be?

Let us start by trying to get a clearer view of the fundamental argument that leads to the conclusion that life is hell. Let me try to present it in as clear a form as possible.

The argument begins by asserting that the human being's fundamental aim is to have an essence or identity that it itself has freely chosen. In brief:

(A) My fundamental aim is to have identity combined with autonomy.

Sartre-Two now points out that:

(B) My identity is my 'being-for-others' (how I look to them, appear in their eyes).

So, he concludes:

(C) My identity depends on how I appear to others.

But then:

(D) If my identity depends on others, it cannot depend on (i.e. be freely chosen by) me.

And so:

(E) The combination of identity and autonomy is 'an impossible synthesis'.

What are we to make of this argument?

No man, to repeat the Duke of Wellington's eminently repeatable remark, is a hero to his valet. For the sake of an aphorism, he of course exaggerated. But his point is a good one: if you want to count in your own eyes as a kind and thoughtful person (or, alternatively, if you want to count as a scurrilous bounder), then you must so count in the eyes of those who have the best, the most intimate knowledge of you. (This, I think, is the point of the *intimacy* of nearly all the relations with others considered by Sartre.) So Sartre's assertion (C) is quite correct: my identity does indeed depend on how I appear to others. In general, to be thoughtful, kind, courageous, and so on, *is* for those who, with regard to the aspect of my being in question, know me best (and are unprejudiced in their judgements) to judge that I am thoughtful, kind or whatever. (Notice that the knowing-me-best-in-relevant-respects requirement takes care of the spy example mentioned on p. 146 above. Though 'others' in general don't take me to be a spy, those who know me best in my professional life do.) Let us call someone who has relevantly intimate knowledge and who makes impartial judgements an 'ideal observer'. What we can say, then, is that for me to be kind, thoughtful, a spy, a waiter or whatever, is for me to be such that an ideal observer (for example, God, were he to exist) would judge me to be kind, thoughtful, a spy, waiter[6] or whatever.

So far so good. The question is, however, does the dependency of my identity on how I look to others mean that it can't depend on me, can't be my own, freely chosen identity, as step (D) in Sartre's argument maintains? Not at all. To see this, consider colour – say, redness. Bearing in mind that the lighting conditions under which things are seen affect their apparent colour (red things seen under blue light look purple), what is it for something to *be* red? It is for it to look red under *ideal* viewing conditions, i.e. standard daylight. So something *is* red if it looks red under ideal conditions, i.e. to an ideal observer. In this respect, then, redness is just like human being-in-itselfness.

But does this mean that I cannot freely choose the colour of my shirt? Does it mean that I have to manipulate the judgement of the observer, or reduce her to a mere 'indifferent' object, so that she can't challenge my choice of the colour of my shirt? Obviously not. All I have to do is to appear in standard daylight wearing a red shirt. Similarly, all I have to do to persuade the ideal observer that a certain trait is an aspect of my identity is to choose that that trait *be* an aspect of my identity – and, of course, make sure, in a disciplined and resolute way, that I live my life in accordance with my fundamental choice.

In a nutshell, Sartre's mistake is to suppose that the dependency of my identity on the 'other's' judgement means that it can't be dependent on my own choice. The truth of the matter is that it is dependent on both. But since the ideal observer's judgement is dependent on me – I can make her judge whatever I want – the latter dependency is no restriction at all on my freedom to choose who I am to be.

Why doesn't Sartre see this really rather obvious point? I think the answer lies in the way he first introduces 'others' and their 'look'.

I am a soldier in time of war crawling cautiously through the undergrowth. Suddenly I hear a twig break behind me. Or suddenly I realise that I am in full view of the farmhouse on top of a little hill, a farmhouse that probably has enemy snipers in it (BN pp. 257–9). Or suppose that I am peeping through a bedroom keyhole (BN pp. 259–60), totally absorbed, 'whether through vice, jealousy or curiosity', in what the man and woman are doing on the other side of the door. Suddenly I hear a noise behind me in the darkened hallway. In all these cases, suggests Sartre, two things happen. First, I suddenly apprehend myself as no longer the looker, the *subject* of looking, but as, rather, the looked at, the *object* of looking. Second, as a consequence of this, I feel suddenly threatened, vulnerable, in the presence of something hostile.[7]

Why should this be so? Because, according to Sartre, the look 'objectifies'. When I look at others, 'I fix the people whom I see into objects' (BN p. 366). When they look at me I am stripped of my 'transcendence', the freedom which makes me a person rather than a thing. I appear in their eyes as belonging to the same category of being as an inkwell – as a 'being-in-itself' rather than a 'being-for-itself' (BN p. 262). To the soldiers in the farmhouse, for example, I am nothing but a dangerous mechanism, a to-be-destroyed enemy soldier. To the looker in the hallway behind me I am nothing but a 'peeping Tom', a 'deviant', malfunctioning piece of human mechanism ripe for psychiatrists and the law courts. Such objectifying is, according to Sartre, the *usual* character of the look: 'This woman whom I see coming toward me, this man who is passing by in the street, this beggar whom I hear calling before my window, all are for me *objects*' (BN p. 252). This is the 'fundamental relation' between myself and others (ibid.).[8]

But now, if I always appear in the look of the other as a mere object, then I *never* appear in that look as the human personality I wish to be – for the simple reason that I never appear as a human personality *at all*. Given this to be true, it seems to follows that in defence of my autonomy I *have to* try either to manipulate the look of the other (as in 'love') or, either metaphorically or literally, to kill her.

The first thing that needs to be said here is that Sartre's claim that the look is always objectifying gains spurious plausibility for the particularly sour set of examples he has chosen. Suppose, for example, he had started off from the look the mother gives her child, the look Jesus gives to Mary Magdalene, the look David gives to Jonathan or the look Juliet gives to Romeo; from, in other words, the various species of the *loving look*. Then a totally different account of human relations and human sexuality would have developed. Since love, 'unconditional' love at least, accepts the beloved for what he is, the other's look would then turn out *never* to be a threat to one's autonomy.

Actually, though, I don't think Sartre's assumption is really the product of an unbalanced set of examples. It is the product, rather, of an inability to think outside the square established by the *éminence grise* of modern French philosophy, René Descartes.

Sartre claims, remember, that the woman, the man and the beggar in the street are, in terms of my immediate experience, nothing but 'objects' for me. This is paradigmatic of my 'fundamental relation' to others in general. Why should Sartre think this? Because, he explains, 'the Other's existence remains purely conjectural' (BN p. 252). In other words, the claim that the look with which we see others is always objectifying turns out to be just Descartes' point that we can never prove that those beings in hats and coats are anything more than cleverly constructed robots (see p. 111 above) – that the 'conjecture', hypothesis or postulation that they are genuine people like oneself is merely something we find useful for explaining their behaviour, on a par with the postulation of quarks and black holes in physics.

Earlier (p. 131 above), I noted that *Being and Nothingness* as a whole is supposed to be an essay in 'phenomenology', a description of the natural, immediate and unreflective experience human beings have of the world. It follows that a claim about my 'fundamental relation' (BN p. 252) to others is not a claim about what I can and can't prove, but a descriptive claim about the natural, immediate and unreflective attitude I in fact adopt to others. But (save with regard to those who have read too much Descartes) it is clearly a very poor piece of phenomenology to claim that the way we respond to others *in general* is to see and treat them as mere objects. What Sartre does here – and in his descriptions of human relations in general – is to offer what is actually the pathology of our experience of others as its anatomy. (The impact of the undoubted insight contained in the pathology can easily lead one to miss this sleight of hand.)

Heidegger (in section 26 of *Being and Time*) is a much more accurate phenomenologist than Sartre on this point. Though 'indifference' is indeed the standard mode of response to people on buses and in the street, it is, for him, not the only, but rather a 'deficient' mode of 'being-with-others'. And even this deficient mode – an even more important point – is different from treating others as mere objects. An object, a piece of firewood, for example, we chop up as suits our needs. The firewood doesn't have any say in the matter. But even someone to whom we are 'indifferent', and who happens to be in our way, we won't chop up (unless we are terrorists or totalitarians). Even those to whom we are indifferent we accord certain rights, which makes our attitude to them fundamentally different from our attitude to objects. In other words, the distinction between people and things, between, in Sartre's language, the for-itself and the in-itself, is fundamental to the phenomenology of human being-in-the-world, fundamental to the 'look' with which we view others. (This, in fact, is what Sartre started off saying (see p. 126 above). But then he somehow lost sight of the point.)

Let us, however, put all this on one side. Let us suppose, for the sake of argument, that the 'Other's' look is indeed always objectifying. Suppose, therefore, that the others, not taking me to be a person at all, will never take me as the person I wish to be, will deny my autonomy. Then the point to be made is that if this is the way the others universally are, then (C) in Sartre's argument (on p. 150 above), the claim that my identity depends on how I appear to others, is simply false. For what we established, remember, is that what my identity depends on is the judgement of an *ideal* – ideally knowledgeable and impartial – observer. Yet if, now, none of the others with whom I share my world *are* ideal, if they see me just as an object rather than as the person I am, then it is *false* that my identity depends on *their* judgement. We can, perhaps, put the matter, picturesquely, as follows. If my world contains nothing but others who objectify me (and such a world is imaginable, for example, the world of a prisoner kept secluded from all but the guards or a patient secluded from all but the doctors), then the only observer on whom my identity depends is God – who, of course, doesn't exist, so it is dependent on no observer at all.

Sartre-Two, as already remarked, is extremely depressing. Life is 'hell' because it is perpetual conflict with others, 'war, all against all'. But it is hell in another sense, too, hell in the sense of being meaningless. Life, as Sartre-Two portrays it, is meaningless because though he appears to allow it a goal – becoming a *causa sui*, a self-creating, self-'naturing' being – it is a goal he portrays as impossible to achieve, and, moreover, one we really know to be impossible. But a goal that is known to be impossible is not a goal at all. Suppose, for example, you have devoted your entire life to the generation of nuclear power by nuclear fusion but that one day it is shown that some law, coiled like a worm deep in the heart of fundamental physics, entails that nuclear fusion is impossible. Then – until you discover some new goal – your life has become meaningless. For a goal to be a genuine, meaning-giving goal one must know, or at least believe, it to be capable of attainment.

Sartre-Two is, then, doubly depressing. According to his 'ontological' investigations, life is both eternal conflict and meaningless. It is no wonder, then, that he says at the end of *Being and Nothingness* that the work is concerned with ontology and not with 'ethics', with what *is* the case rather than with how we *ought* to lead our lives. 'Ontology', he says, 'cannot formulate ethical precepts' (BN p. 625). As a general principle, as we shall see when we come to discuss later Heidegger, this is profoundly false. What is true, on the other hand, is that Sartre's ontology of human being cannot found an account of the good life, for the simple reason that there is, for him, *no such thing* as the good life. To put the matter another way, the question 'What is the right way to live?' makes a presupposition – that life as such is, or can be, worth living. But Sartre denies the presupposition and hence cannot answer the question. Not trying to live well but ceasing to live – suicide – is the rational response to Sartre-Two's account of the hellish structures within which human beings are condemned to live.[9]

Sartre-Two is, then, a nihilist. But he is also, thankfully, a pretty poor arguer. Carefully considered, his argument offers us no genuine reason for believing in the hellish structures that he claims to be inseparable from human existence. Sartre-Two, therefore, is someone we can forget about.

We are still left, however, with the Sartre-One, to return to the topic of the previous chapter. What are we to say about him?

Sartre-One, remember, unlike Sartre-Two, holds that there is no difficulty in choosing the person we are to be by choosing the fundamental 'project' of our lives. Not only *can* we choose our project; we *must* do so. (Even, remember, the choice not to rebel against the identity established for me by my facticity is not an escape from choice, but rather a choosing of that pre-established identity.) The point about this ultimate choice, however, is that, since it is groundless, it and the life that flows from it are meaningless.

Knowing our lives to be thus 'absurd', as we saw (pp. 137–9 above), gives us a 'feeling of unjustifiability', undermines, Sartre seems to say ('Sartre' from now on means, once again, 'Sartre-One'), our ability to take ourselves seriously. It undermines *commitment*. If I know that my life is based on an ungrounded act of fundamental choice, then, when the going gets tough, I have no basis at all for resisting the thought that I should now simply unchoose what I have chosen and make a new act of fundamental choice. To put the point at its most dramatic, no one dies for the sake of groundless choices. (Notice that this is precisely the 'problem of authority' we noted with respect to Nietzsche's view that one's identity is one's own – in effect, groundless – creation.) The result is that, unless we draw the 'veil' of bad faith over this knowledge we have of ourselves, we live our lives at a distance, like actors.[10] We act out a role for a time and then, when the mood takes us, move on to a different role. The result is that, though *the roles* all have a meaning, our lives have none. We become, as it were, 'hollow men', emptiness hiding behind a façade of activity. Knowledge of absurdity generates anguish because it frustrates our fundamental need for meaning.

It is of some interest to compare Sartre's discussion of the absurdity of human life with that offered by Thomas Nagel in an influential essay called 'The Absurd'.[11] Like Sartre, Nagel thinks that our lives are, indeed, absurd. And, also like Sartre, he thinks that we explicitly experience this absurdity when we step out of the 'internal', engaged perspective and into the 'external', spectatorial perspective on our lives. Unlike Sartre, however, Nagel thinks that absurdity doesn't matter. He denies, in other words, the link between absurdity and anguish. On what grounds?

Here he is not entirely clear. On the one hand he seems to say that the absurdity of our lives is just like scepticism about our knowledge of the external world. Just as our knowledge that we can't prove there to be a world outside the mind (we can't *prove* we aren't dreaming) doesn't affect our daily lives in any way at all – we just get on with it – so knowledge of the absurd doesn't have any effect at all on our daily lives and the seriousness with which we take our projects. On the other hand, however, Nagel says that after an encounter with the absurd 'our seriousness becomes laced with irony' (p. 183), but that having to live with irony is something that 'doesn't matter' (p. 185).

With regard to the first answer Sartre would, I think, say that knowledge of the absurd is *not* like scepticism about the external world. For, whereas the latter is confined to idle moments of philosophical speculation, the former is always with us. It produces a permanent 'feeling of unjustifiability'. Freedom constantly 'eats away' at freedom (BN p. 480), undermines our lives. Knowledge of the absurd, in short, is something we at best only ever half repress.

Nagel's second reason for saying that absurdity doesn't matter is harder to assess since he never specifies which of the several meanings of 'irony' he intends. One good meaning, however, is 'detachment', the kind of detachment referred to above as that which distinguishes *acting* a part from *being* that part. If this is what Nagel means, then he is wrong to suggest that the ironic stance to one's life generated by an encounter with the absurd doesn't matter. For what it produces, as I argued, is lack of commitment to the ostensible meaning of one's life, in other words a meaningless life.

Nagel is, then, wrong. If it is really true that our lives are based on groundless acts of ultimate choice, then Sartre is right: our lives are meaningless and, as meaningless, not worth living. But according to Sartre-One our lives *are* based on groundless acts of ultimate choice. Sartre-One turns out, therefore, to be just as depressing, just as nihilistic, as Sartre-Two. The difference is that he is a much more formidable figure, a figure, as we are about to see, much less easy to dispose of.

Is it possible to dispose of Sartre-One's depressing conclusion?

Let us return, first of all, to the question of what the human condition would have to be like for life *not* to be absurd. As we have observed, what would have to be the case is that, rather than being 'prior' to our essences, we would have to *be* those essences. If, that is to say, *Wesen ist was gewesen ist* (essence is what has been), if the essence laid down for me by my facticity is *what I am*, then there can be no question of my having to *choose* my essence, and hence no question of my having to choose it groundlessly and therefore absurdly.

According to Sartre, of course, it is false that *Wesen ist was gewesen ist*. Moreover, we know it to be false – we know the inescapability of groundless choice – so the belief that essence is what has been, the waiter's belief, for example, is always held in bad faith.

For Heidegger, on the other hand, as we saw in the last chapter, my essence *is* determined by my facticity. He puts this, we saw, by saying that what I fundamentally am is determined by my 'heritage'. The fundamental values which are *my* fundamental values are not freely chosen but represent something to which I find myself *already* committed as I grow to adulthood within my native culture, their adoption part and parcel of the process of learning my native language. Whereas for Sartre the self is an isolated Cartesian ego, denuded of all properties save the power of choice (and the capacity to think which such a power entails), for Heidegger the self is an others-implying, 'socially constructed' entity. (We might put this by saying that, whereas Sartre has a 'thin' conception of the self, Heidegger has a 'thick' one.) This doesn't mean that freedom is excluded from Heidegger's picture of things. On the contrary, he insists on it. I *can* fail to act out of heritage, choose to go along with the (usually debased) values of contemporary public opinion. Or I can choose to act out of heritage, choose to be 'authentic', to be, in other words, who I am. The difference from Sartre, however, is that, for Heidegger, what I choose is, not myself, but rather *whether to be* myself. Heritage, he says, is the 'sole authority' (BT p. 391) to which a free being can submit, the reason being that the only authority to which I can submit and still be free, in the sense of following my own will, is myself.

On early Heidegger's view, then, life is never meaningless. There is always a meaning, a meaning that is given to us by the culture out of and within which our selves are constructed. Because that meaning (in Heidegger's language 'destiny') is *given*, there is no question of having to choose it, and hence no possibility of absurdity.

So who is right? Sartre notes correctly that early Heidegger's notion of heritage is really a notion of place (BN pp. 489–96). My heritage is the spiritual place within which, according to Heidegger, I become myself. A way of putting Heidegger's view of the self is to say that, at the deepest level, *I am my place*.

Sartre, however, makes a simple but telling criticism of this idea, arguing that only I make my place *my* place. To someone like Sartre himself, for example, being within a few kilometres of the Eiffel Tower, and all that that implies, is what constitutes 'being there', being in place. But to someone who, though brought up with the same background, decides that, for him, Chicago is 'where it's at', Paris, France, appears not as a homeland but as a kind of prison. Whether, in short, my place is *my* place, whether my heritage is *my* heritage, depends upon my fundamental project, and hence upon my choice, and hence upon my freedom and the absurdity that it brings with it.

This seems inescapable. Just because I am born into a given heritage doesn't make it *my* heritage (as I myself argued on pp. 123–4 above). Heidegger claims that one *is* one's heritage, but the most that can in truth be said is that I have been my heritage up to now. Whether I will continue to be that heritage – part of the communal project that it constitutes – is entirely *up to me*. It depends on the freedom – and absurdity – of my ultimate choice.

So it seems that, in the end, Sartre is right and Heidegger wrong. Life is grounded in the inescapable absurdity of groundless choice and is, therefore, meaningless.

But perhaps this conclusion is too hasty. Perhaps we shall find in later Heidegger the resources to defeat Sartre's depressing conclusion that are absent from *Being and Time*. This is the prospect to which I shall turn in Chapter 15.

What is Sartre's basic problem? What is the real source of his 'anguish'? It is, I think, the death of God. The reason we have to make our own ultimate choices is that God is no longer there to make them for us. This suggests a way of representing Sartre (One) in four sentences. (1) God is dead. (2) Since there is no God to authorise the good, we have to do it for ourselves. But (3) we have no authority over ourselves. Hence (4) we possess no authoritative account of the good, and life is meaningless (and so worthless).

It is possible to see Sartre's later turn to Marxism as the (self-deceiving?) attempt to escape the nihilistic conclusion of this argument by rejecting (1). In Chapter 15, however, I shall suggest that the correct response is to reject (2).

12

Camus

Albert Camus (1913–60) was born into a very poor, working-class family in Algiers, the capital of the then French colony of Algeria. His grandmother and mother were both illiterate. All his life he was subject to bouts of tuberculosis which had the effect of ending a possible career as a professional soccer player (he was a fine goalkeeper). Moving to Paris, he became actively and courageously involved in the Resistance to the Nazi occupation, editing the underground newspaper *Combat*. (As with Sartre, the existential issues about which he wrote arose not out of thin air but out of his life.) He spent most of his working life in Paris, but he retained an intense love for his homeland that is often reflected in his writings. Although belonging, in general, on the political left, his ties to his homeland (where his mother still lived) made it impossible for him, during the Algerian war of independence (1954–62), unambiguously to identify himself with the standard left-wing demand for Algeria's immediate independence. (Given a choice between justice and my mother, he said, I choose my mother.) This led to a break with the by-now-Marxist Sartre, who found Camus' position lacking in the necessary black-and-whiteness. Camus had great personal charm and, with a cigarette permanently in the corner of his mouth, looked (as he knew) like Humphrey Bogart. This no doubt contributed to his enormous success with women. His appetite for sexual pleasure was insatiable and led to his being perpetually unfaithful to both his wife and current mistress. (As we shall see, this and other aspects of his life and personality are reflected in his philosophy.) He was awarded the Nobel prize for literature in 1957, and in 1960 died in an accident in a car driven by his friend and publisher, Michel Gallimard. Both Camus and Gallimard, it appears, were addicted to fast driving.

More famous as a playwright and novelist, Camus is often classified as a mere 'writer' and ignored as a philosopher. The French, in particular, tend to diminish his philosophical standing through invidious comparisons with Sartre's supposed intellectual 'genius'. This seems to me a mistake. Camus' major philosophical work, *The Myth of Sisyphus* (1940),[1] seems to me to contain philosophical ideas at least as important as anything in Sartre.

'There is but one truly serious philosophical problem', Camus writes at the beginning of *The Myth*, 'and that is suicide'; in other words, 'judging whether life is or is not worth living' (MS p. 11). Though startling, the connection he makes here is surely right. If life is really not worth living, then one ought to commit suicide. But if it is, then of course one should not. The question of suicide is thus just a dramatic way of posing the question of life's worth or value.

To say that this question poses a 'problem' is to say that the answer is neither obvious nor straightforward. And to say that is to say that something at least threatens a negative answer to the question. What, we must now ask, is it that makes this threat? And to whom is the threat made?

Starting with the second question, it is important to see that Camus is not interested in something which might make just your or my individual life worthless (the loss of a loved one, a crime for which one can never atone). But neither, at the other extreme (unlike, say, Schopenhauer), does he think that there is something which threatens to reveal the life of humanity in general as worthless. His concern, rather, is historically situated. There is something, he believes, which threatens to reveal the life of *modern Western humanity* as worthless. He calls it 'the absurd'. Though we have met this term before, what it means for Camus is actually somewhat different from what it means for Sartre.

Absurdity, Camus explains, is a disjunction, a disjunction of large – 'absurd' – proportions, between how one wants things to be and how they are or are likely to become. A man attacking a machine-gun nest with a sword is absurd (MS p. 33). Charlie Chaplin (my example, not Camus') is absurd because of the disjunction between the dignity intended by the bowler hat and rolled umbrella and the incredibly undignified things that happen to him – he slips on a banana skin, the wall of a house falls on him. Absurdity in general, says Camus, 'is born of the confrontation between human need and the [as it seems to us] unreasonable silence of the world' (MS p. 32).

But what is '*the* absurd'? What is the fundamental desire in question which reality fails to satisfy? It is, says Camus, a desire for there to be a 'meaning of life' (MS p. 12), 'some great idea that transcends [life] . . . and gives it meaning' (MS p. 15). It is, in other words, the desire, or rather 'need', for an account of the meaning of life of the traditional true-world form. It is the need for, as I have called it, grand-narrative meaning.

For what kind of grand-narrative meaning do we have this fundamental need? In *The Myth* itself Camus identifies our loss of 'values', of 'meaning', with our inability to 'believe in God' (MS p. 7). So the specific grand narrative he has in mind seems to be that of Christianity. But in the 1953 'The artist and his times' he makes the point I made at the end of Chapter 6, that Hegelian Marxism is essentially a translation of the Christian heaven into a naturalistic context, since it postulates 'a miraculous event at the end of time', the coming into being of the communist paradise (MS pp. 187–92). It is for this reason (he is defending himself here against his Marxist critics such as Sartre) that he classifies Marxism as a new 'faith', a 'new mystification' (MS pp. 188–9). So it seems that, in Camus' most considered view, the absurdity of our lives consists in the death, not just of the Christian, but rather of *all* versions of 'God', all true-world narratives.[2]

To say, then, that life is absurd is to point to a radical disjunction between our intense desire that life should have some grand-narrative meaning, on the one hand, and the evident failure of reality to provide such meaning, on the other.[3]

The next question is: why does the realisation that life is absurd threaten suicide? Camus' answer is that it is liable to produce 'the feeling of the absurd' (MS p. 32) or, 'as a writer of today [Sartre, of course] calls it', 'nausea' (MS p. 21).

Camus gives various examples of this feeling which can strike at any time, 'on a street-corner or in a restaurant's revolving door' (MS pp. 18–19). The meaningless pantomime of the man in the telephone booth whose words we cannot hear (MS p. 21); the stranger in the face of the woman one once loved, or in one's own face in the mirror (ibid.); the unanswerable 'Why?' that strikes one as one surveys the circular path of the daily round – rising, breakfast, car, office, meal, sleep, rising, breakfast, et cetera – and makes 'the stage sets collapse' (MS p. 19).

What is common to these examples is alienation, estrangement, disengagement. A life revealed as a 'stage set' is a life that engages me no longer. The woman who has become a stranger is a woman who has lost all value for me. I am as indifferent to her as to the man sitting in the car next to me at the traffic lights. Camus seems to suggest that to be struck by the vivid realisation that life has no (grand-narrative) meaning is to become indifferent to, disengaged from it. (His famous novel *The Outsider* (*L'Etranger*) is an extended exploration of such disengagement. In it, the estranged hero sleepwalks through his life, through a motiveless murder and eventually to his execution.) A deadly 'weariness' (MS p. 19) sets in, a saying 'no' to life (MS p. 14), a longing to get the whole meaningless (yet stressful) pantomime over with, a 'longing for death' (MS p. 14).

One response, then, to the experience of life's absurdity is the conclusion which has suicide as its logical consequence. One treats the experience of 'nausea' as a moment of decisive insight into the truth that life in an absurd world, life without (grand-narrative) meaning, isn't worth living.

Camus' central task is to reject this inference, to show that 'even if one does not believe in God, suicide is not legitimate'; not legitimate because 'even within the limits of nihilism it is possible to find the means to proceed beyond nihilism . . . to live and create in the very midst of the desert' (MS p. 7). More ambitiously, Camus' aim is to show that, actually, life 'will be lived all the better if it has no meaning' (MS p. 53).[4]

A different kind of response to the experience of nausea is what Camus calls 'the leap' (of faith), a term he uses to characterise the position of religious 'existentialists' (MS p. 35) such as Kierkegaard, Jaspers and Leo Chestov. (Given his view of Hegelian Marxism, he would no doubt wish to classify Marxists as 'leapers', too.)

The essence of the leap, as Camus presents it, is the denial of reason. To be sure, the leaper says, reason declares there to be no God, no meaning to life. But what's so great about reason? We can say: 'Reason declares there to be no meaning-giving "beyond", therefore there is none.' But, equally, we can say: 'There is a beyond, therefore reason has its limits.' Moreover we *need* to believe in a 'beyond', otherwise we shall see life as absurd and lapse into 'despair' (MS p. 37).[5]

Camus has nothing but scorn for the leap. He rejects it on two grounds.[6] The first is that it is really nothing but a kind of suicide – 'philosophical suicide'. For what it amounts to is a 'killing' of the fundamental and distinctive part of the human being, reason. In its desecration of reason it constitutes a 'mutilation of the soul', a burning insult to human dignity and 'pride' (MS p. 40). The really important thing, Camus insists, is to *live with* what our reason tells us, not to demean or diminish the human self.

Second, and more importantly, philosophical, just like literal, suicide is unnecessary, is based on a misapprehension. For the truth of the matter is that life's absurdity does *not* entail its worthlessness. Why not?

Camus answers this question by painting a portrait of 'the absurd man': someone who fully accepts life's absurdity, yet lives a life that is, in both his own and our eyes, clearly, indeed splendidly, worth living. As the phrase suggests, Camus presents himself as having a single, unitary account of what it is to live well in the face of the absurd. In fact, however, he has two quite different accounts of the absurd hero. The key word for the first is 'revolt', for the second 'excess'.

The life of 'revolt' is personified by Sisyphus, the hero of Greek mythology after whom *The Myth* is named. Condemned by the gods, for obscure reasons, to push a giant boulder to the top of a mountain whence it immediately roles to the bottom, so that he must do the same thing again and again throughout all eternity, Sisyphus is the 'proletarian of the gods' (MS p. 109). In the first instance, that is, he personifies the endlessly repetitive life of the modern industrial worker. Really, however, he is all of us to the extent that we tread the circular – and hence meaningless – path of everyday life.[7]

Sisyphus, Camus claims, sees his life as neither 'sterile' nor 'futile'. Though he sees no point to his work, this does not render it sterile since 'the struggle to the heights is enough to fill a man's heart'. 'One must', Camus concludes, 'imagine Sisyphus happy' (MS p. 111). Why on earth?

Let us forget about the Greek gods, who rather obscure Camus' main point, and imagine Sisyphus a modern figure, a modern absurd hero. Then Sisyphus is happy because of his 'scorn for the gods' (MS p. 108), in other words, for the cards fate has dealt him. He is happy because, even though he is vividly aware of his fundamental need for meaning, he lives 'without appeal' (MS p. 53), without the 'solace' of comforting 'myths' (MS p. 135). In doing so he is aware of himself as displaying a 'courage' and an 'integrity' that are absent from the character of both the philosophical and the literal suicide.

Sisyphus is a deeply macho hero – 'virile', to use Camus' own language (MS p. 11, footnote). What makes Sisyphus admirable, endows his life with dignity and worth in his own and, Camus implies, our eyes, is his *strength*, the fact that he *hasn't given in*. Continuing to toil without purpose, continuing to live in a world that provides no reason for living, *itself* provides a reason for living. Sisyphus feels good about himself – 'the nobility of my soul', he says (borrowing Oedipus' words), 'makes me conclude that all is well' (MS p. 109) – because he knows himself to be *tough*. He is, as Camus puts it, in 'revolt': 'revolt is the certainty of a crushing fate [life without grand-narrative meaning] without the resignation [literal or 'philosophical' suicide] that ought to accompany it' (MS p. 54).

Though Camus would not perhaps want to put it this way, this is in fact an attempt to show human life to have a meaning (and to be, therefore, worthwhile) in spite of the absence of *grand-narrative* meaning. The meaning of (everyone's) life on this account is 'revolt'. It is revolt, 'man's dogged . . . perseverance' (MS p. 104) with an existence that, given the non-satisfaction of his need for grand-narrative meaning, is thoroughly unsatisfactory, that is the meaning of life. It constitutes 'man's sole dignity' (ibid.), endows his existence with 'majesty'. 'There is', Camus writes, 'no finer sight' (MS p. 54).

The thing, however, that needs to be said about this first account of the absurd hero is that toughness is not enough; not enough to constitute a worthwhile life. *Do* we, in fact, 'imagine Sisyphus happy'? Surely not. Surely our response to his predicament is not admiration but rather *pity*.

Sisyphus is indeed tough. He confronts his fate with his head held high and a proud gait. He is the big boy who never cries. But toughness is not always a virtue. Imagine someone with incurable cancer who has already been through many horrible treatments. He faces a future of ever more intense regimens of chemotherapy for ever shorter remissions. Being tough, he refuses ever to give up the 'battle' against cancer. But is it not possible that his toughness has prevented him from seeing that it is, in fact, time to 'call it a day'? Sisyphus is of course immortal. To make him relevant to the question of suicide, however, he has to be given that option. And given the option it is far from clear that he should not take it. (Note that, if Camus were right, euthanasia would *always* be a mistake.)

Camus' first account of the absurd hero is not, then, convincing. Inappropriate toughness is not a virtue but simply foolishness.[8] The second, however, is more interesting. On this account, absurd heroes are distinguished by a kind of gargantuan appetite, an enormous lust for life. Their lives are marked not by 'revolt', but by the fact that they 'expend' themselves in lives devoted to, by all normal standards, 'excess' (MS p. 78). What counts for them 'is not quality but quantity'. What defines the life of the authentic hero on this second account is an 'ethics of quantity' (MS p. 69).[9] In *The Myth* itself, Camus' central paradigms of the absurd hero of this second type are Don Juan and 'the actor'.

Don Juan (a facet, as we have seen, of Camus' own personality) seduces more women in an evening that most men manage in a lifetime. He does not fall in love or engage in improving conversation. He makes the same speech to every woman since 'to anyone who seeks [mere] quantity in his joys, the only thing that matters is efficiency' (MS p. 68). Where all that matters, in other words, is conquest, it is foolish to depart from the tried and true.

The actor (an element of autobiography is evident here, too) is a 'mime of the ephemeral'. He is someone who, for 'three hours', is Iago and then, for another three, Gloucester, and so on (MS p. 74). Someone who lives like an actor constantly uses up one personality and moves on to the next. Devoted to 'dispersion', his existence represents (here Camus alludes to the Church's traditional disapproval of actors and – especially – actresses) a 'heretical multiplication of souls' (MS p. 78).

It is possible to feel that Don Juan and 'the actor' are not quite the appealing figures Camus takes them to be. In, however, a number of lyrical essays written a few years either side of *The Myth*, specifically 'Summer in Algiers', 'The Minotaur' and 'Helen's exile', Camus develops the idea of 'excess' in what seems to me a considerably more attractive and compelling way.

Written amidst the grimness of wartime and immediately post-war Paris, Camus recalls the Algeria of his youth, recalls, above all, its summertime. He recalls Algeria as a place where 'whoever is young and alive . . . finds occasions for triumph everywhere: in the bay, the sun, the red and white games on the seaward terraces, the flowers and sports stadiums, the cool-legged girls' (MS p. 128). Algeria, he writes, is a place where

> every summer morning seems to be the first in the world. Each twilight seems to be the last, the solemn agony announced at sunset by a final glow that darkens every hue. The sea [Camus' palette, here, seems very close to Van Gogh's] is ultramarine, the road the colour of clotted blood, the beach yellow. Everything disappears with the green sun: an hour later the dunes are bathed in moonlight. There are incomparable nights under a rain of stars.
>
> (MS p. 160)

Algiers, he continues, is a place where one says, not 'go for', but rather 'indulge in' a swim. It is a place where people are not, as in Europe, 'nudists' – those tedious 'protestants of the flesh' – but are simply 'comfortable in the sunlight'. It is a place where people live with Greek '*naïveté*': 'living through the body', the young men, as they run along the beaches, 'repeat the gestures of the athletes of Delos' (MS p. 129). It is a place where one cannot fail to 'participate in [the] . . . dialogue of stone and flesh in tune with the seasons' (MS p. 130). Camus recalls returning to the inner harbour from a day-long canoeing expedition with the friends of his youth: 'how', he asks, 'can I fail to feel that I am piloting through the smooth waters a savage cargo of gods in whom I recognise my brothers?' (ibid.).

How do these beings – at once friends of Camus' youth and reincarnations of the Greeks – live? Like all of Camus' heroes, they live 'without appeal', without appeal to any 'deceptive divinity' (MS 136). In this land where 'a thirty-year old workman has already played all the cards in his hand' (MS p. 132), one lives, like Don Juan and 'the actor', with a lust for experience, with 'a haste that borders on waste' (MS p. 132). In such a land life is 'not to be built up but to be burned up' (MS p. 133). A final remark elevates

Camus' recollections to the status of philosophy: 'I have the mad hope that, without knowing it perhaps, these barbarians lounging on the beaches are actually modelling the image of a culture in which the image of man will at last find its true likeness' (ibid.).

Here, I think it is clear, we have Camus' account of how to live well in an 'absurd' universe presented at its most appealing. What are we to make of it?

One criticism (a criticism one might imagine Nietzsche, for example, making) is that a life governed by the 'ethics of quantity', a life devoted to 'burning up' rather than 'building up', since it lacks any overriding direction or goal, is, in the end, bound to be *boring* and, as such, not worth living. In the end, one might ask, must not Don Juan become bored with his women, must not 'the actor' (like Toad of Toad Hall) become bored with the lives he continually morphs himself into, and must not the 'barbarian gods' become bored with sun and sand? Underlying this objection is the thought introduced in Chapter 7 that while *grand-narrative* meaning is not essential to a worthwhile life – one *can*, then, live well in an absurd universe – meaning in the form of a *personal* meaning, narrative or goal is essential to such a life.

But Camus denies this (MS pp. 56–8). Whereas, he says, 'everyday man lives with aims [and] a concern for justification' of actions in terms of those aims, the absurd hero does not. His life is 'aimless'. From which it follows (to answer a question raised earlier) that when Camus says that life 'will be lived all the better if it has no meaning' (MS p. 53) he means not merely 'no grand-narrative meaning' but rather 'no meaning, period'. Not just a grand, but also a personal narrative is absent from the truly worthwhile life. 'Men with a purpose', says Camus scornfully, live in the city (MS p. 142). They are not to be found on the beaches of his Algerian paradise.

Let us try to be exact as to just what Camus means by describing the life of the absurd hero as 'purposeless', 'meaningless', 'aimless' or goalless. In a certain sense, of course, like everyone else, the absurd hero has to have goals: short-term goals – food, shelter, sleep, etc. – without which he would simply die. But, in the examples Camus gives, he is also allowed long-term goals: to seduce as many women as possible; to experience as great a variety of different lives as possible; or to spend as much time on the beach and as little in the classroom as possible. When, therefore, Camus excludes 'aims' from the worthwhile life, what he means to exclude is not goals as such, but rather goals of a quite specific sort.

> Life is not to be built up but burned up. Stopping to think and becoming better are out of the question.
>
> (MS p. 133)

This tells us what it is that Camus wants to exclude: 'building' or, as the Germans call it, *Bildung*. What is entirely 'out of the question' is 'becoming better', scripting one's life as if writing a *Bildungsroman*, a 'novel of education' in the widest sense of the word (see p. 59 above), a narrative of progression towards a fully realised self. What is excluded is the formation of an ideal conception of the self which then provides the basis for a life conceived as a project of disciplined self-development. It is the exclusion of *this* kind of Germanic, Nietzschean goal that Camus has in mind when he claims that the worthwhile life is goalless.

What is supposed to be wrong with the life of *Bildung*? One of Camus' arguments is that to have 'aims', as 'everyday man' does, is to lack freedom – which he takes to be an obvious feature of the worthwhile life. Having raised himself out of his previous everydayness, the absurd hero realises, he says, that 'to the extent he imagined a purpose to his life, he adapted himself to the demands of a purpose to be achieved and became a slave [to it]' (MS p. 57).

What does Camus mean, here, by freedom? Earlier, I argued that genuinely to have a life-goal is to be *committed* to it. Whatever difficulties I encounter, if it is genuinely my goal, I will not be deterred from its pursuit. There is, however, one exception to this; the case where it becomes obvious that the goal I have set myself is impossible to achieve.

I want to become a first-rate doctor. But I fail my exams. Or kill a few patients. In this case one must abandon one's commitment, recognise that one's goal is, or has become, incompatible with one's facticity. The not merely committed, but rather *obsessed* person, however, is unable to recognise the absolute incompatibility of their goal with their facticity. (The exam results have been faked; it was really someone else's fault the patients died.) For the obsessed person there is *nothing* in their facticity that will convince them that they have to abandon their goal. Whereas for the committed person facticity provides a 'reality-check' with respect to their goal, for the obsessed person it does not. Here, I think, in obsession, we discover what it is to be 'enslaved' by one's goal.

Once, however, the distinction between obsession and commitment is made, it becomes obvious that Camus' argument is not really very good, depending, as it does, on failing to see any difference between the two. The fact of the matter is that the committed (but not obsessed) person *will* be prepared to modify her goal should it become obvious that it is incompatible with her facticity. Becoming a slave to the goal that defines a life of *Bildung* is a danger, but by no means an inevitability.

Camus' main argument against the life of *Bildung* has, however, to do with time.

Camus claims that 'everyday man', the man with 'aims', 'weighs up his chances . . . counts on "some day", his retirement, the labour of his sons' (MS p. 56). He lives, in short, 'in the future'. The absurd hero, by contrast, exhibits total 'indifference' to the future (MS p. 59). He lives in 'the present and the succession of presents' (MS p. 62). What is supposed to be wrong with 'living in the future'?

A hitherto ambitious opera singer, her career interrupted by cancer from which, through a bone marrow transplant, she has now recovered, says in an interview: 'Singing is now no longer my be all and end all. I much more enjoy the sky, walking in the park, the birds, just being alive.' This is the 'barbarian gods' living in a land where 'every morning seems to be the first in the world', being alive to the simple joys of just 'being there', being alive to the extraordinariness of the ordinary. The implication of the singer's remark is that prior to the trauma of cancer the joys of life in the present – and that means the joys of *life*, since in reality, of course, life is always lived in the present – had been sacrificed to a projected future in which she is a famous singer. And, of course, Camus is right: to the extent that one's 'futureness' kills one's being alive to the joys of the present, it is a mistake. Moreover, as Schopenhauer observes, it is a mistake we very commonly make. People, Schopenhauer writes, live

> in the expectation of better things. . . . On the other hand the present is accepted only for the time being, is set at naught, and looked upon merely as the path to the goal. Thus when at the end of their lives most men look back, they will find that

> they have lived throughout *ad interim*; they will be surprised to see that the very thing they allowed to slip by unappreciated and unenjoyed was just their life, precisely that in the expectation of which they had lived.[10]

But 'building' a life towards a goal, it seems to me, does not *have* to kill one's life in the present. One can *both* work at becoming a singer (the interviewee had not, in fact, given up singing) *and* enjoy one's walks in the park, just as one can take the train down the Rhine valley towards one's destination *and* enjoy lunch with a Rhine wine and the passing scene of sunlit vineyards and castles at the same time. Indeed, the walks in the park are almost certain to help make one a *better* singer. Singers who have an experience of life outside singing will, other things being equal, be better singers than those who do not. (The same is true of philosophers.) A properly thought out life of *Bildung*, in short, will budget generously for activity and experience that does not, in any obvious or direct way, contribute to achieving the defining goal of that life.

So, while Camus is right to warn against the kind of obsession with the future that renders one incapable of experiencing the joys of the present, he is wrong to suppose that the life of 'building' *must* take this form. I want now, however, to argue an even stronger point against Camus: not only *can* the building of a life towards a self-defining goal form part of the worthwhile life; it *must* do so.

Nietzsche remarks that the will to power is always the will to more power. One (though not, as I suggested in Chapter 8, the only) thought contained in this remark is the idea that a continual sense of development, growth, ascending movement, self-overcoming, is *essential* to a worthwhile life. It is in the light of this insight that one can see that there really is something seriously wrong with the lives of Don Juan, 'the actor' and the friends of Camus' youth – given that the last are offered as models, not just of youth, but of an entire life. What is wrong with such lives is that they are *static*, without any sense of movement or growth. The Don learns nothing from his seductions; nothing from an earlier affair is carried over into any later one. The same is true with respect to the multiple lives of 'the actor', while the 'surfie' friends of Camus' boyhood are so laid back that they don't even try to become better surfers. ('Stopping to think and becoming better', remember, 'are out of the question'.)

Camus is quite explicit as to the static character of the absurd hero's life. Of Don Juan he says that, like his speeches, he himself is always the same. He is a seducer who 'will not change'. 'Only in novels [*Bildungsromanen*] does one change one's condition or become better' (MS p. 69). But that just means that the life of Camus' absurd hero really is, as we earlier suggested, a life of deadly tedium, a life of *boredom*.

If, then, it is true, as it is, that 'the will to power is always the will to more power', we must conclude that 'building' one's life in the light of a self-defining goal is not just a possible but an *essential* feature of the worthwhile life. For all the many delights of his writing, and for all the credit due to him for looking utterly fundamental issues squarely in the face, Camus is wrong to say that 'life . . . will be lived all the better if it has no meaning'. The worthwhile life *requires* meaning, requires a goal that supplies it with an *at least* personal meaning. (Whether this goal can be *merely* personal or whether it needs to be, in some sense, universal is an issue I shall address in Chapter 15.)

13

Foucault

Michel Foucault was born in Poitiers in 1926 and died of AIDS – possibly the result of engaging in sado-masochistic homosexual practices in San Francisco – in Paris in 1984. By his own account, the liberationist movements of his age, among others, the student uprising of 1968, the Iranian revolution of 1978–9 and the Solidarity resistance to communism in Poland of the 1980s, had a decisive influence on his thinking. So, too, one may surmise, did the generally homophobic character of the times in which he lived. Foucault's influence throughout the social sciences and humanities has been, for the last thirty years, enormous, second only to that of Derrida. Between them, they bear most of the responsibility for the turn, within our universities, to 'postmodernism'.

Given the above biographical data it is unsurprising that the most visible aim in Foucault's writings is the promotion of what he calls 'freedom' (FR pp. 46, 48, 50, 246–7 *et passim*[1]). Why should freedom be a problem?

Recalling (posthumous) Nietzsche's notion that the essence of everything is the 'will to power', Foucault repeatedly insists that the most appropriate model for understanding human society is *war*. Rejecting the view that social phenomena are to be treated as kinds of linguistic *texts* requiring a deciphering of their meaning, he says that 'one's point of reference should be, not the great model of language and signs but to [sic] that of war and battle' (FR p. 56). In any social situation, according to Foucault, there is always the quest for domination, on the one hand, and on the other the desire (or at least the need) to resist. (Actually, Foucault's emphasis on oppression-resistance means that it is not war in general but rather the war of colonisation that is his model. Wars fought to settle border disputes or in competition for hitherto unclaimed land are inappropriate models for Foucault's purposes.)

That which oppresses, Foucault calls variously a 'discourse', 'regime of knowledge', 'regime of truth' and an 'episteme'. These terms seem designed to pick out what, in connection with Hegel, we learnt to call 'shapes of consciousness' (see pp. 59–60 above). They refer, that is, to what are taken to be fundamental, but historically relative, sets of assumptions about the nature of reality and about, in particular, the nature of human beings. Contained in such assumptions is an assumption about what it is to be a 'normal' human being, to be, for example, sane as opposed to mad. Because they thus posit norms of human behaviour, regimes of truth are normative, contain within themselves an 'ethics', an assumption about the right way for human beings to be. (Notice how much, on this account, a regime of knowledge looks like Heidegger's 'the One' (see pp. 112–13 above). A useful 'take' on Foucault's philosophy is to see it as an exploration and development of Heidegger's concept of *das Man*.)

Regimes, Foucault holds, are always the product of power. That is, he seems to hold (in a quasi-Marxist way), they always serve the interests of one social class at the expense of another, and are kept in place by a set of more or less overt 'technologies' or 'disciplines' of control. Sometimes he says that no one is responsible for the coming into being or maintenance of a regime (FR pp. 84–5) and seems to imply that *everyone* is oppressed by regimes of knowledge. Mostly, however, it is, à la Marx, 'the bourgeoisie' whose interests are served and who maintain the regimes. The disciplinary regime of prison and asylum became, in the eighteenth century, the 'dark side' of the *seemingly* emancipatory legislation enacted by 'the politically dominant class', the 'bourgeoisie' (FR p. 211). Moreover, the 'war' metaphor seems to demand an identifiable oppressor as well as an oppressed. It takes two to fight a war.

Foucault's aim is to make us aware of the regimes under which we suffer and to liberate us from them: to, in his own language, encourage 'practical transgression' (FR p. 45). His method is – a term he takes over from Nietzsche – 'genealogical'. It consists in taking some particular discourse/regime, exhibiting its 'descent', and thereby liberating us from it.

What, one might ask, is the connection between knowing the origins of a regime of knowledge and being liberated from it? It is, I think, twofold. First, just to discover that regimes *have* origins weakens their hold over one through their historical relativisation. Foucault emphasises this. Through genealogy, things that seem 'universal, necessary and obligatory' are shown to be, in fact, historically local and 'arbitrary' (FR p. 45). Second, Foucault holds, the origin of regimes of knowledge always lies in power, i.e. in oppression. Theoretically, the genealogy of an ethics might *strengthen* its hold on us – if it turned out to be God's command from out of the burning bush, or if it turned out to be the result of a free and rational compact among human beings wishing to escape the nasty, brutish shortness of existence in a 'state of nature'. But, in fact, Foucault claims, genealogy always reveals not noble or sensible origins, but the ignoble ones of class oppression. One might ask how Foucault knows this to be the case. The answer will become apparent when we turn to his particular applications of the genealogical method.

First of all, to madness. Though one might well assume that the mad have always been confined, their incarceration in fact first began during the Renaissance. From the sixteenth century, claims Foucault, the mad were no longer respected, as they had been during the Middle Ages, as those coming from the alternative 'world of the irrational and bear[ing] its stigmata' (FR p. 136). Initially, the motive for the construction of asylums was to clear the streets of the idle and unproductive, though in times of economic boom the asylums provided a source of cheap labour (FR pp. 124–39). In the nineteenth century there was a move to abolish chains and bars. But that merely meant that the means of coercion took on a subtler guise – being sent to Coventry, for example (FR p. 150) – and in any case the traditional, crude forms of coercion remained in place as a threat of last resort. Freud abandoned the asylum, but still retained its essential structure by elevating the therapist to 'semi-divine' status, by making him the omniscient, silent observer and all-powerful judge (FR pp. 164–6).

Foucault's claim, then, elaborated with a wealth of historical detail, is that both the modern asylum and modern psychotherapeutic practice are oppressive. They are oppressive because, in a word, they seek to 'normalise'.

Since 'normalise' is the central term in Foucault's critical vocabulary, it is worth spending a little time working out exactly what it means. As Foucault uses the word, the primary object of normalisation is a group, a population – usually the entire population of a country (FR p. 341). The aim is to create 'the power of the norm', to – via the 'penalty of the norm' – create 'standardisation', 'homogeneity', albeit a homogeneity that allows for differentiation into the 'fixed specialities' (mother, father, worker, foreman, etc.) (FR pp. 196–7). A population is normalised to the extent it is brought to behave according the relevant (internally differentiated) norm; an individual is normalised to the extent she is incorporated into this process. (Recall Heidegger's talk of the One as 'levelling' the individual down to an 'average' kind of existence.)

In what sense, then, does the asylum normalise? If it 'cures' the previously 'irrational' patient, then the patient herself is normalised. Even, however, if the patient, is not cured, the asylum contributes to the normalisation of the population at large by removing the 'mad' person from the social body. Left at large, they might encourage others to behave in similarly ab-normal ways. Incarcerated, they constitute a sort of negative role model, an example of what happens to you if you depart more than a little from the norm, a warning and a deterrence.

It is easy to see why Foucault views the normalisation of the asylum (and its psychoanalytic extension) as oppressive. His complaint is essentially that of Ken Kesey's *One Flew over the Cuckoo's Nest*, Janet Frame's *An Angel at My Table* and Stanley Kubrick's *Clockwork Orange*. When one works through the superficially impressive array of historical detail, however, one finds a critique that is, at bottom, crude and polemical. Foucault speaks repeatedly of 'madness' and 'the experience of madness'. But there is, surely, no such thing. There are, for example, the criminally insane, the insane who endanger their own lives, the happily dotty, and the 'madness' of genius, what Plato (see p. 12 above) calls 'heaven-sent' madness.

Foucault implicitly treats all madness as being of the last type, the type viewed with awe in the Middle Ages as giving access to a suprarational sphere of reality. Save for occasional flashes in the works of Hölderlin, Nerval and Nietzsche, claims Foucault, 'the life of unreason' – note, again, the assumption that there is only one 'life of unreason' – no longer manifests itself (FR p. 166). But this abolition of distinctions between different types of madness is surely both silly and destructive. Of course we should not try to normalise the harmlessly dotty or the eccentric genius. But what else are we to do with the criminally insane except lock them up and seek to enforce their adherence to those norms departure from which constitutes their criminality?

I turn now to Foucault's genealogical study of sexuality. Two main themes provide the topic of discussion: psychotherapy and the concept of perversion.

Though, from the seventeenth century, says Foucault, there was a taboo on talking about sex in public, in the Catholic confessional you were encouraged to talk about it in detail. The point was that sexual desire personified the guilty flesh and that you had to talk about your sins in detail. This notion that the essential self (the self which, in Christianity, you had to renounce as you gave yourself to God) is largely sexual was taken over by modern psychotherapy. The only difference is that now (the early 1970s) one is encouraged to *embrace* – to *act on* – the desires of this essential self rather than extirpate them. Modern psychotherapy is, then, just the reverse of the Catholic confessional (FR pp. 301–16).

It is not immediately clear why Foucault regards this psychotherapeutic conception of the self as oppressive. But the reason, I think, is that he regards *any* notion of a 'true self' as oppressive since, as we shall see, freedom, for Foucault as for Sartre, is a matter of *creating* rather than discovering a self. What he calls the 'Californian' (FR p. 362) conception of the self is oppressive because it 'normalises' us into beings obsessed with 'getting in touch with their (sexual) feelings', turns us into Californian clichés. This deprives us of the freedom to acknowledge that, in fact, for most of us, 'sex is boring', a mere side-show in our lives. The Greeks, he observes, were much more interested in food than in sex, regarding the latter as an ethical triviality (FR p. 340).

Foucault sees the concept of 'perversion' becoming a force for normalisation in the eighteenth century. (In general, he portrays normalisation not, like Heidegger, as an ahistorical phenomenon present in all human societies, but as something that came into being with the eighteenth-century Enlightenment. Though on the surface preaching reason, liberty, equality and fraternity, the reality, the dark under-belly of the Enlightenment is, for Foucault, the disciplines and techniques of normalisation.) What came about was the 'medicalisation' of sex, particularly unusual sex. Acts became manifestations of personality types – 'homosexual', 'paedophile', 'zoophile' and so on. These labels became exclusionary (FR pp. 316–29). The person so labelled is excluded from 'decent' society, thereby preserving, among 'decent' people, the missionary norm – partly by excluding the abnormal and partly by offering a warning to those tempted by abnormality.

It is not easy to fit everything Foucault says about sex into a coherent whole. The first problem is that, while he is surely right that there is (or rather was in the 1970s – the discussion now seems a little *passé*) a kind of tyranny exercised by many psychotherapists which demanded that one 'let it all hang out' sexually speaking, such tyranny was, surely, exercised only over that relatively small part of the population that was significantly influenced by psychotherapy. The second problem is that if one was to 'let it all hang out', then, if one's desires happened to be 'perverted', one was to let them hang out, too. Yet Foucault says that society exercises a strong normalising pressure *against* 'perverted' sex.

The way to resolve these difficulties is to note that whereas Foucault's central and most important discussions of normalisation concern the normalisation of a national population as a whole – the rivalry of nation states, and the consequent need for as much internal cohesion as possible within a state, is given as the underlying ground for normalisation – the discussion of psychotherapy is focused only on the relatively tiny population of those involved in or influenced by the ideology of psychotherapy. The discussion of perversion concerns the normalisation of a culture as a whole. The discussion of psychotherapy concerns normalisation within a small and deviant subculture of that culture. That Foucault gives no indication of this difference in scale and significance suggests a certain lack of perspective on his part.

One of the major institutions that at least seems to be aimed at normalisation, according to Foucault, is the prison: as well as being an instrument of retribution, it is also, everyone agrees, aimed at retraining the offender into a useful and productive citizen.

What mainly interests Foucault about the modern prison, since he believes this to constitute a central characteristic of modernity in general, is what he calls 'panopticism', 'the gentle efficiency of total surveillance' (FR p. 217). The name is taken from Jeremy Bentham's 1791 design for an ideal prison which he called 'The Panopticon'. That design provided for a tall tower in a courtyard surrounded by the cell buildings, the point being that the prisoners could be kept under constant surveillance, thereby obviating the need for traditional means of prisoner control, chains and violent punishments. People break the rules if they think they can get away with it. But if they know they can't they will hardly ever break the rules.

Panopticism is not just a means of control. It also forms part of a turning of the offender into an object of scientific study. Not only the offender's behaviour in prison but also his biography and the factors leading up to his crime become a matter of study. Penal and psychological theory intersect so that a 'typology' of criminality is set up. The offender is, therefore, no longer merely someone who has broken the law. He becomes, instead, a particular type of person, a 'delinquent' (FR p. 219).

Since the nineteenth century critics, pointing to the permanently high rate of recidivism (re-offending), have charged that the prison system is a failure. In fact, however, claims Foucault, it does not really 'fail' since reform was never its true aim. Rather, its true aim has always been to isolate a particular form (or forms) of human being, namely, 'delinquency'. It aims to expel delinquency from the social body, to preserve it as a permanent underclass, and so to hold it up to us as an ever-present warning, a negative role model, that is permanently present (FR pp. 231–2).

It seems, therefore, that, contrary to what one would expect Foucault to say, the prison neither succeeds nor really tries to 'normalise' the prisoner. Rather, it normalises *us*, the docile run of 'normal', non-criminal people.

What are the practical consequences of Foucault's critique? Given that one major function of the prison is the protection of society from the consequences of crime, he does not, presumably, want prisons abolished. Neither does he voice objections to the idea of retribution, the idea that the offender should 'pay his debt to society'. His critique is focused, rather, on the idea of reform. Does he want a different *type* of reform – one that respects the prisoner's right to privacy and perhaps replaces psychologists and criminologists with philosophers, actors, IT teachers, job-placement specialists – or does he think there is an *essential* incompatibility between prison and reform, that *any* programme of reform must fail? The answer to this question is unclear. One hopes, however, that he intends the first. Even if only a minority are ever saved from recidivism, the effort, surely, is still worthwhile.

Foucault's discussions of the asylum and the prison focused on particular regions of control and normalisation. When he turns to the topic of what he calls 'docile bodies' (FR pp. 179–205), however, these discussions seem to fall into place as contributing to a more general thesis.

The eighteenth century was a time of struggle for power between nation-states. Even when not overtly at war, politics (both political relations with other states and the preservation of internal peace and order) was a continuation of war by other means (FR p. 185). This, of course, represented nothing new. What was new, however, was that, in pursuit of pre-eminence, states subjected the 'bodies' of their citizens to a unique kind of control (a kind of control Foucault takes to be definitive of the epoch created by the Enlightenment, i.e. modernity in general). The reason for this was that state power depended on economic power, which depended on efficient and reliable labour power, which depended, in turn, on 'docile bodies'. (Foucault speaks, here, of 'bodies' rather than of 'people', I think, to emphasise the fact that, to modern capitalism, people *are* nothing but 'bodies' – more or less efficient productive units.)

There is, Foucault points out, a natural 'rhetoric' to the body of a soldier – a 'military air'. What the eighteenth century realised was that this was not the prerogative of a military aristocracy: it did not need to be inborn, but could be produced by training. The humblest peasant could be trained to the 'automatism', in other words, 'docility', of the soldier.

The training of docile bodies did not stop with the military. The eighteenth century had a 'military dream of society' as a whole: 'Politics, as the technique of internal peace and order, sought to implement the mechanism of the perfect army, of the disciplined mass, of the docile, useful troop . . .' (FR p. 185). The key to such a politics lay in the surveillance and disciplining of every detail in the individual's life, in a 'microphysics' of power (FR p. 183). Napoleon's aim, for example, was 'to embrace the whole of this vast machine [of the state] without the slightest detail escaping his attention' (FR p. 185).

The techniques of this 'microphysics' were many and various. Foucault organises them, however, under two headings: 'hierarchical observation' and 'normalisation of judgments' (FR p. 188).

'Hierarchical organisation' is just panopticism. Foucault introduces this new term, however, I think, to make the point that whereas Bentham's Panopticon involved a single gaze directly viewing every prisoner, military panopticism works through hierarchical delegation: the corporal keeps an eye on the (not so private) private and reports to the sergeant who reports to the lieutenant, and so on.

The military camp is organised for hierarchical observation. But so, too, is, for example, the workers' housing estate, built on the model of the camp, and the school where half-doors on the lavatories (FR p. 191) mean that, even here, the individual cannot escape surveillance.[2]

One of the major techniques of 'normalisation of judgments' we have already discussed: exclusion. The asylum and the prison normalise the population by excluding and isolating the 'lunatic' or 'delinquent'. Other techniques of normalisation operate not in this indirect way but directly on the docile-body-to-be. The eighteenth-century state was riddled with micro-systems of discipline. The workshop, for example, had an elaborate system of light physical punishments and petty humiliations to deal with 'incorrect' attitudes and behaviour such as lateness, chatter, making vulgar gestures, impoliteness, insolence, impurity (FR p. 194). In the school, the national examination secured both normalisation and hierarchical observation on a national scale (FR p. 197).

Normalisation and panopticism work in tandem. Normalisation operates by establishing docile norms and penalties for those who offend against them. Panopticism ensures that, there being nowhere to hide, norm-breakers will be seen and disciplined. It ensures that the sanctions established by normalisation will only rarely be invoked. Since 'big brother' sees one's every move, one knows there is no chance of getting away with norm-breaking. Panopticism renders the system of control perfect.

As I have said, Foucault's most visible aim appears to be freedom, freedom from the regimes of 'knowledge' ('knowledge' about, for example, what it is to be sane rather than mad, decent rather than delinquent, straight rather than sexually deviant). Since every regime of knowledge is an instrument of power by means of which some élite group or class threatens to dominate us – to 'normalise' us into 'docile' (Nietzsche would say 'herd') animals – resistance – or, as Foucault calls it, 'transgression' – is a permanent task. Since 'everything [every regime of knowledge] is dangerous . . . we always have something to do. So my position leads not to apathy but to a hyper- and pessimistic activism' (FR p. 343).

What, however, is the point of resistance? What is so bad about being dominated? What is so good about being free of domination? Why is 'freedom' valuable?

One answer, hinted at in the above remark that, as Foucaultians, 'we always have something to do', would be that there is actually nothing particularly valuable about freedom as such. It is just, it might be said, that critique and transgression keeps at bay the Schopenhauerian boredom of life. The positive message of Foucault's philosophy would then be that, to give meaning to our lives, we should adopt, as our life-project, the persona of the critic (or 'pessimist'). (As the ex-wife of a friend of mine once said of him, 'It doesn't matter what it is, he's against it'.) This, however, is not a very good answer. First, because if everyone followed Foucault's advice and became a critic there would be no power-knowledge regimes left to resist and nothing left to do save commit suicide out of boredom. And, second, because there is something intrinsically unsatisfying about the life of the eternal critic. Our fundamental impulse, that is to say, is surely to create, to construct. This is why we find real satisfaction in 'deconstruction' only when it is a preliminary to construction. We need then, if possible, to discover some other answer to the question of why we should accept 'freedom' to be of such central value.

Foucault talks at considerable length about the 'ethics' of the ancient world (see especially FR pp. 340–51). The key concept was, he maintains, 'care of the self'. This, however, meant something different in the Graeco-Roman period than it meant to the Greeks of the fourth century BC. To the latter, to Plato for example, you cared for yourself – got your soul in order, achieved self-mastery, mastery over your unruly desires (the 'black horse' we discussed in Chapter 1) – in order to be in a fit condition to care for the community as a whole.[3] For the former, however – Foucault is thinking, here, mainly of the Stoics – everyone is to care simply for himself. There is no ulterior end to care of self (FR p. 348).

So far as I can tell, Foucault is strongly attached to the conception of ethics that he attributes to the Stoics. The Platonic conception, I think, strikes him as too bossy, too potentially oppressive. Everyone, he thinks, should take care of himself or herself, and leave everyone else alone to do the same. Care for community does not seem to figure in Foucault's ethical outlook.

The goal of self-care, self-mastery was, for the Stoics, says Foucault, aesthetic. Though agreeing with Plato on a life of sexual austerity, for them, the point was simply that (according to their taste) sexual incontinence was *ugly*. The point, then, is to live a *beautiful* life, to live one's life, in effect, as an artwork. The trouble with modernity is that art is excluded from life:

> What strikes me is the fact that in our society, art has become something which is related only to objects and not to individuals, or to life. That art is something which is specialised or which is done by experts who are artists. But couldn't everyone's life become a work of art? Why should the lamp or house be an art object but not our life?
>
> (FR p. 350)

Hence (to relate Foucault, finally, to our central theme) when it comes to giving meaning to our lives Foucault's view is that we are to become works of art. The meaningful life is not a matter (as the 'Californians' think) of discovering 'the truth about desire, life, nature, body, and so on' (FR p. 350). It is not a matter of being 'authentic', of being true to a real, given but repressed self. (Foucault attributes this view to Sartre, which is extraordinary, given Sartre's antipathy to Freud and the unconscious.) Rather, it is a matter of being *creative* (FR p. 351).

This, of course, is essentially a rerun of Nietzsche's view (see Chapter 7 above) that we are to construct our lives as works of art with ourselves as the 'heroes'. Foucault acknowledges this, and makes particular reference to section 290 of *The Gay Science* (FR p. 351), which reads as follows:

> *One thing is needful.* – To 'give style' to one's character – a great and rare art! It is practiced by those who survey all the strengths and weaknesses of their nature and then fit them into an artistic plan until every one of them appears as art and reason and even weaknesses delight the eye. . . . In the end, when the work is finished, it becomes evident how the constraint of a single taste governed and formed everything, large and small. Whether this taste was good or bad is less important than one might suppose, if only it was a single taste. . . .

(Notice that giving a unified 'style' to one's life offers an account of Foucault's otherwise unexplained notion of 'beauty'.) Hence when we ask for Foucault's account of how to live with meaning in a God-deserted universe his answer is the same as Nietzsche's.

What this means is that, for all its prominence, freedom is not Foucault's ultimate value. Rather, beauty, that is to say art, is. Better put, the *creation* of oneself as a beautiful artwork is what Foucault takes to be ultimately valuable. Since creation is by definition free activity, freedom seems, for Foucault, to be valuable as a means to beauty. If we are to create ourselves as beings who are, in Nietzsche's words, 'new, unique, incomparable' (GS 335), we must, of course, free ourselves from the clichés established by the regimes of knowledge that surround us.

As what kind of an artwork is one to create oneself? That is entirely up to the individual. Ethics is a matter of 'personal choice' (FR pp. 248, 361). Notice that there is no inconsistency in Foucault's saying that 'everyone' (see the quotation on p. 183 above) should create themselves as a work of art and that ethics is a matter of personal choice. One's 'ethics', as Foucault conceives it, *is* the artwork one creates oneself as. That one should create oneself as an artwork is the recommendation that one should *have* an ethics.

I am going to offer three major criticisms of Foucault's philosophy. The first concerns the 'war' model of society, the second and third the idea of creating oneself as an artwork.

Foucault presents his accounts of domination through normalisation as an analysis of the order of society created by the eighteenth-century Enlightenment: an analysis, in other words, of modernity. But actually, one might ask, has not normalisation *always* been with us, as prevalent in the Graeco-Roman world Foucault seems so much to admire as in the modern age? Is not the pressure to conform to some historically specific 'regime of knowledge' in fact an *a priori* or necessary feature of human existence, as Heidegger takes 'the One' to be?

Now, it turns out that, in fact, Foucault *does* believe that domination through normalisation is an omnipresent feature of human existence. This becomes at least relatively clear in the course of a discussion of the 'war' model in a 1983 interview conducted in the University of California at Berkeley.

The question is raised as to whether Foucault's view of politics as 'essentially domination and repression' (in other words, 'war') is not excessively 'bleak'. Should not at least the 'fictional possibility' of 'consensus' be allowed (FR p. 379)? In other words, is not collective action aimed at a common goal without there being relations of domination and repression within the collectivity at least conceivable? Can we not adopt it as an at least theoretically attainable 'goal' (ibid.)?

Not so, replies Foucault. Even within the seemingly consensual group 'the problem of power relations remains' (FR p. 378). The most that can be allowed is the use of consensuality as a 'critical principle': 'one must be against non-consensuality' but 'one must not be for consensuality' (FR p. 379). Since, in other words, the overcoming of relations of domination and oppression is not an even 'fictional possibility', to be 'for' consensuality would be entirely futile.

This discussion makes it clear – though Foucault would never use this word – that what he in fact believes in is a *metaphysics* of 'war' (otherwise put, posthumous Nietzsche's metaphysics of 'will to power'), a supposedly universal account of the essence of human relations elevated to the status of a necessary truth. For Foucault, it is *impossible* for any society or social group to escape the war model. In an early work, Foucault says that dreams reveal 'radical liberty' to be the human essence.[4] But equally, it seems, it belongs to the human essence to deny that freedom to others. This is what human relations are all about: the quest for ever more complete domination, and the quest for liberation. Oppression and resistance. In a word, a power struggle. Foucault's metaphysics, it seems, is indistinguishable from the metaphysics of posthumous Nietzsche.

This – the elevation of the war metaphor to a metaphysics – seems to me to turn Foucault's often illuminating exposures of particular regions of domination into a thesis that is empirically false, even obviously so. As anyone who lived through the London Blitz or has played in a football team or string quartet knows, 'consensual' action is not merely a theoretical possibility but an actuality. And because it is so obviously false it lends an unpleasant air of cynicism, even paranoia, to Foucault's philosophy.

At the end of the Berkeley interview the interviewers make Foucault realise that his insistence that relations of domination and subjection are internal to even the most seemingly consensual group relies on a confusion between subordination and oppression. (The captain of the rugby team makes the lineout calls, the first violin of the string quartet gives the leads, but that does not at all mean that either oppresses their fellows.) As a result, Foucault retreats to saying that he offers no 'general analysis' of human relations but merely analyses particular areas of oppression (FR p. 380).

Two comments are in order here. First, the remark is an *ad hoc* response to finding himself in a corner and contradicts what he had said earlier in the interview. Second, since it is the synoptic eye, the view to the general that is the hallmark of philosophy, to the extent that he puts his weight behind this remark, Foucault reduces himself to the status of a historian-sociologist, ceases to have any claim to be a philosopher or to be interesting to philosophers.

My first criticism of Foucault is, then, that his 'war' model is either false or philosophically uninteresting. My second concerns the idea of creating oneself as an artwork.

We are, Foucault says, with Nietzsche, to live 'beautiful' lives, to give 'style' to our characters. We are, through the kind of 'self-mastery' prized by the Stoics, to create ourselves as a literary unity à la Nietzsche.

But what is to be the *content* of this artwork? How am I to select among the indefinitely many possibilities available within the limits of my facticity? Am I to constitute myself a poet or a tax consultant, a saint or a sinner?

Foucault has an interesting fourfold taxonomy of 'ethics'. Ethics has, he says, (1) a topic (for example, erotic desires), (2) a mode of authority (for example, reason, God's command or a cosmological order), (3) an itemisation of the means of self-transformation (modes of self-discipline, 'asceticism' in a broad sense) and (4) a *telos* – what one is to be transformed into (for example, something pure, beautiful, free or immortal) (FR pp. 352–5). The thing to notice with respect to his own account of ethics, however, is that category (2) is absolutely empty. Time after time he insists that the kind of person I am to be is grounded in nothing other than, or beyond, my 'personal choice' (FR p. 361).

But this returns us to Sartre's problem of absurdity. Since I have no ground for preferring one choice to the other *it does not matter* which choice I make. And, since whatever choice I did make (by, in effect, tossing a coin) did not matter, it does not matter either whether or not I stick with my choice if and when it calls for sacrifice and perseverance. In other words, as we have observed before, groundless choice cannot provide a basis of *commitment*. No one dies for ungrounded choices.

My second criticism is, then, that, like all thinkers in the Nietzschean tradition, Foucault cannot provide an account or explanation of ethical commitment. But commitment is a salient feature of the ethical life. People are, to varying degrees, *committed* to their ethical codes. Commitment, indeed, is the point of ethics – if 'duty' never required the overcoming of 'desire', never required 'self-mastery', there would be no point in having a sense of duty.

Something, therefore, is missing from Foucault's ethics, something to do with grounding ethics in something other than personal choice.

In sum, then, my second criticism is that Foucault cannot deal with what I earlier (p. 95) called 'the problem of authority'. And the third is that, with nothing to add to Nietzsche's account of living one's life as an artwork, he cannot deal either with what I called 'the problem of the immoral script' (ibid.) If there is nothing to ground the living of one life rather than another apart from 'personal choice', then there is no reason to prefer the life of a saint to that of a sinner, that of an AIDS researcher to that of a mafiosa.

In sum, then, in spite of his influence and stellar reputation, Foucault is neither a very interesting nor a very original philosopher – though he may have some significance as a historian-sociologist. His answer to the question of the meaning of life (like his metaphysics) is essentially a repetition of Nietzsche and, being of this character, it is inadequate in the same ways.

14

Derrida

Jacques Derrida, born in 1930 – like Camus, in Algeria – has had an enormous influence within the contemporary university, sometimes over philosophers but most decisively within literature departments. Extremely good-looking and media-savvy, he has become a 'star' even outside the university. His influence has not, however, been universally welcomed. In 1992 the proposal to offer him an honorary degree at Cambridge University (normally an entirely pro-forma affair) was vigorously and publicly opposed by a sizeable number of members of the University. By the end of this chapter it will be obvious how I think the members of the University should have voted.

I propose to discuss two themes. First, '*différance*' (spelled with an 'a' instead of the 'e' usual in both French and English), something Derrida identifies as his greatest claim to importance in the history of philosophy, and then 'deconstruction', a term coined by Derrida that has since passed into general use and assumed a much wider and vaguer meaning than the meaning he himself intended.

The concept of *différance*, as Derrida acknowledges, grows out of the 'semiotics' (theory of signs) of Ferdinand de Saussure (1857–1913). Its meaning consists in a number of claims Derrida makes about it which can be set out in the form of an extended series of inferences. I shall give numbers to the individual steps in this series.

(1) As Saussure shows, says Derrida, difference (with the usual 'e') is the condition of any sign's (word's) possessing meaning. The meaning of a word is not, as the 'classical' view holds, atomic, but is, rather, holistic. The meaning of a word is determined by its interaction with other meaningful words, by the role it plays in language as a whole. And, of course, to possess a distinctive meaning, the

word must have a distinctive role, one that is *different* from the role played by every other word. *Différance*, says Derrida, embraces difference in this sense. It is, therefore, the fundamental presupposition of all meaning, 'the movement according to which language, or any code or system of referral in general is constituted.'[1]

Thus far, *différance* seems to embody good, if not particularly original, sense. (Analytic philosophers such as Frege, Wittgenstein, Quine and Sellars have each, in their own way, emphasised that meaning is holistic; in fact one would be hard-pressed to find anyone at all, writing after about 1950, prepared to defend Derrida's so-called 'classical' view.) The basic point is that a child who reliably utters the sound 'rabbit' in the presence of rabbits but has no mastery of, say, 'animal', 'fur', 'food' or 'pest', as well as more remote expressions like 'not' and 'if . . . then', has not yet learnt the meaning of 'rabbit'. If she does not understand 'A rabbit is an animal', which in turn requires understanding 'an animal is not a plant', and so on, she has yet to master the word.

(2) Language, Derrida now claims, produces that which is 'present' (D p. 13). Specifically, since to be something present is to be different from everything else, language 'spaces' things out, puts gaps or boundaries between them. (A boundary is where something *starts*, not where it stops, remarks Heidegger.) Language, that is to say, supplies the identity – and therefore difference – conditions for what 'presences'; tells us, for example, what is figure and what background.

But since, Derrida now claims, *différance* produces language it follows that it produces the things that 'presence', i.e. that it 'spaces' them out as the things they are. 'Spacing' is one of the central functions of *différance*.

(3) To be a present thing is to have a past and a future. (To be present, for example, as a sapling is to be something that was a seed and will be a tree.) So language, as an essential part of its production of what is present, 'temporises' i.e. 'temporalises' what is present. It 'defers' part of its being to the past and part to the future. (Derrida puns here, in a rather obscure way, on the French verb *différer*, which can mean both 'to defer' and 'to differentiate'.) Language, therefore, temporalises what 'presences'. And, since *différance* is what produces language, fundamentally it is *différance* which temporalises that which 'presences'. This is another essential characteristic of *différance*: not only does it 'space'; it 'temporalises', too.

Hence (4), *différance* is the origin of space and time.

What are we to make of this apparent pulling of a very large rabbit out of a rather small hat? On a certain reading, the movement of thought from (2) to (4) is perfectly in order. It is, that is to say, *true* that the world shows up, 'presences', differently to different linguistic communities. And it is true that, without the 'spacing' and 'temporalising' effect of language, reality would not show up as a space–time world at all. So it is true that the fact that things 'presence' to us and the way they 'presence' are dependent on our language. Hence, if Derrida is right about the relation between language and *différance*, the spatio-temporal organisation of reality is dependent on *différance*.

Of course, the fact that the that and the how of reality's *presencing* to us is dependent on language does not at all mean that reality itself is. The latter claim would be absurd since it would entail that nothing at all existed prior to linguistic humanity's appearance on the scene.

We need, then, to make a sharp distinction between:

(*a*) Language produces the spatio-temporal organisation of reality;

and

(*b*) Language produces space and time.

Which of these does Derrida mean to claim? It is, I think, impossible to tell. He often produces the language of (*b*) (e.g. at D p. 13) – revelling, one suspects, in the grand effect it produces – but it always remains open to him to say that (*b*) is only intended as an elliptical way of saying (*a*).

What, now, about (1) in the foregoing chain of reasoning, the claim that it is *différance* which produces 'language, or any code or system of referral in general'? What *is différance*?

Once again, I think, a 'deconstruction' (of which more shortly) of Derrida's writings discloses two views which I shall call (A) and (B).

(A) *Différance* is, says Derrida, 'older' than Heidegger's 'Being' (D p. 26). It is the origin of space and time. So, really, it is God, the god of numerous creation myths who creates the world through difference, through setting things apart: earth and sky, dry land and sea and everything that lives on the land, in the sky, or in the sea. It is, in fact, Heraclitus' *polemos* (strife or war). (That *différance* so strongly calls to mind Heraclitus' fragment 53, 'strife is the father of all . . .', can hardly be accidental.) Of course, this God of *polemos* is a god about whose intrinsic nature nothing can be said. As the presupposition of all language, *différance* is 'unnameable' in language (D p. 18). (This is actually a terrible inference; grammar is a presupposition of all language, as are people, but a language can, of course, talk about its own grammar and about people – but let us not dwell on this point.) So *différance* is ineffable, the object of a kind of 'negative theology' (D p. 6).

(B) Having raised the idea of a negative theology, Derrida, at a different point in '*Différance*', denies he subscribes to one. *Différance*, he says, is not an origin or cause of anything. It is not an authority; he is, rather, devoted to abolishing all authority. *Différance* is not at all like Heidegger's Being: there are 'no capital Bs' for us, says Derrida. We *accept* the 'death of God' (D pp. 21–2).

But what, then, on this deflationary account, *is différance*? Let us return to its Saussurian kernel. Following Saussure, Derrida observes that the existence of meaningful words depends on difference: on there being differentiation, differences, between the roles played by words within the network of language. This is true. Equally true, however, is that semantic difference depends on there being meaningful words. For, in general, 'there is difference' entails 'there are things that are different'. This means that 'there is (semantic) difference' and 'there are meaningful words' are *equivalent* statements. Semantic difference, therefore, is not temporally or causally prior to language. It simply *is* language, with one of its essential features selected for special attention. *Différance*, then, on this second account, does not designate an origin of language but rather simply highlights an important feature of anything that is to count as a language.

Account (A), when the chips are down, is not an account Derrida really wishes to subscribe to. For what it amounts to is metaphysics of the grandest sort, and 'metaphysics' is absolute anathema to Derrida. (In *On Spirit* he claims that what got Heidegger into Nazism was the 'metaphysical' character of his earlier philosophy.) One can only conclude that the hints of account (A) are present purely for reasons of showmanship, to provide Derrida's writings with a rhetorical lustre, an air of quasi-Greek profundity.

Given this, what, finally, does the claim that, since (*a*) language produces space and time and (*b*) *différance* produces language, it follows that (*c*) *différance* produces space and time really amount to? It amounts to the claim that language, the essential feature of which is differentiated roles for the words it contains, produces our spatio-temporally organised *experience* of the world. This is true but hardly original, hardly justifying of entry to the pantheon of great philosophers. Long before Derrida, Heidegger put the insight into one sentence: 'When we go to the well we go through the word "well".'

What, to turn now to the second major term in Derrida's philosophy, is 'deconstruction'? The notion is based on a view about the meaning of words which Derrida calls 'dissemination'. Dissemination is more than mere 'polysemy'. Polysemy is 'a multiplicity of meaning, a kind of ambiguity' which none the less belongs to a given 'regime of meaning'. Dissemination includes that kind of multiplicity of meaning but also another kind: that which transcends any given regime of meaning.[2] So, for example (I think), while the difference in the meaning of 'cut' in 'cut the cake' and 'cut the cards' exhibits polysemy – both meanings operate within that 'regime' which has to do with dividing up physical objects – the occurrence of 'cut' in 'to cut a former friend' exhibits the dissemination of the word's meaning, since we have moved to the 'regime' that has to do with human relations. The essential thing about dissemination is, then, as I shall put it, multidimensionality. The claim that the meaning of a word or text is disseminated is the claim that it has many *trans*dimensional meanings – indefinitely many, since, claims Derrida, a word's meaning exceeds not just a single regime of meaning but any finite set of such regimes (FP p. 98).

The meaning of a word is, we saw earlier, constituted by its role in language. But what we now see is that that role is indefinitely multidimensional. Since texts are made up of words it follows, therefore, that any text is indefinitely multidimensional in meaning. And what follows from that is that any interpretation which claims to present *the* unique and complete meaning of a text is mistaken. Deconstruction, the deconstruction of a particular text, is the demonstration of this general thesis in a particular instance.

At first sight, the general thesis looks to be absurd, since it seems to entail the impossibility of communication. King Edward I was known as 'the hammer of the Scots'. And Nietzsche spoke of himself as 'doing philosophy with a hammer'. So, it seems, when Bert, on the building site, says 'Pass the hammer, Jim', Jim has no idea whether he wants a king, a pen or a thing for knocking in nails. This of course is ridiculous. Normally, human conversation is smooth and unproblematic, untroubled by any kind of ambiguity. But – this is Derrida's point – the reason it is so is that it generally takes place against a shared but unspoken background 'regime of meaning' (elsewhere Derrida calls it a 'centre') which blocks out all other regimes. Bert and Jim communicate without difficulty because they share the unspoken assumption that their discourse occurs (not within the dimension of English history or German philosophy but rather) within the dimension of equipment.

Derrida says that 'deconstruct' is 'intended to translate a word such as *Abbau* [literally, "unbuild"] in Heidegger . . . it's a matter of gaining access to the mode in which a system or structure, or ensemble, is constructed or constituted' (FP p. 97). So what deconstruction does is to disclose the particular 'regime' or 'centre' on which a discourse is based but which normally escapes attention. Speaking of Western science and philosophy, in particular, Derrida says that it always presupposes a 'centre, which is, by definition, unique and constitutes the very thing within a structure which, while governing the structure, escapes structurality'[3] and usually, therefore, articulation.

Deconstruction, then, articulates a 'regime' or 'centre'. And by making us aware of the possibility of other 'centres' it makes us aware of the possibilities of meanings within the text other than the ostensible, received or socially sanctioned meaning that is ascribed to it. What is the point of this?

One of Derrida's famous (or infamous) remarks is 'There is nothing outside the text'.[4] As before, let us assume that Derrida is not asserting that nothing existed before human, text-making creatures came into being. What he is emphasising, then, is that there is nothing *in our experience* save that which is determined by language. The way reality shows up for us is entirely determined by the language we speak. But, having understood dissemination, we now know that our language is inexhaustibly rich. So, therefore, is our world. Hence deconstruction calls us away from the claustrophobic 'logocentrism' (FP p. 104) of supposing that we (or the natural scientist) possess, or might possess, complete and final knowledge of reality.

'Deconstruction', claims Derrida, is 'a means of carrying out . . . [a] going beyond being, beyond being as presence, at least' (FP p. 97). It is a means, that is to say, of overcoming the idea that the world as it is 'present' to us in everyday experience or in natural science constitutes the totality of what there is.

To escape the claustrophobic illusion of completeness, to realise what Derrida calls our 'non-knowledge', opens us up to the infinite wonder of things and is, therefore, no doubt, spiritually improving.

Yet Derrida claims more than this for deconstruction. He claims that it is 'political', 'transgressive' and 'dangerous' (FP p. 95). There must, therefore, be more to deconstruction than we have yet discovered.

I think that when Derrida calls deconstruction 'dangerous', etc., he is speaking of it not in general, but specifically in its application to major, life-shaping texts belonging, mainly, to literature, the human sciences and philosophy. Like all texts, texts such as these possess a hidden 'centre'. But, with respect to many, and perhaps all, of the texts belonging to this genre, something else if true: the centre involves a pair of opposite terms, where one is valued positively and the other negatively. Thus, in Plato, for example, one finds Being opposed to becoming, in Christianity spirit opposed to flesh, in Kant the intellectual opposed to the sensory, in Marx the worker opposed to the capitalist, in Schopenhauer the male opposed to the female, with, in each case, the first valued positively, the second negatively.

Derrida suggests that to deconstruct a philosophical text is to 'reconsider all the pairs of opposites on which philosophy is constructed' (D p. 17). As with the deconstruction of any text, one articulates the hidden centre which in this case involves articulating the hidden opposition and hidden valuation. And then one 'reconsiders' it. With regard to Plato, for example, one might point out that the negative evaluation of 'becoming' involves focusing on its association with 'instability', 'disorder' 'imperfection', and shutting out that alternative centre – or perspective – in terms of which 'becoming' connotes 'excitement', 'growth', 'development', while 'being' stands for 'tedium', 'stiffness' and 'decline'. Deconstruction of a philosophical text is a matter, then, of (*a*) exposing the hidden centre, with its hidden opposition and valuation, on which the text rests and (*b*) constructing an alternative centre according to which the valuations are reversed. One does not, it seems to me, have to affirm this new centre as *the correct* centre – if one does one becomes a target for deconstruction oneself. One rather inhabits it 'playfully', as a temporary device for exposing the centre to be deconstructed.

Let me give an example of what I take to be deconstruction at work. One prevalent narrative – i.e. 'text' – has it that parents are boring, oppressive, conservative and unadventurous. (This was a particularly powerful narrative in the 1960s when, following Abby Hoffman's advice, one never trusted anyone over 30.) It is against this background that Milos Forman, a recent and grateful immigrant to the United States after the Russian invasion of Czechoslovakia in 1968, made his film *Taking Off*. In the film, the Middle American parents of runaway teenagers (teenagers who have run away from home, no doubt, because they understand their parents to be boring, oppressive, etc.) form a kind of support group. Initially, suited and tied, twin-setted and pearled, they appear just as the narrative says. But then, having decided that to understand their children they must try marijuana, they turn out to be amazingly unconventional, given to free love, all-night parties, naked dancing, in general to much wilder adventures than anything one imagines their run-away children (about whom they have by now completely forgotten) to have got up to. This, if I understand Derrida, is a perfect example of the disclosure of a suppressed level of meaning belonging to the word 'parent' (parent = human being, *homo ludens*, the man who plays) which results in an inversion of the opposition on which the adolescent narrative depends.

So why, then, when applied to the right kinds of texts, is deconstruction 'dangerous', 'transgressive'? Because, in a word, it reduces what presents itself as the complete and final truth as a mere 'take' on things, a perspective in relation to which there are indefinitely many alternative perspectives. The difference between 'the truth' and 'a perspective' is that, whereas it is *compulsory* to adopt the former ('I know it's true but I don't believe it' makes no sense), it is *optional* whether or not one adopts the latter ('I know that's a possible interpretation but it's not mine' makes perfect sense). Deconstruction can be dangerous because it can destroy the power of a text.

I have included Derrida in this study because he is the most famous living philosopher – to date, over five hundred books have been devoted to his work – with a reputation for great profundity. So surely, one would think, Derrida has something important to say that bears on the question of the meaning of life. The question is: what?

The answer lies, if anywhere, in the notion of deconstruction, something Derrida tends to present as an ongoing task, a way of life, a warrior existence devoted to overcoming 'logocentricism' in all its forms, which include 'European ethnocentrism' and 'phallocentrism' (FP p. 104). The deconstructive life is, then, devoted to resisting oppression, the root of which has to do with 'texts' rather than with the police: referring to the 1968 student revolution,

Derrida once remarked that deconstruction is more important than taking to the streets.

Like Foucault, then, Derrida is concerned with resistance to oppression, the repression exercised by, in Foucault's language, 'regimes of knowledge' of which we are normally unaware. But what are we to do with our freedom, once achieved? Foucault has, at least, a kind of answer to this question: we are to construct ourselves as works of art, choose, in Sartrian terms, a fundamental project to live by. As Sartre emphasises, however, choosing a project is choosing a 'world' – a world impregnated with evaluative oppositions. If, for example, I commit myself to environmentalism, then tree-preservers are valued positively and unbridled forest-loggers negatively. Hence there arises, in Derrida's language, a 'text', in other words, something ripe for deconstruction. But if it is deconstructed, then my life loses its meaning. (Notice that deconstructive theory is *itself* a text with its own oppositions: 'logocentricism' versus multiplicity of interpretation, for example. If *every* life-shaping text can and should be deconstructed, then the warrior existence of the deconstructer itself loses meaning.)

The moral of this is that deconstruction cannot contribute to a meaningful existence, since meaningfulness starts only where deconstruction ceases. This is not to say that *attempted* deconstruction cannot be incorporated into a meaningful life. Avoiding two-dimensional stereotypes, considering alternative points of view (the timber-logger does, after all, have a family to feed) is clearly all to the good. But the fact is that one's life is meaningful only to the extent that one's personal narrative together with its oppositions *retains* its power over one, only to the extent that it *resists* deconstruction.

Derrida's philosophy is devoted to the deconstruction – destruction – of the power that 'texts' have over us. But life is meaningful precisely to the extent that some text has such power. His philosophy is, therefore – for all its reputation of significance and profundity – not merely unhelpful to the quest for a meaningful life but positively antithetical to it. Derrida's philosophy, far from being an antidote to the nihilism of postmodernity, is a manifestation of it. Derrida belongs to the problem, not to its solution.

15

Later Heidegger

Grand-narrative, end-of-history, 'true-world' philosophies offered, as we saw, a meaning of life that is universal, the same for all human beings at all times and in all places. Though there is no necessary reason why this should be so – nothing in logic says that a universal meaning to life can be provided only in terms of a grand-narrative, end-of-history structure (a point to which I shall return) – the death of God, in all his forms, has, *de facto*, meant the death of the attempt to discover a universal meaning, the abandonment of the quest to discover anything that could count as *the* meaning of life. With the exception of posthumous Nietzsche's view that the meaning of life is power (which doesn't really count since posthumous Nietzsche never existed), post-death-of-God philosophers are generally agreed that there is no meaning of *life*, that life as such is meaningless; 'chaos' (Nietzsche), 'absurd' (Camus).

Given this agreed point of departure, the most common response to the resulting threat of, as Nietzsche calls it, 'nausea and suicide' (GS 107) is to suggest that the fact that *life* is meaningless in no way entails that *my life* is meaningless. A distinction is drawn, that is to say, between *universal* meaning and *personal* meaning, and the suggestion is made that the absence of the former does not entail the absence of the latter. It is further suggested that, while it is indeed true that life needs meaning to be worth living, personal meaning will do just as well as universal meaning to secure such worthwhileness. (The exception here is Camus, who, as we finally understood him, argues – in the end unconvincingly, I suggested – that a worthwhile life can't have any meaning (either universal or personal) since any meaning cuts one off from the vibrant joys of just being in the world.) This is the position adopted by (later) Nietzsche, Foucault, and, one might guess (since his outlook is in general close to that of Foucault), is the kind of thing that would be said by Derrida, too. It is, moreover, the position of those Sartrians who choose to sanitise Sartre by ignoring the darkness in his thinking, his nihilism. One is to give personal meaning to one's life by, in Nietzsche's language, creating oneself as a work of art, in Sartre's, by choosing oneself as a 'fundamental project'.

Early Heidegger takes a different tack. The meaning of one's life, for him, is established not personally but communally. None the less, he, too, joins in the general consensus that there is no such thing as a universal, community-transcending meaning of life, no meaning written into the condition of being a human being as such. In effect, then, post-death-of-God philosophy's response to the question 'What is the meaning of life?' is not to answer it, but rather to claim that (like, for example, the question 'How old is your hippopotamus?') it contains a false presupposition: the presupposition that there is such a thing as '*the* meaning of life'.

The exception to this rule of modern, 'Continental' thinking is the later Martin Heidegger. (As already mentioned, Heidegger speaks of a radical 'turn' in his thinking as having begun in about 1930, about three years after the publication of *Being and Time*, so by 'later Heidegger' I mean his writings from 1930 until his death in 1976.) For later Heidegger, as I read him, there *is* such a thing as the meaning of life. This is why I have reserved this final and concluding chapter for him. Though chronologically prior to Foucault and Derrida – as we progress, the reader may recognise the origin of some of the ideas that appear in their work – Heidegger, it seems to me, has something unique to say about the meaning of life, something which sets him apart from – and above – all the other post-death-of-God philosophers we have considered.

Later Heidegger's thinking begins – this, at least, is one point of entry – with a discussion of technology; with, in particular, a contrast between ancient, paradigmatically Greek, technology on the one hand, and modern technology on the other.

Compare and contrast the old wooden bridge, which lets the river run its course, lets it remain a river, with the modern hydro-electric dam which turns it into a reservoir. Or compare the ancient farmer who harvested those crops that were natural and native to his region with the modern agro-business which, through the use of artificial fertilisers, pesticides and genetic engineering, compels the land to yield whatever the market demands. Or compare the ancient woodcutter, who took what he needed but allowed the forest to remain the forest, with the modern timber company which clear-fells the native forest and replants with fast-growing exotic pines. It seems that, whereas ancient technology lived in respectful rapport with nature, modern technology is a kind of 'setting upon',[1] a rape or violation of nature. It seems that whereas ancient technology had a kind of gentleness to it, modern technology is, as E. F. Schumacher has called it, 'violent' technology.[2]

What explains this contrast between Greek technological practice and that of modernity? Fundamental to any kind of technology is the notion of causation. In its modern conception, Heidegger points out, causation is *making happen*, centrally, *manufacturing*. For the Greeks, on the other hand, causation, being responsible for the existence of something, is 'bringing forth', 'bringing forth out of concealment into unconcealment', a 'letting of what is not yet present arrive in its presencing' (QCT pp. 10–11). Thus the ancient wood-turner, for example, required himself to 'answer and respond to all the different kinds of wood and the shapes slumbering within the wood', the ancient sculptor thought of himself as 'releasing' the figure already present within the marble.

Greek technology was, then, not the self-assertiveness of 'making' but rather the gentleness of 'bringing forth'. What, however, to repeat the question, is the ground of this gentleness?

A fundamental Heideggerian axiom, roughly put, is that how you see the world is how you act: 'He who knows what is . . . knows what he wills in the midst of what is.'[3] How, then, did the ancient Greeks experience the world?

At the basis of the Greek understanding of reality is the notion of *poiesis*, a word which means 'bringing forth' (and also 'poetry'). The Greeks distinguished two types of bringing forth. First, *physis*, unaided bringing forth, as when a bud bursts into flower. Second, *techne* (the origin of our word 'technology'), which occurs when nature's 'blossoming' is aided by the hand of the craftsman or artist – the Greeks drew no distinction between the two, classifying both as *technites*.

In the Greek experience of reality – or 'Being' as Heidegger calls it – the relation between natural and human activity looked, then, the way it is shown in Figure 15.1.

The question remains, however, as to *why* the Greeks saw their own technological activity as – when conducted in a proper manner – continuous in the above way with nature's own creative activity.

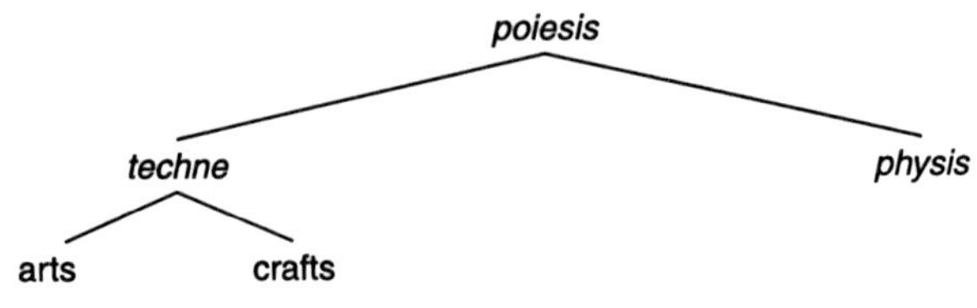

Figure 15.1

Why did the Greeks understand their own 'building', understood in the widest sense of the word, as continuous with, and a completion of, nature's own 'building'?

The model for *poiesis* is *physis*, the rising forth of the spring from the rock, the plant from the seed or the blossom from the bud. But, while the flower bud is, of course, visible and known, the, as it were, 'world bud' is utterly mysterious, incomprehensible. And, by virtue of its creative power, breathtakingly awesome.

The Greeks, then, experienced their world as created and sustained by an incomprehensible but overwhelmingly powerful force. More exactly, they experienced it as the self-display of the simultaneously self-concealing divinity 'earth'; as Sophocles called it, 'the most sublime of the gods'. The Greek cosmos was 'touched by the exciting nearness of the fire from the heavens'. It was a numinous world, a holy place.

With respect to Greek technological practice this had two consequences. First, since the fundamental order of things is divine, towards that order one shows respect and reverence. Towards, that is, the major structural features of 'the Origin' 's self-expression (its, as it were, performance artwork), towards great rivers, forests, mountains, species of animal and cultures ('peoples', Heidegger calls them), one's fundamental stance will be one of conservation. Second, where (as is inevitable) one does produce changes to the way things are, such changes will be the gentleness of 'letting what is coming arrive' rather than the violence of making. Better put, they will be a matter of allowing the divine Origin of things to complete its creative self-disclosure *through* one's own creative activities.

In a word, the gentleness of the Greeks' technology was grounded in the fact that their world disclosed itself to them as a sacred place.

Before proceeding with the exposition of Heidegger's philosophy, it will be as well to confront a criticism that is commonly raised against his portrait of the Greeks. The criticism is that it *sentimentalises* them. In reality, it is claimed, far from being the nice bunch of 'Greens' of Heidegger's myth, the Greeks were very like us, their technology every bit as violent, though of course on a smaller and less powerful scale.

The issue, here, is a historical one. Fortunately, however, it is not necessary to enter into a (probably unresolvable) historical dispute. For the fact is that Heidegger's 'Greeks' can fulfil the role they are required to perform in his thinking even if they are partially, or even totally, mythical. They are introduced, that is, (*a*) to provide a contrast that will highlight the violence of modern technology and (*b*) to provide an intimation of the kind of world-experience that is necessary to overcome such violence. And these functions they can perform even if they are entirely fictional. All that is required is that they should represent a *possible* community and a *possible* form of technological practice, not that this possibility has ever been historically actualised. What is really important about Heidegger's Greeks is that they represent a possible *future*, not that they represent an actual past. I shall continue to speak as if Heidegger's Greeks actually lived. It should be borne in mind, however, that remarks of the form 'The Greeks did such-and-such' are always translatable into statements of the form 'We could become a community who do such-and-such'.

Greek technology is, then, a conserving and bringing forth of nature. Modern technology, by contrast, is a 'setting upon', an attack upon, and violation of, nature. Many thinkers, both lay and professional, have looked with disquiet on the violence of modern technology. What is unique to Heidegger, however, is his identification of the 'essence' of modern technology – and, he holds, of modernity in general – the essential ground of its being the way it is. As the essence of Greek technology is a mode of world-understanding (a 'metaphysics', if you like, though Heidegger would not wish to use this word), so, too, is the essence of modern technology. Heidegger calls this mode *das Gestell*, which, because it is very hard to translate ('Enframing' in the standard translation; 'the set up' or 'the frame up' would be better but are still not quite right), I shall leave untranslated.

Gestell, says Heidegger, is that mode of world-understanding in which 'the real reveals itself as resource' (QCT p. 23). 'Resource' is used here in an unusually broad way to cover not just things like oil, water or electricity, but also the machines that operate on, and are powered by, such resources. Not just the machines, but also the beings that operate such machines: already in 1946 Heidegger noticed the appearance in the language of the sinister phrase 'human resource' (PLT p. 111). *Gestell*, then, is that mode of world-understanding in which everything – human beings included – shows up as resource; as, again in a very broad use of the word, 'equipment' to be deployed in technological activity.

There is, however, something missing from the characterisation of *Gestell* as it has been presented to date. The issue concerns the topic of work.

Work, conceived not as the opposite of leisure but in a broad, philosophical sense as any kind of intentional production of change in one's natural or human environment, is the human condition. All humans, Heidegger observes, of whatever culture or historical epoch, work. Not only do human beings work; they work nearly all of the time (except when they are asleep, and occasionally even then). 'Doing', as opposed to simply 'being', is, as Heidegger puts it, the 'everydayness' of human existence. But work requires that the world be experienced in work-appropriate ways – as resource. You cannot knock in a nail unless the wood–steel combination is grasped as a hammer; you cannot build a Greek temple unless the side of the hill is grasped as a potential quarry of stone; and neither can you organise the building of the temple unless your masons, sculptors and painters are grasped as human resources. The trouble with *Gestell*, as we have so far described it, is in short that it characterises *every* historical epoch, ancient Greece included. Heidegger, on the other hand, offers *Gestell* as the essence, *uniquely*, of modernity. There must, therefore, be more to *Gestell* than has so far met the eye.

Heidegger says that when *Gestell* 'holds sway' it 'drives out every other possibility of revealing' (QCT p. 27). What this suggests is that *Gestell* is not just the disclosure of things as resource: it is their disclosure as *nothing but* resource, *pure* resource. The Greek architect saw the hillside as a potential quarry. But he *also* understood it as a hillside and, as such, part of the divine order of nature's *poiesis*. Hence he was careful, in determining the site and scale of the quarry, to allow the hillside to remain itself. But where the hill shows up as *nothing but* a quarry, or as, let us say, a piece of 'real estate' ripe for 'development', there is nothing to slow, limit or guide the, as Heidegger puts it, 'unconditional self-assertion' (PLT

p. 111) of the technological will. Modern technology is, then, violent technology. It violates both non-human and human nature, not because modern humanity (or some self-serving élite within it) is especially wicked, but because, as a culture, it is afflicted by a peculiarly one-dimensional way of experiencing reality.

Lying before us, now, is a contrast between the 'gentleness' of Greek (or 'Greek') technology and the violence of modern technology. But why should we be interested in it? No doubt to some, already Green, eyes there is something very attractive about Heidegger's Greeks and something very unattractive about the modernity of Heidegger's portrait. But attractiveness is not a philosophically significant quality – *truth* is what we are interested in.

Heidegger, however, argues more than the attractiveness of Greek technological practice and the world-experience on which it is based. He argues, in effect, its *correctness*. The Greek experience of nature as *poiesis* is based on 'insight into that which is' (QCT p. 46), while the technological practice of modernity is based on a kind of blindness or illusion. To follow the argument for this, we have to enter the seemingly forbidding domain of Heidegger's philosophy of truth and 'Being'.

What is truth? According to both philosophical tradition and common sense, truth is 'correspondence', correspondence to 'the facts'. 'Bridget is a nurse' is true if and only if it is indeed a fact that Bridget is a nurse. What, however, tells us what the facts are? The traditional answer is that you just look and see. Let us, then, apply this simple procedure.

I say, pointing to the river, 'You'll never bathe in that again'. You, having bathed there every summer and firmly intending to continue the practice, dispute this. Actually, however, what I was referring to was not the river, but the particular body of water in front of us which is about to move off downstream and be replaced by a new body of water. This example may seem far-fetched – as it is. But it makes the point that simple word–object correlation, pointing, is not sufficient to establish what is being talked about, and hence not sufficient to establish what the relevant facts are against which statements are to be checked for correctness. Normally, of course, conversation flows entirely smoothly, but that is because there is a – usually unnoticed – background assumption as to the kinds of entities – for example, objects rather than the ever-changing stuffs that make them up – that are under discussion. Heidegger calls such inconspicuous background assumptions 'horizons of disclosure', occasionally, following Nietzsche, 'perspectives'.

Heidegger does not deny that truth is correspondence. His point is that the possibility of the world's showing up in such a way that true or false statements can be made about it – the possibility of its being, as I shall say, 'intelligible' – depends on horizons of disclosure; depends on, as Heidegger puts it, 'truth as disclosure'. (From now on when I talk about 'truth' without modification I mean truth as disclosure.)

Disclosure, says Heidegger, is always simultaneously 'concealment' (PLT pp. 53–4). Horizons conceal the intelligibility that would be revealed by other horizons. That, after all, is their point – how they make unambiguous communication possible. (The universal paranoia towards 'regimes of knowledge' or 'regimes of meaning' displayed by Foucault and Derrida seems to miss this entirely necessary and legitimate function of horizons of intelligibility.) Heidegger calls that which truth conceals 'the mystery'. Because of its hidden depth, because behind truth is concealed a hidden 'reservoir of the not yet revealed' (PLT p. 60), truth is 'uncanny', 'awesome' (PLT p. 68).

Initially, this is a puzzling inference. For, although, for example, the object horizon occludes the constituent-stuff horizon for the time being, the latter is certainly a horizon I can come to inhabit if I choose. By 'horizon', however, Heidegger means *ultimate* horizon. This, embodied in the language we speak, represents the ultimate limit of what, to us, is intelligible. It is, so to speak, the horizon of all our horizons.

Since it would be mere arrogance to assume that the limits of intelligibility for my historical–cultural epoch constitute the limits of intelligibility *per se*, we are forced to conclude that, in addition to what is intelligible to us, reality – 'Being' – possesses an infinite 'plenitude' of 'facets' (PLT p. 124) which would be intelligible to us were we to inhabit horizons beyond our ultimate horizon, but which, in fact, are entirely unintelligible to us. This is what makes Being an unfathomable 'mystery'.

One further point. The language we speak, together with the horizon of disclosure it embodies, is no human creation. It cannot be, since we need to possess language *already* in order to think, to plan, to form intentions – in short, to create. Language happens through human beings but not by human intention. Hence it and the world it discloses is something we *receive*, something, as Heidegger puts it, 'sent' to us. By what? All we can say is that it is sent by the real: by, that is to say, 'Being'. Being gives birth to a language and a linguistic community and so, as it were, kindles itself a light, enters the realm of intelligibility.

Being, then, has two essential characteristics. First, it discloses itself, becomes intelligible as a world (the world of the Greeks, the world of the Jews, the world of the Middle Ages and so on) by 'sending' language. But, second, it conceals itself: remains, though 'near', at the same time infinitely 'far'. (Being is, in Wim Wenders' words, 'Far Away so Close'.) These two characteristics, however, creative self-disclosure and self-concealment, are precisely the two essential characteristics of the Greek understanding of their world as nature's *poiesis*. The conclusion is, therefore, that intuitively and poetically the Greeks achieved a fundamentally *correct* understanding of truth and Being.

What this means is that Greek technological practice, 'guardianship' Heidegger calls it (*techne* or bringing forth contained within the fundamental limits of conservation), is not just attractive. It is, rather, the *correct* way for human beings to be in the world. Since the world *is* the holy place the Greeks took it to be, then, whether we realise it or not, respect and reverence, guardianship, is the correct way of being in it.

How, then, did we fall into modern technological practice, into the practice of violating, desecrating nature? Heidegger's answer is contained in one word, the word 'metaphysics',[4] a word he chooses with an eye to the traditional metaphysician's claim to have discovered *the* nature of ultimate reality.

What is 'metaphysics'? One way of describing it is to say that it consists in thinking – either explicitly or implicitly – that there is no more to truth than correspondence. It is the failure to realise that the world as one experiences it is disclosed and conditioned by a particular horizon of disclosure, a horizon that simultaneously occludes indefinitely many other horizons and conceals, therefore, indefinitely many other worlds. Metaphysics is, as I shall call it, the 'absolutisation' of some particular horizon of disclosure into *the* (one and only) way that reality is. Otherwise put, metaphysics is 'oblivion' to 'the mystery', oblivion to the awesome darkness that is the other side of our illumination of Being. To use an image Heidegger himself deploys at one point (PLT p. 124), the illusion that is metaphysics is like the illusion that the moon is a flat, illuminated disc. (PLT p. 124).

Heidegger's choice of the term 'metaphysics' is in some ways unfortunate, since it makes it look as though the phenomenon it describes is a philosopher's vice, confined to a few professional 'metaphysicians'. In fact, however, a powerful tendency towards the 'oblivion' of metaphysics is inherent in all human beings. The reason for this lies in two facts. First, that, as we have seen, work is the normal, the 'everyday' state of human beings. And, second, that *Gestell*, the reduction of things to *nothing but* resource – in other words, *a form of 'metaphysics'* – is the natural horizon that one inhabits during the process of work. This is a point Heidegger had emphasised in *Being and Time*. Let us distinguish the 'being-in-itself' of things – those properties they have independently of us and our technological activities – from their 'being-for-us' – those properties (being a hammer) they have which are dependent on our technological activities. *Being and Time*'s point is that in normal technological activity only the being-for-us of things shows up. The carpenter, for example, is unaware of the type of wood used in the shaft of his hammer, unaware of the pattern formed by the grain, unaware of the shiny coolness of the head, unaware of the faintly acrid smell of the steel in the head. All he is normally aware of is 'the thing for knocking in nails'. In normal technological activity, as Heidegger puts it in a later work, the being-in-itself of things 'disappears into usefulness' (PLT p. 46).

The *threat of Gestell*, of 'metaphysics', then, surrounds every historical epoch. Why, then, is its 'world-historical' take-over unique to modernity? What saved the Greeks? In a word, according to Heidegger, 'the festival', the authentic 'holiday' (holy-day).[5] What is that?

First, a break from work. The modern holiday is typically not really that at all, but is part, rather, of the work-system – a period of stress-relief designed to return one to the workforce as an even more efficient productive unit than before. The authentic holiday, on the other hand, is genuine time out from work, a genuine stepping out of the 'everydayness' in which things show up as pure resource.

A stepping out of everydayness into what? Partly, when he talks of 'the festival' Heidegger has in mind the gathering in the Greek temple, at the Olympic Games or in the medieval cathedral. Principally, however, what he is interested in is the mood or mode of world-disclosure[6] that may well be inhabited by many of the participants on such occasions but is, in fact, independent of them. The, as I shall call it, 'festive' mood is something one may, as an individual, inhabit on any occasion but, equally, something one may never inhabit, whatever communal gatherings one participates in. In this mood man steps, says Heidegger, into 'the full breadth of the space proper to his essence' (QCT p. 39).

This stepping out of the narrowness of *Gestell* and into the breadth of a proper space involves two things. First, instead of being shut down to their being-for-us, things show up in their 'ownness', in other words, their being-in-itself. In the festive mode of disclosure, therefore, we step into the *fullness* of the world that is disclosed to us by the language, by the 'clearing of Being', that we inhabit. The wooded hillside, that is, shows up not merely as a store of building material but also as a hillside that is home to the flora and fauna that inhabit it. Second, we step into an intuitive sense of our world as nature's *poiesis*. We step, that is, out of 'the dull overcastness of the everyday' and into 'the radiance' that comes from an intuitive apprehension of the infinite depth, the boundlessness of Being. And we step, too, into 'the wonder that around us a world worlds, that there is something rather than nothing, that there are things, and we ourselves are in their midst'. We step, in other words, into an apprehension of our world as something *granted* to us, something which, rather than being *of course* there, is something which *might not have been*, something fragile and precious. As a result, we experience a profound sense of 'gratitude', gratitude for the 'clearing', for illumination, for light, gratitude that there is something rather than nothing. This is what makes the festive state *festive* – a celebration.

Each aspect of this stepping out of *Gestell* and into a proper spaciousness is important to being a 'guardian'. That things show up in their being-in-itself is essential to our knowing *how* to care for them: unless something shows up in its 'ownness', as a forest rather than as a mere supply of timber, one cannot possibly care for it as a forest. And unless something shows up in the holy 'radiance' of *poiesis* one will not be *motivated* to care for it. (One may, of course, be moved to preserve a forest for the sake of the tourist dollars it represents, but that is merely a subtle form of exploitation, not genuine guardianship.)

What, then, we lack, and what, both as a culture and as

individuals we need to recover, is the festive mode of world-disclosure. (According to Heidegger, art, art that renders the world transparent to the blue depths of *poiesis*, has here a crucial role to play.[7]) Until we cease to be 'workaholics' we will continue to be imprisoned by *Gestell* and will continue with our violation of nature.

To summarise and make explicit the relevance of the foregoing discussion to the main theme of this book: in distinction from all the other post-death-of-God philosophers we have discussed, Heidegger does think that there is a meaning to life as such, a task which belongs to, constitutes the 'essence' (QCT p. 28, PLT p. 147) of the human being as such.[8] This is the task of being the 'guardians' of our world, of living in such a way that the changes we make to it are always 'bringings forth' rather than violations, bringings forth that are always circumscribed by the will to conserve the fundamental order of things that is granted to us. (Of course, the ways in which different human beings can best be guardians are as diverse as the different facticities in which they find themselves.)

The human being as the guardian of its world stands in the starkest of contrasts to modern man as its exploiter. This is why Heidegger speaks of the transition of our culture as a whole from exploitation to guardianship as 'the turning' (QCT pp. 36ff.). The transition of our culture as a whole from violence to guardianship is a turning from modernity to a *genuinely* postmodern age.

Many of us, as individuals, have already understood something like guardianship as the meaning of our lives. We already recycle refuse, oppose genetically engineered food, oppose World Bank-funded irrigation schemes that destroy valleys and villages, oppose IMF schemes that turn Third World farmers into slaves of First World multinationals, make our houses, in Frank Lloyd Wright's words, 'of' rather than 'on' the hill. But what is important about Heidegger is not that he believes in these things, too. What is important and unique about him is that he enables us – given the correctness of his philosophy of Being and truth – not merely to *believe* guardianship to be the meaning of life, but rather to *know* it.

In Chapter 11, at the end of my discussion of Sartre, I left hanging in the air a fundamental problem. Sartre argues, remember, that who I am, my fundamental 'project' or set of fundamental values, is the product of my free but groundless choice. Being groundless, however, that choice and the life that flows from it is, he says, 'absurd', meaningless.

If we are to escape this depressing conclusion, I suggested, then one's fundamental project needs to be given to one *in and with* one's facticity. Rather than 'existence' being 'prior to essence', essence must be inseparable from existence. To avoid meaninglessness, our existence must be, as one might put it, always already 'essenced'.

Early Heidegger, the Heidegger we met in Chapter 8, seemed initially to offer the promise of showing this to be the case. I do not choose (and hence do not groundlessly, absurdly, choose) my fundamental project, he seems to demonstrate, because that project is constituted by my 'heritage', a heritage I find myself '*already* in' as I grow to adulthood within a given culture. This, together with the details of my particular facticity, gives me my fundamental project. In *Being and Time*, '*Wesen*' really is '*gewesen*'.

Yet Sartre, as we saw (pp. 158–9 above) has a simple but telling objection to this claim. That I am born into a fundamental set of values does not, of necessity, make them *my* values. Though brought up in France, someone who thinks New York to be 'where it's at' may feel herself thoroughly alienated from the French cultural and ethical tradition. To be or not to be (in a more than legalistic sense) French is, therefore, inescapably a matter of choice.

The question that is now before us is: does later Heidegger do any better than earlier in resisting the argument for Sartrian absurdity? Does he have any greater success at showing that we have an 'essence' that is given to us *along with* our 'existence', an essence that we possess completely independently of any choices we might or might not make?

Later Heidegger, as we have seen, claims that we all, simply by virtue of being human beings, have, in Sartre's language, a fundamental project: to be guardians of our world. This – Heidegger even uses Sartrian language to make the point – is our 'essence' (QCT p. 28). To a Sartrian, of course, this claim is as a red rag to a bull. Guardianship, she will respond, like any other fundamental project, is a matter of foundational choice (and therefore groundless choice – though she may choose not to dwell on this point). Whether I am to be a conserver of things or an exploiter of resources is absolutely up to me. To pretend otherwise is nothing but 'bad faith'.

In considering this, let us ask first of all what this 'world' is of which human beings are to be, according to Heidegger, the guardians? It is, first of all, the fundamental order of things, natural and human, in the midst of which I find myself. Heidegger calls this fundamental order 'the fourfold of earth, sky, divinities, and mortals' (PLT pp. 149–50, 178–9) – roughly speaking, land, climate, community-creating customs personified by the lives of 'divine' figures (roughly 'role models'), and ourselves.[9] But world is something else, too, something the Greeks indicated by calling it nature's *poiesis*, and Heidegger by speaking of it as the self-disclosure of the self-concealing 'mystery'. The world is, we have seen, a holy place. We might put this by saying that it has five dimensions: the four dimensions of the fourfold plus the dimension of the holy. (Heidegger actually uses the metaphor of 'dimension', here, a metaphor which he takes over from the poet Friedrich Hölderlin (see PLT p. 221).)

But since the world is a holy place it follows that *we have no choice* but to stand to it in a relation of respect and reverence. For the holy simply *is* that before which one bows down in awe. If, in one's actions, one does not reverence the world, then one simply *does not understand* its holiness. If one becomes its exploiter rather than its guardian, then, as we have seen, one is a victim of that intellectual and spiritual blindness which Heidegger calls (in his special sense of the word) 'metaphysics'.

Another word Heidegger uses in place of 'metaphysics' is 'forgetfulness of Being'; forgetfulness of the depth, power, might, majesty and mystery of Being. (Forgetfulness of Being, to repeat the metaphor Heidegger takes over from Rilke, is like taking the moon to be a flat, illuminated disc.) Sartre's philosophy – though he does not always highlight this characteristic – is profoundly nihilistic, a philosophy of despair. We now understand why this is so, what is the source of Sartrian despair. It is precisely 'forgetfulness of Being'. The reason, that is to say, he thinks we cannot escape the absurdity of basing our lives on groundless choice is that – archetypal modern man that he is – he has lost the feeling of awe: the understanding of reality as so awesome as to take our breath away. Less metaphorically, he has lost the sense of the world as a place whose sacredness deprives us of both the necessity and possibility of *choosing* whether or not to become its guardian.

Bismarck (of all people) once said one should never trust a man who is insensible to the wonders of nature. What he had in mind, I think, is the fact that for post-death-of-God humanity nature represents one of the few avenues to the experience of awe that still remains open. But Sartre, like Socrates (though profoundly unlike

Camus), hated nature. The edges of his world were the edges of Paris. Heidegger, on the other hand, lived his entire life in and around the Black Forest, and wrote much of his philosophy in a simple ski-hut in a clearing in its midst. This, I think, explains a lot. Philosophy, as someone wisely remarked, is usually autobiography.

One final remark.

Earlier I referred to Heidegger as, along with all the other figures discussed in Part II of this book, a 'post-death-of-God' philosopher. But, it might be asked, isn't Heidegger's 'Being' – particularly in view of the fact that it is written with a capital 'B' – actually just another name for God? Isn't, in fact, the fundamental difference between Heidegger and the Nietzscheans that, whereas they think that God is dead, he believes him to be still alive? In so far, then, as the truth about the meaning of life is to be found in Heidegger, doesn't that truth really consist in the discovery that, after all, God *didn't* die?

Yes and no. Heidegger denies many times that Being has anything to do with the God of traditional Christian theology. He has nothing but scorn for a theology that seeks to diminish God's majesty and mystery by endowing him with a nature determined by 'articles of faith and Church dogmas' (being a first cause, being wholly benevolent, an intelligent designer and so on). On the other hand, as we have seen, Being is clearly, for Heidegger, an object of reverence and awe, the object of *religious* feeling. So Being surely is *some* kind of a God, a fact confirmed by the title of Heidegger's final address to the public at large (a 1966 interview with the German magazine *Der Spiegel*), 'Only a God can save us'. Since he argues, as we have seen, that only the overcoming of 'oblivion of Being' can save us, 'Being' and 'God' must be the same.

Specifically, I think, what Heidegger believes in is not the 'god of the [Christian] philosophers' but rather the 'God of the poets'. He believes, in particular, in Friedrich Hölderlin's 'unknown God' who approaches us in the sight of 'familiar' things (PLT p. 225): a God who, unlike the God of traditional Christian theology, is genuinely mysterious and so genuinely 'far away', but one who is also, again unlike the Christian God, 'the nearest of all', immanent in the world, 'so close' to us. It is with this God, Hölderlin's and Wim Wenders's God, that Heidegger identifies Being.

But this is not the God we have been discussing so far. Throughout this book, 'God' has been used as a synonym for 'true world'.

To affirm a God in this sense is to affirm a true world and the grand, apocalyptic narrative of which it is the conclusion.

This, it is important to see, Heidegger does *not* do. Although he affirms a meaning of life that is both universal and discovered (rather than chosen), it is not a grand-narrative meaning. There is no 'end of history' in Heidegger, no crossing the rainbow bridge into a final paradise. Rather, the task of guardianship is ongoing and endless.

Earlier, in discussing Schopenhauer (pp. 42–3 above), I suggested that the penalty for defining one's life in terms of a goal that is extinguished by its achievement is boredom. But to define human life in terms of a goal that constitutes an 'end to history' *is*, surely, to define it in terms of a goal that is so extinguished. It would seem, then, that the 'end of history' means, in fact, not entry into paradise but rather entry into boredom. Hence the fact that Heidegger is no grand narrator, that in *this* sense God is dead for him, too, speaks in an important way in favour of his philosophy.

Further reading

Chapter 1

R. E. Allen *Studies in Plato's Metaphysics*, London: Routledge & Kegal Paul, 1965.

R. Kraut (ed.) *The Cambridge Companion to Plato*, Cambridge: Cambridge University Press, 1992.

Chapter 2

P. Guyer (ed.) *The Cambridge Companion to Kant*, Cambridge: Cambridge University Press, 1992.

R. Walker *Kant*, London: Routledge & Kegan Paul, 1978.

Chapter 3

J. E. Atwell *Schopenhauer: The Human Character*, Philadelphia, Pa: Temple University Press, 1990.

C. Janaway *Schopenhauer*, Oxford: Oxford University Press, 1994.

J. P. Young *Willing and Unwilling: A Study in the Philosophy of Arthur Schopenhauer*, Dordrecht: Nijhoff, 1987.

Chapters 4, 7 and 8

A. Nehamas *Nietzsche: Life as Literature*, Cambridge, Mass.: Harvard University Press, 1985.

R. Schacht *Nietzsche*, London: Routledge & Kegan Paul, 1983.

J. P. Young *Nietzsche's Philosophy of Art*, Cambridge: Cambridge University Press, 1992.

Chapters 5 and 6

F. C. Beiser (ed.) *The Cambridge Campanion to Hegel*, Cambridge: Cambridge University Press, 1993.
T. Pinkard *Hegel's Phenomenology: The Sociality of Reason*, Cambridge: Cambridge University Press, 1994.
C. Taylor *Hegel*, Cambridge: Cambridge University Press, 1975.
A. Wood *Karl Marx*, London: Routledge & Kegan Paul, 1981.

Chapter 9

H. Dreyfus *Being-in-the-World*, Cambridge, Mass.: MIT Press, 1991.
S. Mulhall *Heidegger and 'Being and Time'*, London: Routledge, 1996.
J. P. Young *Heidegger, Philosophy, Nazism*, Cambridge: Cambridge University Press, 1997.

Chapters 10 and 11

A. Danto *Sartre*, London: Fontana, 1975.
I. Murdoch *Sartre*, London: Vintage, 1999.

Chapter 12

P. McCarthy *Camus*, New York: Random House, 1982.
D. A. Spritzen *Camus: A Critical Examination*, Philadelphia, Pa: Temple University Press, 1988.

Chapter 13

H. Dreyfus and P. Rabinow *Michel Foucault: Beyond Structuralism and Hermenutics*, Chicago, Ill.: University of Chicago Press, 1983.
L. McNay *Foucault: A Critical Introduction*, New York: Continuum, 1994.

Chapter 14

R. Gasché *Inventions of Difference: On Jaques Derrida*, Cambridge, Mass.: Harvard University Press, 1994.
I. Harvey *Derrida and the Economy of Difference*, Bloomington, Ind.: Indiana University Press, 1986.

Chapter 15

J. P. Young *Heidegger's Philosophy of Art*, Cambridge: Cambridge University Press, 2001.

—— *Heidegger's Later Philosophy*, Cambridge: Cambridge University Press, 2002.

Notes

Introduction

1 Here, and from now on, I abandon the 'scare quotes' round 'true world'. Whenever the phrase occurs, however, they should be imagined to be there, lending it a tone of mild irony.

2 The basic definition of 'metaphysics' is 'the study of what ultimately exists'. Sometimes, however, philosophers emphasise the etymological components of the word – meta-physics, above-the-physical – so that the word is used in a more restricted way (particularly by nineteenth-century Germans) to mean 'the study of the (putative) supra-natural world'. A third use of 'metaphysics', which will not appear until Chapter 15, is introduced by Heidegger. In this book the first of these three uses will be by far the most common.

3 If I know someone has drunk a slow-acting, but invariably fatal, poison, I may correctly say 'You're dead' even though you are, in fact, still alive. When Nietzsche announced the death of God in 1882, he spoke with the prescience of the seer. He knew perfectly well that Marxism – 'socialism', as he called it – was a perpetuation of the idea of God by other means: he called it God's 'shadow'. But he also knew that this form of the idea had to 'die', too. It is, therefore, no objection to Nietzsche to point out that 'God's' death-throes did not completely end until the fall of the Berlin Wall (the final and visible collapse of communism) in 1989.

4 'Life' is not the same as 'my life'. While 'life is meaningful' entails 'my life is meaningful', on the surface, at least, it would seem that my life might be meaningful even if life as such were not. I shall return to this point later on.

Plato

1 *Plato's Phaedrus*, trans. R. M. Hackforth, Cambridge: Cambridge University Press, 1952. References are to the so-called Stephanus numbers given in the margins of this (and every) Plato translation.

2 I have somewhat simplified the structure of the dialogue at this point.

3 It is hard to think why the Forms of colours, smells and sounds should not be equally present in sense experience. (That there should be such Forms is required for the theory of Forms to function as a theory of linguistic meaning.) Socrates ought to mean, here, that beauty is unique among the 'moral' Forms, the Forms (justice, wisdom, temperance, courage and so on) that are Forms of *values*.

4 In the *Meno* Plato 'proves' that knowledge is really recollection by getting a slave boy to solve a mathematical problem even though Socrates has done nothing but ask him questions – the so-called 'Socratic method'.

5 Michel Foucault, whom we shall meet in a later chapter, comments:

> it's very significant that when Plato tries to integrate love for boys and friendship he is obliged to put aside sexual relations. Friendship is reciprocal and sexual relationships are not reciprocal: in sexual relations you can penetrate or you are penetrated.

Lack of reciprocity, he adds, was, for the Greeks, not a problem so far as women were concerned. But it was with regard to boys since they were future citizens and should not, therefore, be used as sex objects (*The Foucault Reader*, ed. P. Rabinow, London: Penguin, 1991, pp. 344–6). This passage seems to tell us something about the Greeks, and something about Foucault himself.

6 In the *Timaeus* the world is the creation of a divine craftsman who, following the model of the Forms, attempts to reproduce their perfection in his creation. Forced, however, to work with inadequate and unstable materials (matter), which he did not create, he cannot do so.

Kant and Christianity

1 *Critique of Pure Reason*, trans. N. Kemp Smith, London: Macmillan, 1964. References are to the numbers given in the margins ('A' refers to the first German edition, 'B' to the second).

2 On 'deconstruction' see Chapter 14 below.

Schopenhauer

1 *The World as Will and Representation*, 2 vols, trans. E. F. J. Payne, New York: Dover, 1966, hereafter referred to as WR I, volume I, and WR II, volume II.

2 *Parerga and Paralipomena*, 2 vols, trans. E. F. J. Payne, Oxford: Clarendon Press, 1974, vol. II, pp. 614–15.

3 This last point, as we shall see, is an affirmation of 'the eternal recurrence of the same', a doctrine often thought to have been invented by Nietzsche.

4 I think that Tennessee Williams must have read Schopenhauer, since there is a very similar lamentation over the fate of turtles in *Suddenly Last Summer*.

5 Not all games are trivial or pointless. Important games like football have, it seems to me, the function of gathering the community together in a clarifying celebration of itself. But that is another story.

6 Since the Sanskrit texts were translated (into English) for the first time during Schopenhauer's lifetime, he was the first major Western philosopher to have access to Buddhist (and Hindu) thought.

7 For interesting but complex reasons he regards suicide, as it occurs in the West, as, in fact, an *affirmation* of the will, of life (though not, of course, of the suicide's own life). See WR I section 69.

8 In my book on Schopenhauer, *Willing and Unwilling: A Study in the Philosophy of Arthur Schopenhauer*, Dordrecht: Nijhoff, 1987, I have suggested that Schopenhauer, particularly later Schopenhauer, can be read as proposing a *three*-part metaphysics – phenomenon, will and thing in itself – whereby he *denies* the identity of the will with the thing in itself. Will, while meta-physical, above physics, falls short of being the thing in itself. Such a reading would resolve the above

inconsistency. Here, however, I have not proposed this reading because it is not how Nietzsche read him, and is not the solution to the inconsistency Nietzsche proposes. Here, that is to say, my prime concern has been to present Schopenhauer's ultimately ambiguous philosophy in such a way as to reveal where the younger Nietzsche is 'coming from'.

Early Nietzsche

1 BT refers to *The Birth of Tragedy*, trans. W. Kaufmann, New York: Vintage Press, 1966. The numbers refer to sections, not to pages.

2 *On the whole* Nietzsche removes this inconsistency. Sometimes, however, he suggests that the primordial unity itself is 'ever suffering and contradictory and has need of rapt vision and delightful illusion to redeem itself' (BT 4). The child-artist creates the world in order to distract itself from its own pain. This messes everything up. It is inconsistent with 'individuation is the primal cause of evil' (BT 10) and makes it incomprehensible why anyone should find 'metaphysical comfort' in identification with the primordial unity – it re-creates, that is to say, the Schopenhauerian inconsistency that has just been resolved. Moreover, the reference to 'delightful illusion', with its suggestion that the primordial unity is an *Apollonian* artist, indicates a confusion in Nietzsche's mind between the two senses of 'Apollonian'. The only 'artwork' the primordial unity can create is the Apollonian world, in the *mundane* sense of the word. All it can create is the 'dream'. Apollonian art, however, is that world raised to a state of glory. It is a dream *within* a dream which only *human* artists can have. Conceived as an artist, in fact, the primordial unity is *neither* an Apollonian *nor* a Dionysian artist. Nietzsche's categories do not cover this case.

3 Kant himself thought that we could have the negative knowledge about the thing in itself that it is non-spatio-temporal. In the 'Transcendental Dialectic' of the *Critique of Pure Reason* he argues that insoluble 'antinomies', paradoxes, arise from the supposition that time and space have mind-independent reality – for example that space is both finite and infinite, that the world both had a beginning and has always existed. While these arguments are of great interest, it is pretty obvious that they cannot finally be sound: contemporary science, while

containing many perplexities, does not find itself driven into intolerable antinomies by assuming, as it does, the reality of space and time.

Hegel

1 Hegel PS refers to Hegel's *Phenomenology of Spirit*, trans. A.V. Miller, Oxford: Oxford University Press, 1977. The numbers refer to paragraphs, not to pages.
2 Two-dimensional or three-dimensional shapes? Surely the latter. Beings that see a three-dimensional world two-dimensionally get wiped out before they can reproduce themselves. But if the latter, then interpretation of immediate, two-dimensional, retinal experience is involved. Hegel's apparent positing of a purely 'sense-datum' experience as the first human encounter with the world is actually highly implausible.
3 Einstein's famous remark, apropos of the indeterminism of quantum physics, that 'God does not play dice with the universe' is an expression of the project of discovering exceptionless laws of nature that Hegel attributes to reason.
4 There is a puzzle here. Human behaviour is the paradigm of reason-exhibiting behaviour. But human behaviour is governed only by tendencies, not by exceptionless laws. Why, then, should the discovery of reason in nature demand the discovery of *exceptionless* laws?
5 I am not sure that this is true. Certainly one requires culture to *articulate* Stoicism as a philosophical doctrine, but one can, surely, be an inarticulate Stoic, can live the Stoic life, without being able to articulate the principles on which it is based.
6 Hegel argues that certainty with respect to one's independence/freedom requires 'recognition' by another. But absolute spirit has no 'other'. Can it, then, possess certainty of its freedom/independence? This, I think, exposes a serious problem of consistency in Hegel's thinking.
7 For example, an arrow never reaches its target because to cover the whole distance it must cover half, and a quarter and . . . an infinite task that could only be completed in infinite time, i.e. never.
8 Things that look red in one light look brown in another, so there aren't really any coloured things at all.
9 Dreams are qualitatively indistinguishable from waking states,

so you can never really know you are awake rather than dreaming.

10 The idea of the true world, we argued, entered *philosophy* with Plato. What Hegel is discussing, however, is its entry into *history*, its becoming the shape of consciousness that is definitive of a historical epoch.

11 It is possible that Hegel is influenced here by George Berkeley's argument against John Locke. Locke had distinguished between 'primary' and 'secondary' qualities. The former – shape, size and weight, for example – are genuinely 'in' objects, 'material substances', but the latter – colour, taste, sound, for example – are only subjective impressions in the mind. One cannot, for instance, say that an *object* is red because (as the sceptics knew) in a different light it may look brown. Berkeley pointed out, however, that the same relativity arguments apply to so-called primary qualities – what looks round to one person looks oval to another – and concluded that Locke's 'material substance' is (in Hegel's word) a mere 'vacuum'. Notice that the vacuous 'material substance' looks to be a reappearance of the 'pin-cushion' view of 'substance' that appeared on p. 61 above.

Hegel (continued), with a postscript on Marx

1 There is a serious problem of consistency between Hegel's second and third histories. The third history, we have just seen, *begins* with the 'happy' state. This is, therefore, the first state, the first social condition that succeeded the pre-social 'state of nature'. According to the second history, however, the first social condition that succeeded the universal war of the 'state of nature' was the 'master–slave' society. That, of itself, is not a problem. For ancient Greece was, throughout its history, a slave-owning society. The problem is, however, that, while the third history pictures the Greek as a thriving, 'happy' person, the second (see p. 65 above) pictures the slave-owner as a decadent, alienated individual, worse off, even, than the slave he exploits and terrorises. I do not know the explanation of this apparently glaring inconsistency, nor how Hegel would seek to remove it.

2 Notice that the shift from the 'happy state' to that of 'legal status' seems, from the point of view of 'absolute knowing', a clearly *regressive* transition. The picture of history as

ever-onwards-and-upwards dialectical progress seems to have become, here, entangled with another: history as the recovery of a lost paradise.

3 Notice that Hegel seems to subscribe to a form of psychological egoism. Human action is always motivated by self-interest. Such action can, however, be aimed at the good of the whole since, sometimes, what the individual identifies as her primary self *is* the whole. This premiss is nowhere defended and might well be challenged.

4 Hegel seems to have lost sight of the rural serfs.

5 And Greece. In Plato's sketch of the ideal state in the *Republic*, craftsmen are the lowest of the social classes, public servants the highest. Since the Gymnasia of Germany and the public (private) schools of Britain were, until the middle of the last century, founded on the study of, above all, Greek, valorisation of public service and contempt for wealth survived until quite recently in an important segment of European society.

6 The battle cry of the Revolution, 'liberty, equality, fraternity' was, in fact, taken from Rousseau's *The Social Contract*.

7 This questionable impulse survives, as we shall see in Chapter 13, in the works of Michel Foucault. Since Foucault was mightily impressed by Hegel it is strange he did not see Hegel's point that the impulse represents a relatively primitive level of thinking.

8 Unlike Christianity, of course, Hegelianism offers no salvation to the *individual* soul. You and I, as individuals, will not be there at the end of time. But, then, Hegel will say, if one has understood him properly, one will see that one's *true* self is not the individual but rather the collective soul, spirit.

9 As an 'essential' phenomenon, art, Hegel claims in his 1828–9 *Lecture of Aesthetics*, 'died' with the Greeks. It is dead for us because we have moved on to something better – science. There is something basically impoverished about Hegel's conception of the human being – perhaps because he led such a boring, ivory-towered life.

10 Some scholars distinguish between Marx as, in his own way, a prophet of the end of history and Marx as a diagnostician of the ills of capitalism. While conceding that the 'Hegelian' Marx is a dead duck they suggest that the latter Marx remains an important figure with a great deal of insight into the way we are now. I am not here concerned to dispute this latter claim (though I actually believe that, even as a mere diagnostician, Marx is a

seriously flawed figure.) My claim that Marx is a dead duck refers only to the Hegelian Marx.

11 Trans. B. Fowkes, New York: Random House, 1977.

12 This was seen by Camus (see further Chapter 12 below) who rejected communism (thereby falling out with much of the left-wing French intelligentsia) because he saw that it was a religion, 'a faith . . . a new mystification', and therefore, in his eyes, a cop-out in the face of the 'absurdity' of life.

Later Nietzsche

1 In this chapter I shall introduce the following abbreviations for Nietzsche's works:

EH *Ecce Homo*, trans. R. J. Hollingdale, Harmondsworth: Penguin, 1979.
GM *The Genealogy of Morals*, trans. W. Kaufmann and R. J. Hollingdale, New York: Vintage, 1968.
GS *The Gay Science*, trans. W. Kaufmann, New York: Vintage, 1974.
TI *Twilight of the Idols*, in *The Portable Nietzsche*, trans. and ed. W. Kaufmann, New York: Penguin, 1976.
Z *Thus Spoke Zarathustra*, also in *The Portable Nietzsche*.

Unless otherwise indicated, numerals refer to sections rather than to pages.

2 Nietzsche also makes the point that to attribute 'heartlessness and unreason' (à la Schopenhauer) to the world is just as much an anthropomorphic projection as its opposite (GS 109).

3 From Maj Sjöwall and Per Wahlöö's detective story *Die Terroristen*, German translation (from the Swedish) by E. Schultz, Reinbek bei Hamburg: Rowohlt, 1977, p. 150.

4 'Theoretical' skill, I take it, is the ability to construct a life-story, 'practical' skill – something close to 'self-discipline' – the ability to live by that story.

5 As we observed in Chapter 3 (note 3) the idea of eternal recurrence occurs in Schopenhauer – who doesn't represent it as an original idea of his own. What came to Nietzsche, we must suppose, was not the idea itself but rather the particular use of it which I am about to describe.

6 My life includes my experience and knowledge of the world around me. It includes the-world-from-my-point-of-view. This,

I think, is the point of the reference to the spider in the moonlight.

7 Honoré Gabriel comte de Mirabeau (1749–91), French revolutionary politician and orator, much loved on account of his eloquence and integrity.

8 A reputation that has *some* (but not much) foundation in Nietzsche's writings, as we shall see in the next chapter.

9 Recall *The Birth of Tragedy*'s explanation of why dreams epitomise the beautiful: 'in our dreams we delight in immediate understanding of figures; all forms speak to us; there is nothing unimportant or superfluous' (BT 1).

10 In the 'Epilogue' to my *Nietzsche's Philosophy of Art* (Cambridge: Cambridge University Press, 1992), I argue that Nietzsche's forgetting was, in fact, not the genuine, *übermenschlich* forgetting he so much admired but rather repression.

11 The quotation and the biographical facts that follow are taken from Peter Conradi's *Iris Murdoch: A Life* (New York: Norton, 2001), movingly reviewed by Stuart Hampshire (who obviously knew Murdoch) in *The New York Review of Books*, vol. XLVIII, no. 18, Nov. 2001, pp. 24–6.

12 See, further, p. 109 below.

Posthumous Nietzsche

1 Martin Heidegger, *Nietzsche*, 4 vols, trans. D. Krell, New York: HarperCollins, 1991, vol. I, pp. 8–9.

2 *The Will to Power*, trans. W. Kaufmann and R. Hollingdale, New York: Vintage Press, 1968. I shall use the abbreviation WP to refer to this work, with numbers referring to sections, not to pages.

3 See Bernd Magnus, 'The use and abuse of *The Will to Power*', in *Reading Nietzsche*, ed. R. Solomon and K. Higgins, New York: Oxford, 1988, pp. 218–35.

4 A useful summary of the main conclusions of the vast *Nietzsche* study mentioned in note 1 is to be found in 'Nietzsche's Word: "God is dead"' in *Off the Beaten Track*, trans. Julian Young and Kenneth Haynes, Cambridge: Cambridge University Press, 2002, pp. 157–99.

5 Heidegger does not say this to glorify the Nazis but rather to point to the horror implicit in Nietzsche's metaphysics. Though himself an early supporter of Nazism, Heidegger had, by 1943,

rejected Nazism and become, within the limits imposed by the fact that his Nietzsche lectures were delivered under the observation of Gestapo spies, a savage critic. For at least a decade after the Second World War, Nietzsche, perceived as the philosopher of Nazism *par excellence*, was unteachable in Anglo-Saxon universities. There is a certain complex irony in the fact that while the 'Nazi' Heidegger was largely responsible for the reading of Nietzsche as a Nazi, his stance towards the 'Nazi' Nietzsche was one, not of sympathy, but of extreme antipathy. I have discussed this whole issue in Chapter 5 of my *Heidegger, Philosophy, Nazism*, Cambridge: Cambridge University Press, 1997.

6 Another alternative, to return to the Apollonianism of *The Birth of Tragedy*, might be to cover over the 'terror and horror' of existence with illusion. But that, we argued, is unlikely to constitute a successful long-term strategy.

Early Heidegger

1 *The Dream of Reason: A History of Western Philosophy from the Greeks to the Renaissance*, by Anthony Gottlieb, New York: Norton, 2001.

2 *Being and Time*, trans. J. Macquarrie and E. Robinson, Oxford: Blackwell, 1973, hereafter referred to as BT. Numbers refer to pages in the seventh German edition (given in the margins of the translation), not to the page numbers in the translation itself.

3 Notice that Heidegger here seems to declare a great deal of German metaphysics – Hegel's 'universal spirit', the Schopenhauerian/Nietzschean 'primordial unity' – inauthentic.

4 Notice that whereas Nietzsche assumes it to be a matter of free choice who one is to be, Heidegger assumes that one *discovers* who one is. Why he makes this assumption will become clear shortly.

5 In the 1930s, influenced by his reading of *Antigone*, Heidegger assimilates heritage to Sophocles' 'unwritten law divine', the law to which Antigone appeals in resisting the unjust laws of the state. Much more plausibly than Hegel's account of 'divine law' as the law of the family (see pp. 71–2 above), Heidegger reads it as being the most fundamental understanding of the proper way to live possessed by a culture. See further

my *Heidegger's Later Philosophy*, Cambridge: Cambridge University Press, 2002, chapter 7, section 2.

6 Notice that both heritage and current opinion consist in a sense of what 'one' does (or 'we' do). Both, in fact, are aspects of 'the One'. *Das Man*, is, therefore, internally complex and almost always divided against itself. It is an ambiguous phenomenon, the source of inauthenticity, but also of the possibility of authenticity.

Sartre

1 Trans. H. E. Barnes, New York: Philosophical Library, 1956, hereafter referred to as BN.

2 Sartre claims that 'existence precedes . . . essence' is a quotation from Heidegger (BN p. 438), but this is a fiction, the result, perhaps, of Sartre's apparently quite poor command of German. What Heidegger actually says is that 'the essence of Dasein lies in its existence' (BT 42), where 'existence' is used in a technical sense to mean that the question of whether or not to be authentic is an inescapable 'issue' for Dasein, a choice it cannot avoid making (BT 12). But, though *this* is a matter of choice, the question of *what it is* that constitutes my authenticity, what it is, in *Sartre's* sense that constitutes my 'essence', is, as we saw in the last chapter, determined by my facticity, specifically by 'heritage', and has nothing to do with choice. Heidegger is not an existentialist, and Sartre disguises the fundamental opposition between the two of them by claiming to be following Heidegger's lead.

3 Sartre explores the problem of action in the absence of genuine commitment in a quartet of novels called *The Paths of Liberty* written during the same period as *Being and Nothingness*. In Shakespeare's *Hamlet*, the hero remarks that 'conscience [thinking deeply about things] does make cowards of us all', makes us unable to act. The only way he can act is impulsively, on the spur of the moment, without any gathering of reasons. It is the same for Sartre's characters. The only way they can act – get married, join the communist party, die a soldier's heroic death, stab a knife into the back of one's hand – is by performing an *act gratuit*. They act without reasons because they secretly know that the search for reasons ends in action-paralysing absurdity.

4 Bad faith of the relevant sort. Along with the Paris waiter, Sartre's other example of bad faith which sticks in the mind is that of the coquette who wishes to enjoy the flattering attention of her admirer without quite – or quite yet – admitting that anything to do with physical sex is in the air (BN pp. 55–6). Here, Sartre points out, bad faith consists in a denial not of freedom, but of embodied facticity – the woman pretends to herself that she is a purely spiritual being and has nothing to do with the body whose hand the man is holding. Fascinating and insightful though it is, this example seems to me to have nothing to do with the main line of Sartre's argument. And in fact, given that 'bad faith' just means 'self-deception', there are, as we shall see in the next chapter, several other types of bad faith discussed by Sartre that have nothing at all to do with evading the 'anguish' of freedom.

Sartre (continued)

1 Sartre uses the phrase 'becoming an in-itself-for-itself' (BN pp. 90, 362) to describe this goal, but this is one of those ambiguously plastic pieces of technical terminology which make it hard to see what he is up to. In one meaning it might be used to express the desire of, for example, the gambler or the waiter to relegate the anguish-causing phenomenon of free choice to the past, so that from now on one's nature is as absolutely fixed as that of an oak tree (see p. 140 above). But on the other hand it is often used to express the project of becoming a *causa sui*, where it expresses the desire for, not a fixed nature but rather a freely chosen one. Because the phrase is confusing, I shall avoid using it.

2 That is, the self 'in itself'. Just as, for Kant, objects or things divide into the 'appearances' of things and 'things in themselves' (see Chapter 2 above), so the self divides into the self as 'appearance' and the self 'in itself'.

3 Needless to say, this autobiographical flavour has given rise to a plethora of articles devoted to exposing Sartre's 'sexism'.

4 Notice that 'indifference' towards all but the beloved must be how the lover tries to make himself 'alone in the world with the beloved'.

5 *Phaedrus* 230d:

> **Phaedrus** You, my excellent friend, strike me as the oddest of men . . . never leaving town to cross the frontier nor even, I believe, so much as setting foot outside the walls [of Athens].
> **Socrates** You must forgive me, dear friend; I'm a lover of learning, and trees and open country won't teach me anything, whereas men in the town do.

Sartre, remember, said he never felt at home anywhere except in a fifth-floor Paris apartment.

6 Of course, with respect to being a waiter and many similar aspects of identity, there is no 'inner circle' of expertise. Anyone, virtually, can tell as well as anyone else that someone is a waiter.

7 Notice that here (and also with respect to the anguish that is said to accompany the experience of freedom) Sartre assumes a given emotional response to be universal to human beings – which contradicts his official position that emotions are always the product of free choice (see pp. 133–4 above).

8 Notice that this is essentially the 'indifference' which earlier appeared as the attitude of the disappointed lover. So the special stratagem adopted by the disappointed lover now appears as a universalising of the standard attitude to others, a refusal to make any exceptions to it.

9 The final pages of *Being and Nothingness* preview a prospective book which, Sartre claims, will take up the question of ethics. Unsurprisingly, it was never written.

10 As we saw in the last chapter (note 3) Sartre's *Paths of Liberty* novels do allow for apparent acts of commitment. Brunet becomes a communist, Mathieu dies a heroic (and futile) death resisting the Germans. Since Sartre holds, however, that we all really know our lives to be meaningless, he is committed to viewing all such acts as being made in bad faith. From the perspective of *Being and Nothingness*, they have to be viewed as *pretences*, rather than authentic acts, of commitment.

11 In *The Meaning of Life*, ed. E. D. Klemke, New York: Oxford University Press, 2000, pp. 176–85.

Camus

1 Trans. J. O'Brian, London: Penguin, 2000, hereafter referred to as MS.

2 Notice that whereas 'absurd', in Camus, means 'absence of grand-narrative meaning' – which leaves open the possibility that life, or at least my life, might have some other type of meaning – 'absurd', in Sartre, means 'meaningless', period. This is why I said that one should not identify the two philosophers' use of the word. (On the other hand, given my suggestion at the end of Chapter 11 that the 'death of God' is at the root of Sartre(-One)'s notion of absurdity, they are not unrelated, either.)

3 Or, rather, reality as we understand it. For Camus, I think, absurdity is a disjunction between how we want the world to be and how we *take* it to be. How it *actually* is seems to me irrelevant to the question of whether life is, in Camus' sense, absurd.

4 A crucial question is whether 'no meaning', here, means merely 'no *grand-narrative* meaning' or, more challengingly, 'no meaning *at all*'? Later on in this chapter, I shall attempt to answer it.

5 In the *Critique of Judgment* (trans. J. C. Meredith, Oxford: Clarendon Press, 1973, pp. 450–3), Kant argues that virtuous atheism is impossible on the ground that unless one believes in a benevolent governor who steers history in the direction of moral perfection, unless one believes that history is 'on the side of' virtue, one will lapse into moral despair, will lose the will to virtuous action. Such despair, I suggest, is akin to Camus' and Kierkegaard's 'feeling of the absurd'.

6 Curiously, he ignores the fact that it is not at all obvious that one *can*, having confronted the abyss of absurdity, simply *decide* to believe in God (or Marx), any more than one can simply decide to believe that 2+2=5 or that Germany won the 1966 World Cup.

7 Notice that, though Sisyphus is immortal and we are not, this does not matter from the point of view of the personification: just as there is nothing but repetitive activity in Sisyphus' life, so there is nothing but that in our everyday lives.

8 Plato makes this point in the *Protagoras*. People who dive into wells, he says (today he would have talked about bungy jumping), are not truly courageous but simply foolhardy. True courage, he concludes, must always be accompanied by the knowledge of when it is appropriate to engage in tough or risky action and when it is not.

9 Reverting for a moment to the first account of the absurd hero, Camus says that, providing they 'know' the absurdity of life and 'mask nothing', 'the chaste man' or the 'civil servant' can be

absurd heroes (MS p. 84). Since such figures are paradigms of moderation, this shows that 'excess' plays no essential role in the life of 'revolt'. Similarly one can be devoted to 'excess' without being in 'revolt'. Though someone *might* be both in revolt and devoted to excess, this just shows that someone might qualify as an absurd hero on both of Camus' accounts, not that he has one, unified account of what it is that makes one an absurd hero.

10 *Parerga and Paralipomena*, 2 vols, trans. E. F. J. Payne, Oxford: Clarendon Press, 1974, vol. II, pp. 285–6.

Foucault

1 *The Foucault Reader: an Introduction to Foucault's Thought*, ed. P. Rabinow, London: Penguin, 1984, hereafter referred to as FR.

2 In the 'prep' school part of my school – if I may be allowed a personal reminiscence – there were no doors at all on the lavatory cubicles. One graduated to half-doors when one graduated to the 'upper' school.

3 Foucault is thinking, here, of the philosopher-king of the *Republic*, rather than the more retiring philosopher of the *Phaedrus*. Like everyone who thinks, Plato changed his mind from time to time.

4 'Dream, imagination and existence', *Review of Existential Psychology and Psychiatry*, vol. 19, no. 1, 1984–5, pp. 51–2.

Derrida

1 '*Différance*', in *Margins of Philosophy*, trans. A. Bass, Chicago, Ill.: University of Chicago Press, 1982, pp. 1–29, p. 12, hereafter referred to as D.

2 *French Philosophers in Conversation*, by R. Mortley, London: Routledge, 1991, pp. 97–8, hereafter referred to as FP.

3 *Modern Literary Theory: A Reader*, ed. P. Rice and P. Waugh, London: Arnold, 1996, p. 150.

4 *Of Grammatology*, trans. G. Spivak, Baltimore, Md: Johns Hopkins University Press, 1998, p. 158.

Later Heidegger

1 *The Question Concerning Technology and Other Essays*, trans. W. Lovitt, New York: Harper & Row, 1977, p. 16, hereafter referred to as QCT. Since they are drawn from a wide variety of sources, I have, in this chapter, not always given references for quotations. For a list of the full range of texts on which the chapter is based, see the abbreviations page of my *Heidegger's Later Philosophy*, Cambridge: Cambridge University Press, 2002.

2 *Small Is Beautiful*, London: Sphere, 1974.

3 *Poetry, Language, Thought*, trans. A. Hofstadter, New York: Harper & Row, 1971, p. 67, hereafter referred to as PLT.

4 French 'postmodern' philosophers such as Foucault and Derrida all acknowledge Heidegger as their intellectual father. (Whether he would recognise them as his children is quite another matter.) It is because he introduced the use of 'metaphysics' to denote a fundamental error – he called (posthumous) Nietzsche 'the last metaphysician' – that the word figures as a term of abuse in postmodern French philosophy.

5 Heidegger's discussion of 'the festival' is almost entirely confined to texts which have not been translated into English. For references, see my *Heidegger's Later Philosophy*, pp. 55–62.

6 As mentioned in the Introduction, one of Heidegger's insights is that moods are not inner sensations but rather the way the world as a whole is disclosed. Boredom, for example, is the disclosure of everything as drab and dead, joy the disclosure of everything as sparkling, fresh, newly minted.

7 See my *Heidegger's Philosophy of Art*, Cambridge: Cambridge University Press, 2001, chapter 4.

8 Charles Larmore correctly describes the foundation of liberal political thinking as the assumption that people must live together in spite of the fact that 'there are many valid forms of human self-realisation', since 'man's essence does not provide any firm point of reasonable agreement on which a universal ethics can be founded' (*The Morals of Modernity*, Cambridge: Cambridge University Press, 1996, pp. 122, 54). If Heidegger is right, therefore, there is something deeply wrong with modern liberalism and the foundations of liberal democracy.

9 For a full discussion of the fourfold, see my *Heidegger's Later Philosophy*, chapters 7 and 8.

Index

CPSIA information can be obtained at www.ICGtesting.com
Printed in the USA
LVOW071950100113

315247LV00011B/280/P